AMERICA'S

ENDEMIC PROBLEM

AND THE WORLD'S COMPLICIT SILENCE

EBSEN WILLIAM
AMARTEIFIO

DIPLOMA IN JOURNALISM BSc (HONS)
BUSINESS MANAGEMENT RMN

MS Moods Media, LLC

1309 Coffeen Avenue STE 1200 Sheridan, Wy
+1 312 212 3899 U.S.
https://www.istrategae.com/

AMERICA'S ENDEMIC PROBLEM AND THE
WORLD'S COMPLICIT SILENCE

ISBN (Paperback): 979-8-9859096-6-1

Printed in the United States of America

DEDICATION

This book is dedicated to human beings of all races who have suffered or are suffering inequality, racial or social injustice in our world: Whether it was the gross human rights violations in bygone era of Apartheid South Africa, inhumane treatment by dictatorships or even some elected governments the world over, humanity should be acutely concerned. May the Good Lord grant all victims patience and fortitude to prevail.

Crucially may He grant eternal peace to those who have lost their lives through police and state sponsored brutality. We seek protection, love and comfort for those who have survived and especially the young left motherless or fatherless.

The rest of humanity to acknowledge the ultimate sacrifices the fallen have made and honour their memory. We should all be our brother's keeper.

I also dedicate this book to the memory of my father, George A. Amarteifio, a pharmacist, who died on December 19th,1971. He was the inspiration behind my fourth book, 'Humanity and The Nature of Man.' I used that book to officially launch a charity, 'The George A. Amarteifio Foundation' at the Upper Norwood Methodist Church, London SE19 in 2013.

I founded the charity in 1997. We have been send- ing medical products to mainly the Korle-Bu University Teaching Hospital, Ridge Regional Hospital and Ningo Community Hospital, all in Accra, Ghana.

My father was a kind and generous person. Morality and especially Christian values were his priorities. He strongly believed that humanity would overcome countless hurdles if human beings learnt how to live with each other and one another.

CONTENTS

PROLOGUE

The Transatlantic slave trade in the early 17th, Century deprived Mother Africa of an estimated 12 to 15 million of her sons and daughters who were transported to the Americans and the Caribbean. The first arrivals were taken to the James Town colony in America in 1619.

Shackled African slaves were grouped in cramped conditions in slave ships. The conditions quickly became unhygienic giving rise to a number of diseases. The arduous journey through the middle passage made a very difficult experience traumatic for all the African slaves.

Thousands died during the transit. Those who had fallen ill and were deemed not well enough to survive the difficult journey were, together with the dead, jettisoned. Insurance papers were then duly completed by slave masters for compensation. Some slaves still shackled committed suicide en masse by drowning. They had decided that it was the better option than to complete the journey and endure an even more inhumane treatment.

On arrival in the Americas and the Caribbean, the African slaves endured the indignity of being lined up in 'marketplaces,' assessed individually by prospective buyers and eventually becoming the property of the wealthy and powerful in society. Many of these African slaves were responsible and proud patriarchs and matriarchs in their respective households. They were also respected, and therefore influential elders in their various African communities.

Working in the plantations became the next dimension of the suffering of the Africans. In the scorching sun and in very difficult conditions, they worked for hours on end. Any hint of dissent or rebellion was bru- tally quelled. Even pregnant women were not spared the drudgery of plantation work. Consequently, infant mortality within the African population was high. Again, as it was during the transit, disease and illness were rife.

The wealthy, the powerful, the influential and no fewer than twelve American Presidents owned slaves. The White House was built by slaves from 1782 to 1800. Many other landmarks in America built by slaves include Capitol Hill, New York Stock Exchange, and Harvard University.

It took almost 250 years of free African labour before slavery was finally abolished in 1865. The American Congress outlawed the trade in slaves in 1808 but in the south the domestic trade went on regardless. It was vital to their economy. The resistance of the Southern States delayed the eventual abolition of slavery by two decades. It was this dogged resistance of the southerners who advocated the right to continue with the practice which plunged America into the Civil War starting from April 12th,1861, and ending on May 9th, 1865. The war gave the African slaves the opportunity to contribute positively to the Union effort. The African slaves were initially tasked with cooking, washing, digging trenches and cleaning in the Confederate side. In the Union section, the recruited African slaves proved their mettle. They endeared themselves to their white commanders. The Confederates were outnumbered by the Union Army with the recruitment of the African slaves.

Congress passed a Bill authorizing equal pay for black and white soldiers in 1864. When the war ended in 1865, about 180,000 (about 90,000 from the Confederate states) had served as soldiers in the Union Army. The number accounted for 10% of the total Union Force. The percentage of blacks in the Navy in 1861 was about 6%. The following year recorded a massive jump to 15% of the enlisted black men. Many who joined were from the east coast of America.

Abolition of slavery, Citizenship and the Right to Vote were formalised respectively through the 13th, 14th and 15th Amendments of the American Constitution. The years were 1865, 1868 and 1870. President Abraham Lincoln who presided over the abolition of slavery, rightly and humanely said, "If slavery is not wrong, then nothing is wrong." A heartfelt declaration.

The hurdle of abolition had been overcome, but as the Jamaican Reggae singer Jimmy Cliff beautifully sang, there were "many rivers to cross." The next hurdle emerged in the form of segregation- the Jim Crow laws. African American opposition was intense and resolute, but the self-righteous racists were (totally) entrenched in their ideology. One of the countless highlights of the segregation era was the refusal of George Wallace, the Democratic Governor of Alabama, to allow two African Americans enrol in Alabama University. It was June 11th, 1963, and only the intervention of President John F. Kennedy, no less, saved the day. He ordered the National Guards to protect the two African Americans. Hostility did not only come from elected officials, but some members of law enforcement, some members of the judiciary and sections of the public were equally hostile. The Jim Crow laws were a bane in the daily lives of the African Americans. The psychological scars persist. The struggle of African Americans for com- mon acceptance and decency jolted the con- science of majority of white Americans.

The Jim Crow laws were a thorn in the flesh of the African American. but thankfully the beginning of an American awakening proved invaluable during the Civil Rights Era spanning almost one hundred years. The first Civil Rights Act was in 1866 and the last 1965. The intent and resolve of the African Americans were unquestionable. The stalwarts of the Civil Rights Movement; personali- ties like Rev. Dr Martin Luther King, Rosa Park and John Lewis suffered immensely, some fatally, for having the temerity of advocating for basic human rights. Whether protests were peaceful or otherwise, on numerous occasions they were met with the same brutality by either the police or national guards. In sections of soci- ety especially the south, arbitrary lynching of African Americans by white mobs became a spectator sport. Families with children were often in attendance.

Some whites who dared question the barbaric act were dubbed, "nigger lovers." Some even faced the same fate. However, the political will and especially the moral will of many Americans were crucial in clearing some social hurdles.

Many rivers were crossed but sadly more hurdles to surmount. What has been a stumbling block for decades in America, is police brutality towards especially blacks, and other minorities. The practice is replicated but to a lesser extent in countries like the UK, France, Brazil, and Australia. During the era of Apartheid South Africa, the inhumane treatment was part and parcel of the regime's machinery to subjugate the majority black population.

Then in America, on May 25th, 2020, there was the public lynching of African American George Floyd by white American police officer, Derek Chauvin; with the entire world watching. The suffering of the African on American soil since 1619, was all encapsulated in 9 agonising minutes (shy of 14 seconds). The political world might have been in a stupor, but the citizens of Mother Earth were moved and lodged their horror through countless demonstrations. Amid the clam- our for justice for all humanity, the Black Lives Matter Movement, formed in 2013, gained global prominence. Once again, the conscience of the world received a timely nudge; public and many private establishments (including influential public figures) came to the fore and instituted practical and financial policies to redress social and racial inequalities in society. Notable among them were Bank of America, Bank of England, Royal Bank of Scotland, Barclays Bank, HSBC, Lloyd's of London, Amazon and Apple.

A lot has been achieved by the African in America in four centuries of struggling. However, rivers abound to be crossed. Despite all the doom and gloom, Black America has excelled in a relatively short period in education, diverse professions including law, sports and entertainment to enrich the United States of America in every sense of the word. Just think about it. The year 2008 delivered the cherry on the cake- the American Presidency. Wonderful! What a momentous and inspiring feat by Barack Obama, not forgetting the crucial contribution of decent and fair-minded white Americans.

About 250 years of free African labour to the Americas and some European powers cannot be discussed without the subject of Reparation. Political decisions by governments of different complexions effortlessly secured attractive compensations for countless families and individuals who had to free their slaves after the abolition of the trade and practice of slavery. However, the mere mention of "Reparation" for descendants of slaves, sends shivers down the spines of politicians. They lack the political will and the overriding moral consideration to improve the lives of fellow man.

The importance of Africa to the rest of the world cannot be overstated. Howard W. French of the New York Times wrote in the Guardian, "The creation of the modern, interconnected world is generally credited to European pioneers. But Africa was the wellspring for almost everything they achieved- and African lives were the terrible cost." French added in the Guardian's 'The Long Read,' "Without African peoples trafficked from its shores, the Americas would have counted for little in the ascendance of the west. African labour, in the form of enslaved people, was what made the development of the Americas possible. Without it, Europe's colonial projects in the New World are unimaginable."

The writer accentuated his point by quoting W.E.B Du Bois, "It was black labour that established the modern world commerce, which began first as a commerce in the bodies of the slaves themselves."

On slavery, when the need for rescue was (acutely) desperate, the Quakers, William Wilberforce and associates – they were all white human beings- demonstrated the moral courage against massive odds to highlight the plight of the African. Their stance awoke the innate humanity of the masses, and a movement was formed. The Abolition of Slavery Movement.

I believe in humanity. There are countless examples to prove that if majority of the white population in the US and Europe knew the extent of the barbarity of slavery in the plantations, the inhumane trade and equally vile practice, would have been abolished a considerable period before the mid-19th, Century. A notable example, in 1863, just before the abolition of slavery, an African slave who became known as 'Whipped Peter,' survived one of the worst forms of inhumanity imaginable in a Louisiana plantation. The perpetrators were white slave owners, John and Bridget Lyons.
When Peter escaped, he was pursued by slave hunters with bloodhounds. Having survived days on the run, he made it safely to the Union domain. Matt Roper of the Daily Mirror reported that when 'Whipped Peter' removed his shirt, the web of raised criss-crossing scars, "sent a thrill of horror to every white person present, but the few blacks who were waiting, paid little attention to the sad spectacle, such terrible scenes being painfully familiar to them all."

The human being can be Hellishly Heinous withal HEAVENLY HUMANE. May the Good Lord help all of us to earnestly eliminate the former and GRACIOUSLY ELEVATE the latter. Great Redeemer Come And Redeem Adam's Helpless Race. We Solemnly Pray.

CHAPTER ONE

AFRICA THE BIRTHPLACE OF HUMANITY

The continent of Africa is regarded as the birthplace of humanity and the cradle of civilization. Scientific research indicates that all human beings have African ancestors. In the early 17th Century, the Transatlantic Slave Trade took sons and daughters of Mother Africa to the New World. In America they endured the desolation of working in plantations, the horrors and pain of lynching, the schism of segregation, the intense and traumatic struggle for civil rights, the repulsive racial inequality, the hatred in public hostility and decades of unbridled police brutality. These are the lot of the black man. The political world, a constant spectator; but in silence.

A detailed study of African history shows that Africa was not the 'Dark Continent.' and Africans were not (and still not) inferior to Europeans. Europeans used the description 'dark' because in my opinion they knew nothing about Africa. The term-Dark Continent- first emerged in the mid- 19th Century. According to com/geography/africa/website, the term was most likely used for the first time by American explorer and journalist, Henry Stanley. On the whole the term stuck in the west because of "the mysteries and savagery they expected to find in the interior." If they knew nothing about Africa, there was no justification also to refer to Africans as inferior. This was the term which many Europeans used to justify slavery.

Thomas Jefferson, the 3rd President of America stated, "All men are created equal," before the Declaration of American Independence on July 4th, 1776. American historian, Jack Rakove was reported to have explained that Jefferson did not mean individual equality, but that American colonists, as a people, had the same right to self-government as other nations. Fair enough! The Good Lord created all humanity. The difference we all see is mere skin colour. Is there any universally agreed crite- ria to define inferiority and superiority as far as human beings are concerned? The Atlantic Slave Trade was and remains the largest forced migration in world history.

Prior to the arrival of European slave traders on African soil, majority of African societies were in their own respective stages of development. They were civilized, effectively organized and technologically capable.

Egypt was at the fore of many great African civilizations. It lasted thousands of years and made a mark in the fields of science, medicine, technology, mathematics and the arts. Egyptian civilization was already 2,000 years old before the city of Rome was built.

In West Africa, the kingdom of Gana (Ghana) was a vast empire which covered an area the size of Western Europe, between the ninth and thirteenth centuries. The trading was in gold, copper and salt. The empire was very advanced and prosperous. Ghana was compared to a medieval European empire. There were a number of powerful local rulers who were under the jurisdiction of a King or Emperor. The Ghanaian ruler was reported to have had an army of 200,000 men.

NOK- one of the earliest kingdoms in West Africa belonged to the Nok people. They were farmers, potters and metal workers who settled near River Niger around 500BC.

IFE AND BENIN- The kingdom of Ife developed in the rain forest in the 600s. The art and religion of Ife had an influence on the culture of Benin. These two kingdoms were driven by the Yoruba people. The people of Ife were noted for their magnificent work in bronze, brass, copper, wood and ivory.

Benin emerged in the 900s with her power, most evident between the 1400s and 1600s. The people of Benin were very skilled in ivory carving, pottery, rope and gum production.

MALI- The kingdom of Mali, from the thirteenth to the fifteenth century, covered much of West and North-East Africa. During the peak of her development, in the fourteenth century, the kingdom was 2,000 kilometre wide. There was an organized and profitable trading in gold dust; and agricultural products, which were exported north. Cowrie shells were used as currency; and gold, copper and salt were traded.

SONGHAY KINGDOM- The kingdom grew very powerful and prosperous between 1450 and 1550. The kingdom had a well -organized system of government, a developed currency and imported fabrics from Europe. The kingdom's city of Timbuktu became one of the most important places in the world. Libraries and universities were built. Scholars and poets and artists from other parts of Africa and the Middle East used the city as a meeting place.

ASHANTI KINGDOM 1701-1894: One of the last king-doms in Africa was the Ashanti Kingdom which was founded in 1701. The kingdom covered present -day Ivory Coast, Central Ghana and present-day Togo. It had Dahomey Kingdom in the north and Dahomey in the east. The Ashantis were famous for their work in gold. They were also fierce warriors.

KINGDOMS IN AFRICA BERFORE COLONIZATION- In Central Africa- The Kongo Kingdom (1400-1800), the Luba Empire (1585-1885), it occupied marshy grassland of the Upemba Depression in what is now Southern Democratic Republic of Congo. Lunda Empire (1660-1887), Democratic Republic of Congo, north-eastern Angola and north-western present-day Zambia. The central state of the empire was in Katanga.

EAST AFRICA- Buganda (1,300 to present). home of the Buganda people of Uganda. The medieval Swahili city-states.

HORN OF AFRICA- Ancient land of Punt (2,500 BC), Opone/Xafun (1000 BC - 5th Century AD), Kingdom of Aksum (1st Century - 9th Century), Kingdom of Belgin 9th Century, Sultanate of Mogadishu (10th Century - 16th Century) and Ethiopia Empire (1137 - 1974).

NORTH AFRICA- Kingdom of Kemma (2500-1500 BC), Ancient Egypt (3100- 650 BC), Kingdom of Kush (1070 BC- 350 AD) and Nobatia Kingdom (350 - 650 AD).

SOUTH AFRICA- Zulu Kingdom, Maravi Kingdom and Kingdom of Mapungubwe.

Most of the African Kingdoms in time came to an end and were then replaced by new kingdoms.

African gold especially from the great empires of West Africa -Gana (Ghana), Mali and Songhay boosted the economic fortunes of European nations in the 13th and 14th Centuries. European interest focused on the wealth of West Africa. The availability of gold in the region gave rise to the voyages of early European explorers.

SLAVERY IN AFRICA- There were forms of slavery in Africa prior to the arrival of the Europeans. People were temporarily enslaved for crimes committed, as prisoners of war or failure to settle debts. In some cases, slaves could work to gain their freedom. Children of the enslaved were not regarded as slaves. The Transatlantic Slave Trade which started in the 17th Century was there- fore different to what preceded it amongst Africans. Nevertheless, it does not absolve the African practice of immorality.

CHARTER TWO

HOW THE SLAVE TRADE STARTED

In the 15th Century, Portugal and later seven other European countries, Britain, France, Spain, Germany, Denmark, Italy and the Netherlands eventually infiltrated the continent of Africa. The first African slaves arrived in Portugal in 1441. In the 1480s, Portuguese ships transported African slaves on to sugar plantations in the Cape Verde and Madeira Islands in the eastern Atlantic. The Spanish took African slaves to the Caribbean after 1502. The Netherlands became the leading traders in slaves in the 1600s. In the 17th Century as a whole, the English and French controlled about half of the Transatlantic slave trade; taking majority of the slaves from West Africa between Senegal and the Niger Rivers.

The Portuguese kidnapped Africans and in bondage, took them to Europe. The Portuguese expansion was driven by first, Prince Henry, the Navigator and later King John The First's objective in gaining a foothold in the Gold-producing areas in West Africa. The Trans-Sahara trade routes between the Kingdom of Songhay and the North African traders yielded Europe with gold coins which were used to trade with India for spices, silk and other luxuries in high demand on the European market.

The major trade routes were between the Sahara Desert, the Western-Central Africa and the port trading centres all dotted along the Mediterranean Sea. The trade route from Timbuktu across the Sahara to Sijimas was also important. Camels which were first domesticated by the Berbers of North Africa at about 300 CE were used for the long journey across the desert. The camels were well fattened before each journey. A typical caravan moving three miles per hour took about 40 hours to cross the Sahara. The Sahara Desert covers about a third of the area of the African continent.

THE TRANSATLANTIC SLAVE TRADE

It is estimated that between 12-15 million African slaves were taken to the Americas and the Caribbean between the 16th and the 19th centuries.

This trade in humans was the second category of what was termed the Triangular Trade. The first category involved arms, textiles and wine shipped from Europe to Africa. The third angle of the trade involved sugar and coffee from the Americas to Europe.

Conservative figures indicate that no more than a few thousands of Africans were taken to the Americas before the beginning of the 17th Century. The growth of sugar plantations in the Caribbean and the Chesapeake Region in North America was attributable to the demand of slave labour. It is estimated that 60% of slaves ended up in the Americas during the 18th Century.

Unquestionably the effect of the slave trade on African countries was dire. The fittest, healthiest and the youth were taken. Among this group were notably women of childbearing age and young men. The elderly disabled and those considered unsuitable were left behind. This 'wholesale enforced evacuation,' needless to stress, affected the economic development of the coun- tries throughout West Africa and other affected coun- tries in the continent. Food production- farming- was one of the areas of economic activity which suffered immensely.

The kidnapping and banditry of the European slave traders put fear into the rest of the African populace. No doubt the Europeans had African accomplices- tribal Chiefs and warlords- some of whom were hoodwinked into selling fellow Africans down the river. Besides kid- napping and banditry, tribal wars contributed to cap- tives being sold into slavery.

Slaves taken from the interior of Africa endured jour- neys on foot covering as many as 300 miles (485 km). It is estimated that between 10-15% died on the way to the coast. Some captured Africans found suicide an option rather than to be taken over the big ocean to an unknown far- away place.

THE ATLANTIC PASSAGE OR THE MIDDLE PASSAGE

The transit from Africa to the Americas and Caribbean was fraught with unimaginable difficulties. Hundreds of slaves were chained and cramped into tiny tiers below decks for the arduous journey of 5,000 miles (8,000 km). The ceilings were low. The heat was unbearable. The air, predictably, stuffy. The slaves were allowed only a few hours a day out, still in chains for much needed fresh air and the stretching of cramped limbs. The slaves suffered, as a result, from severe dysentery and dehydration. In a typical case in 1781, in a bid to stop an infectious disease spreading even more, one Captain Collingwood was responsible for 132 sick African slaves being thrown overboard the slave ship zone.

It is estimated that between 15%-25% of the slaves could not survive the journey. This included the sick and those who died on board. Another group included those who envisaged even more brutality at the unknown destination. Like those who committed suicide on route from the interior of Africa to the coast; this group committed suicide en masse by jumping into the ocean, shackles and all and drowning. Slave drivers duly completed insurance forms to receive compensation for all slaves 'lost' during the difficult middle passage. The suffering and punishment meted out to the African slaves by the slave masters were graphically spelt out in the autobiography of a freed West African slave, Olaudah Equiano in 1789.

The continued suffering of the slaves included routine rape of the African women by their slave masters. There were odd occasions when African slaves insurrected and took over the command of slave ships. A nota- ble example was in 1839 when a slave named Joseph Cinque led a revolt of 53 illegally purchased slaves on a Spanish slave ship, Amistad. The captain and two members were killed. The US Supreme Court ultimately ordered the return of Africans to their homes.

During the American Revolution 1775-1783, there was an overwhelming support among the Northern American colonies to stop the importation of more slaves. Despite the objective of the Northern states, Congress inclined to the wishes of the Southern states, stalled for two decades before making the importation of slaves, illegal. In 1808 the law was enacted in Congress with little opposition. However, the Caribbean smugglers persisted often violating the law until it was enforced by the Northern blockade of the South in 1861 during the American Civil War.

Britain outlawed slavery throughout its Empire in 1833. Brazil outlawed the slave trade in 1850, though the smuggling of new slaves did not end until the country finally enacted Emancipation in 1888.

In the plantations, the mournful songs of the African slaves revealed the suffering they went through and still enduring in bondage. Their songs also reflected how they and their descendants have adopted Christianity.

Examples-"Sometimes I feel like a motherless child." "Nobody knows the trouble I have seen." "Steal away." "Swing low, sweet chariot." "Go down Moses." "He's got the whole world in His hands." "Every time I feel the spirit." "Let us break bread together on our knees;" and "Wade in the water." The slaves eagerly looked forward to Sundays, the only day most of them were free to worship and praise their God in prayer and sonorous hymns.

When the Emancipation Proclamation was signed in 1863, the conclusion of the American Civil War and the Ratification of the 13th Amendment to the Constitution formally abolishing slavery in 1865, it was reported that most slaves shunned the music of their masters.

The old Negro Spirituals were resurrected by a group of students from the newly founded Fisk College of

Nashville, Tennessee. The Fisk Jubilee Singers toured and raised money for their institution which needed a lot of financial assistance. The group took the Spirituals to parts of America which had not heard of Negro folk songs. The well-trained musicians performed during their tours of Europe in the 1870s in front of Royalty. The success of the Fisk Jubilee Singers paved the way for other black colleges to form touring groups. The professional Jubilee Singers enjoyed successful tours around the world. Consequently, collections of plantation songs were published to meet the grow- ing public demand. Many pieces of American music notably Blues, Jazz and Gospel have their roots in the African Negro Spirituals. The songs of the plantations, the serene and sometimes the sonorous sounds of the Spirituals boosted the protesters during the Civil Right marches of the 1950s and 1960s.

CHAPTER THREE

THE SCRAMBLE FOR AFRICA

Africa had suffered severely from slavery. The next stage for the Europeans was the Scramble for Africa between 1881- 1914. It was also known as the Partition of Africa or the Conquest of Africa. It was the inva- sion, occupation, division and colonization of Africa by European nations. The main players were Portugal, Britain, France, Spain, Italy, Germany and Belgium. In 1914, the beginning of the First World War, 90% of the African continent was under European control. Only three countries, Ethiopia (then known as Abyssinia), Liberia (occupied by returned slaves) and the Dervish State (part of the present-day Somalia); were free from European colonial rule.

The main objective for the scramble was for European powers to improve their economies by controlling commodities and vital trade routes. The scramble for Africa happened four decades after the first Industrial Revolution. The industrial revolution was the focus of new manufacturing processes in Europe and the United States between 1760-1840.

In 1884, at Portugal's proposal, fourteen European countries met in Berlin (Berlin Conference 1884) regarding the division of Africa. The initial aim of the conference was to agree that the Congo River and Niger River estuaries and basins would be considered neutral and open to trade. At the time of the Berlin Conference, only the coastal areas of Africa were colonized by the European powers.

During the conference which lasted until February 26th, 1885 (three months), the Colonial European powers 'haggled' over geometric boundaries in the interior of Africa without considering the prevailing cultural and linguistic boundaries of the indigenous African population. The countries at the conference included Austria, Hungary, Belgium, Denmark, France, Germany, Britain, Italy, The Netherlands, Portugal, Russia, Spain, Sweden-Norway (unified from 1814-1905), Turkey and the United States. The Conference ended with the continent of Africa being divided into fifty irregular countries.

During the time of colonization, Europe was suffering from economic depression with the major players-notably Britain, France and Germany- losing money. The Europeans viewed the abundance of Africa's raw materials as a source for making money. The cheap African labour provided ivory, palm oil, wood, cotton and gum. These raw materials boosted the next stage of the European Industrial Revolution.

European missionaries made inroads (deep) into Africa arousing a keen interest within their respective countries. Warfare within the continent was rife so the missionaries depended on their respective countries for protection and when necessary, intervention. The British explorer, David Livingstone contended that civilization of Africans could be achieved through good governance and education. Livingstone strongly believed that trade, good governance and education were compelling factors in alleviating or even ending human suffering in Africa. Christianity would be the channel for moral principles, while education and commerce would be the spur for Africans to produce their own goods to foster trade with Europe. In the pursuance of this objective, an effective and legitimate governing system was imperative. It would also create the condition for the civil rights of the people to be established.

David Livingstone's empathy for the African problem was vivid. His prognosis - practicable. His compassion, laudable. David Livingstone was a slavery abolitionist. In the biography by Jay Milbrandt, 'The Daring Heart of David Livingstone: Exile, African Slavery, And the Publicity Stunt That Saved Millions,' Milbrandt wrote, "Livingstone was passionate about ending the brutal trade in East Africa. In fact, the closing of the slave markets in Zanzibar, highlighted in the statement above, was one of the greatest achievements of his career, which unfortunately he did not live to see."

The referred statement was, "To all our subjects who may see this, also others, may God save you, know that we have prohibited the transport of slaves by sea in all our harbours and have closed the markets which are for sale of slaves throughout all our dominions. Whoever therefore shall ship a raw slave after this date will render himself liable to punishment and this, he will bring upon himself. Be this known." The notice was posted on a Custom House in Zanzibar on June 5th, 1873, about a month after David Livingstone's death.

The Africans were known to have loved and adored David Livingstone. The scientist and explorer's medical discoveries included using quinine for the prevention and treatment of malaria. An endearing speech made by an African about the Great Explorer was- "A white man who treated black men as his brothers, and whose memory would always be cherished all along the Rovuma Valley after we were all dead and gone. A short man with a bushy moustache, and a keen piercing eye, whose words were always gentle, and whose manners were always kind, whom as a leader, it was a privilege to follow, and who knew the way to the hearts of all men."

Henry Morton Stanley was sent by the New York Herald to go to Africa and find David Livingstone. Notable among Livingstone's expeditions, was to find the headwaters of the Nile. Stanley was not able to convince the famous explorer to return to "civilization", but during a span of four months, he had a series of interviews with him. Stanley who was described as not particularly religious, wrote about Livingstone, "His religion is not of the theoretical kind, but it is a constant, earnest, sincere practice. It is neither demonstrative nor loud, but manifests itself in a quiet, practical way, and is always at work… In him religion exhibits its loveliest features; it governs his conduct not only towards his servants – religion has tamed him and made him a Christian gentleman."

The seven main colonial powers had by 1900 colonized a considerable part of Africa. These were Britain, France, Germany, Belgium, Spain, Portugal and Italy. Having decentralized and 'centralized' states, the European powers began establishing colonial state systems. The colonial state was the apparatus of administrative domination which was used by the European powers to exploit the colonies.

The Europeans took advantage of rivalries between African chiefs and between Kings. These rulers were competing fiercely to be the richest and most powerful in their respective areas or regions. The European powers were successful in teaming up with one group against the other and ultimately gained overall control.

Natural disasters were other factors which contributed to the relatively easy colonization of Africa. In 1895 many regions were affected by drought, the result of scarcity of rain. Food production was seriously affected causing the deaths of people and animals. A plague of locusts also destroyed the few crops which were produced. In the 1890s, cattle plague broke out with devastating effect- cattle, goat and sheep perished in large numbers. Human fatality was extremely high as a result, making the Africans unable to resist the Europeans in their quest to carve up the continent. The Europeans used force and violence through powerful weapons in the pursuit of their objectives. The Africans, needless to point out, could hardly match the fire power of the Europeans.

In the late 1890s, an epidemic of smallpox dealt a blow to the Africans. The Europeans had already experienced it in Europe therefore they were immune. Numerous Africans died or were too weak to fight back colonization.

The only independent countries in Africa, as already stated, were Ethiopia (Abyssinia) and Liberia which had been occupied by returning free slaves from the

United States. The spoils of the 'carve up' were as detailed below.

1. BRITISH COLONIES- Lesotho (colonial name Basutoland), Botswana (Bechuanaland), Kenya and Uganda (British East Africa), Somalia (British Somaliland), Gambia (The Gambia), Ghana (Gold Coast). Nigeria, Zambia (Northern Rhodesia), Malawi (Nyasaland), Sierra Leone, South Africa, Zimbabwe (Southern Rhodesia) and Swaziland.

2. FRENCH COLONIES- Algeria, Chad, Gabon: Republic of Congo, Central African Republic (All known as French Equatorial Africa): Benin, Guinea, Mali, Ivory Coast, Mauritania, Niger, Senegal and Burkina Faso (Also known as French West Africa), Djibouti (French Somaliland), Madagascar, Morocco and Tunisia.

3. GERMAN COLONIES- Cameroon (Kamerun): Tanzania, Rwanda and Buruni (German East Africa), Namibia (South- West Africa), Togo (Togoland).

4. BELGIUM COLONY- Democratic Republic of Congo (Belgian Congo).

5. PORTUGUESE COLONIES- Angola, Mozambique (Portuguese East Africa), Guinea-Bissau (Portuguese Guinea).

6. ITALIAN COLONIES- Eritrea, Libya and Somalia.

7. SPANISH COLONIES- Rio De Oro (Western Sahara, disputed territory claimed by Morocco), Morocco (Spanish Morocco), German East Africa was divided between Britain and Belgium. Belgium took

Rwanda and Burundi with Britain taking control of Tanganyika.

Independence saw Tanganyika and Zanzibar become present day Tanzania.

8. GERMAN COLONIES- The end of the First World War 1914-1918 saw all the German African Colonies taken away and made Mandate Territories by the League of Nations (Now United Nations). This meant that they were supposed to be organized for independence by the allied powers which were Britain, France, Belgium and South Africa.

German Kamerun was more sizeable than modern day Cameroun. It extended into present day Nigeria, Chad and the Central African Republic. After the war most of German Kamerun went to France with Britain taking control of the piece of land adjacent to Nigeria. When Independence was achieved, the British Cameroons decided and joined Nigeria while Southern British Cameroons joined Cameroon. The German South-West Africa was controlled by South Africa until 1990.

In 1884, Togoland comprising of what is now Togo and most of what is now the Volta Region of Ghana (approximately 29,867 sq miles) 77,355km2, was a German Protectorate. In 1914 during the outbreak of the First World War, the British and the French joined forces and took Togoland from the Germans. The East became Togo, and the West (Volta Region) was taken by the British and added to the rest of (Ghana) then Gold Coast.

Present day Somalia is made up of what were formerly Italian Somaliland and British Somaliland. Morocco- there is still a dispute over Morocco's borders. The country was made up initially of two separate colonies: French Morocco and the Spanish. Spanish Morocco lay on the northern coast near the straits of Gibraltar, but Spain also had two separate territories (Rio De Oro and Saguia EL-Hamra) just south of French Morocco. Spain combined these two colonies into Spanish Saharan the 1920s. In 1957 Spain gave up much of what had been Saguia El-Hamra to Morocco. Morocco continued to claim the southern section and in 1975 seized control of the territory. The United Nations recognizes the south- ern section, which is often called Western Sahara, as a non-self- governing territory. The African Union recog- nizes it as the Sovereign of Sahara Arab Democratic Republic (SADR). However, the SADR controls only a section of the territory known as Western Sahara.

CHAPTER FOUR

AFRICAN KINGDOMS BEFORE COLONIZATION

A system of governance through kingdoms or empires was in operation throughout the African continent before European colonization. The following are worthy of consideration.

1. THE SONGHAY EMPIRE- The Songhay Empire (1460-1591) was a state which controlled the western Sahel in the 15th and 16th Centuries. It was one of the largest states in African history. The state was known by its historiographical name which was derived from the then dominant ethnic ruling elite, the Songhai. Sunni Ali established Gao as the capital of the empire. Timbuktu and Djenne were other notable cities in the empire active during the Trans-Sahara Trade.

    The Songhay Empire replaced the Mali Empire (1240-1645) as the most important state in West Africa. The empire covered modern Southern Mauritania and Mali. The sudden expansion of the Songhay Empire, from a small kingdom along the eastern side of the bend of the River Niger occurred during the reign of Sunni Ali (1464-1492). The empire enjoyed economic prosperity throughout the 16th Century. However, having been seriously weakened by civil wars, the Songhay was attacked and became a part of the Moroccan Empire in 1591.

2. THE MALI EMPIRE- The Mali Empire was situated along the savannah belt between the Sahara Desert to the North and the forests of southwest- ern part of West Africa, which was often referred to as the Sudan Region. The empire became prosperous through its control of local and external trade in notably gold and salt from the mid- 13th Century. However civil wars, the bane of many of these African kingdoms and empires contributed to the collapse of the Mali Empire in the 1460s. Other contributory factors were the opening up of competing trade routes elsewhere, an attack by nomadic Tuareg of the Southern Sudan and the Mossi people. The Mossi people then controlled the lands south of the Niger River. The rise and sudden expansion of the Songhay Empire overshadowed the Mali Empire. It was therefore left with only the western corner of what was once its huge territories. The arrival of the Moroccans in the 17th Century ended what was left of the great Mali Empire.

3. EGYPTIAN EMPIRE- Two major kingdoms sprang up along the Nile River around 5500 BC. King Narmer (AKA Meves) was credited for merging the Upper Egypt and Lower Egypt Kingdoms to form what is recognized as the beginning of the Egyptian Civilization. Egypt was one of the first civilizations to invent writing. The ancient Egyptians were scientists and mathematicians. They invented the 365 days-a-year calendar. Some of the achievements

of ancient Egyptians include quarrying, surveying and construction techniques which supported the building of the huge pyramids, temples, obelisks (tall pillars set up as monuments), a system of mathematics, a practical and effective system of medicine, irrigation systems and agricultural production techniques.

The rich soil of the Nile boosted agricultural production. The most important crops were wheat, flax and papyrus. Flax is a blue-flowered plant, the stem of which can be used to make textile fiber. Papyrus is a water plant which looks like reed. The ancient Egyptians made paper from it. The sale of the wheat throughout the Middle East and the manufacture of linen for clothing from flax boosted the Egyptian economy. Mineral exploitation of the Nile valley and the surrounding desert regions was one of the many economic activities. Religion played a key role in the lives of the ancient Egyptians. Ancient Egypt featured prominently in the Christian Bible.

During the years of the decline of the empire, Egypt was conquered by the Sasanian Persian army between 618-628 AD. The Roman emperor Heraclius recaptured it between 629-639 AD. The empire was finally captured by Muslim Rashidun army in 639-641 AD, which ended Roman Rule.

4. LUNDA EMPIRE- The Bantu-speaking African state was founded in the 16th Century in the region of Upper Kasai River -situated in present northern Angola and the western part of the Democratic Republic of Congo. The Empire was founded by invaders who came west from Luba despite the Luba people having previously lived in the area.

Between 1600-1750, groups of Lunda adventurers formed numerous satellites (Kasaje, Kazembe, Luba-Landa states). The empire had a centralized base, a ring of provinces closely linked to the capital and an outer ring of independent provinces which paid tribute. There was also a fringe of other autonomous kingdoms which shared a common Lunda culture. The boundaries were therefore only loosely defined.

The Lunda people traded with both the Arabs on the Indian Ocean and from about 1650, the Portuguese on the Atlantic. The main exports included slaves and ivory. The imports included guns and cloth. The Lunda Empire attained the peak of its powers by the 1850s. This period (1850s) brought about incursions by the neighbouring Choklue people which weakened the empire. In 1884, Portuguese troops arrived from Angola in the west; followed in 1898 by Belgians from the Congo Free State in the north-east. The Lunda Empire was partitioned between the Portuguese and the Belgians. Guerrilla warfare against the Congo Free State continued until 1909 when the Lunda leaders were captured and executed.

5. ETHIOPIAN EMPIRE- The Ethiopian Empire also known as Abyssinia began with the creation of the Solomonic dynasty by Yekuno Amlak from around 1270. The empire covered the current area of Ethiopia and Eritrea. The empire ended in 1974 when the Emperor, Haile Selassie was overthrown in a Marxist-coup.

In 1896, an invading Italian army was defeated by the Ethiopians. The Italians controlled Eritrea and were able to add Italian Somaliland. In 1935, Italian soldiers under the command of Marshal Emilio De Bono successfully invaded Ethiopia (second Italo-Ethiopian war). The war lasted seven months before declaration of victory by the Italians. The invasion was condemned by the League of Nations (UN). Ethiopia then became part of Italian East Africa until it was liberated in 1941 by allies in North Africa.

In 1951, Eritrea was given to Ethiopia by the United Nations on condition it would have special status as an autonomous province. In 1961 however Haile Selassie singularly revoked the arrangement. This brought about a 30-year War of Independence. The overthrow of Emperor Selassie in 1974 did not end the war. The Leninist-Marxist regime continued until in 1993. Eritrea was internationally recognized as a sovereign state.

Ethiopia was administered from 1935 to 1941 as part of a colonial administration but did not benefit from the same legal status as other African colonies. The overthrow of Haile Selassie in 1974 by Mengistu Haile Mariam led to the establishment of a one-party Communist state. The imprisonment and eventual death of Haile Selassie on 26.08.1975 marked the end of the Ethiopian Empire.

Economic activity of the Ethiopian Empire centered on the exportation of gold, ivory and frankincense to the Muslim world. The empire was also involved in the Inter-Continental Slave Trade.

6. BUGANDA KINGDOM - Buganda Kingdom was established in the 14th Century under the first king Kato Kintu, the founder of Buganda's Kintu Dynasty. Buganda became one of the largest and most

powerful kingdoms in East Africa in the 18th and 19th Centuries.

During the Scramble for Africa 1881-1914, British imperialism prevailed, and it lost its independence. Buganda became the center of the Uganda Protectorate in 1894. The British adopted Uganda which is the Swahili term for Buganda. Buganda with its capital Lubanga became a major pro- vider of cotton and coffee. They were also trad- ers dealing in millet and banana. They kept live- stock, practised weaving and pottery. There were also iron mongers and blacksmiths. The kingdom of Buganda was officially restored in 1993 after it was abolished in 1966 by Uganda's first Prime Minister, Milton Obote. Buganda is now a monarchy with a substantial degree of autonomy from the Ugandan state. The King of Buganda, known as The Kabaka, is Muwenda Mutebi the Second. He is recognized as the 36th Kabaka of Buganda. He has been king since the restoration of the kingdom in 1993.

7.   THE ASHANTI EMPIRE- In the 17th Century, Osei Tutu, the Ashanti King (1695 -1717) and his adviser, Okomfo Anokye declared the importance of the Ashanti Golden Stool as a sole unifying symbol of the Ashantis. The Stool is sacred and believed to contain the spirit/soul of the people. The king was instrumental in the massive expansion of the king- dom. In 1701, the powerful Ashanti army conquered Denkyira. This earned them access across to the Gulf of Guinea and the Atlantic Ocean, coastal trade with Europeans, especially the Dutch.

The Ashanti Empire started in 1670 and ended in 1957, when the then Gold Coast gained independence from Britain and became Ghana. Brong Ahafo, Central, Eastern, Greater Accra, Western and Northern Regions were added to the Ashanti Empire to form the present-day Republic of Ghana.

During the height of the Ashanti Empire, it was estimated that the population numbered 3m. It had its own efficient social, political and military establishments. The Ashantis, equipped with European firearms inflicted heavy casualties on advancing British troops. In some cases, the British were beaten. It took a hundred years of fighting until the British prevailed in the face of stiff resistance from the proud Ashantis.

Gold mining was the most important economic activity of the Ashanti Empire. Other economic activities were, pottery, cloth weaving, manufacture of spears, fishing hooks, farming implements and swords by blacksmiths. The hundred-year war between the Ashantis and the British was from 1807 to 1900. In 1900, between March 28th to late September, the British and the Ashantis were engaged in another war dubbed, 'The War of The Golden Stool.' The British were eventually victories.

Consequently, the Asantewaa (Queen) and other leaders were exiled to the Seychelles to join the Ashanti King Prempeh the First. In 1902, Britain finally designated the Ashanti Kingdom a Protectorate. The Ashanti Kingdom regained self-rule on 31.01.1935. The Ashanti Kingship was restored in 1957 (Ghana's Independence) with Prempeh the Second at the helm.

8. THE ZULU EMPIRE- The Zulu Empire of South Africa covered the coast of the Indian Ocean from the

Tugela River in the south to Pongola River in the north. It was founded by Shaka (1787-1828), whose father was a Zulu chief, and his mother the daughter of a neighbouring clan. The empire ended in the Zulu War of South Africa in 1879. It was a sustained two-year political activity and bloodshed aimed at dislodging the final obstacle to British imperial power in Southern Africa. This British victory on July 4th, 1879, avenged the defeat on January 22nd, the same year as the Battle of Isandlwana.

King Ketchwayo Ka Mpande (1826-1879) was the leader of the empire during the Anglo-Zulu war of 1879. He had succeeded his father King Mpande in 1873. The British had issued an ultimatum to King Ketchwayo, but he refused. The ultimatum was for him to dismantle his efficient military system within 30 days and pay reparations for alleged insults. The king's confidence in the ability of his strong assembled army of 40 to 60,000 men was central to his refusal. In the ensuing war, the British were victorious and subsequently divided Zululand into thirteen provinces. The traditional region of Zululand is the northeastern section of present day KwaZulu Natal (formerly Natal) Province. The defeat and division spelt the end of the Zulu tribe and therefore the empire.

Prior to the arrival of Europeans in the 15th and 16th centuries, trade within African cities, king- doms or empires was well organized. Trade routes were managed and protected as they generated wealth and power.

Respective cities, kingdoms or empires had communities and societies functioning accordingly.

Communities were managed by elders within family groups. In societies, a hierarchy of senior elders, respected public figures reporting to and advising sub-chiefs, chiefs and even kings.

The sub-chiefs, chiefs and kings had their own spokes persons who in turn had a group of advisers assisting them manage the everyday lives of the people under their authority. There were small local courts to handle disputes. A case would only go to court when all levels of arbitration within a household, a community or one community against another have been exhausted. Decisions taken by courts controlled by sub-chiefs, chiefs or ultimately the king, were binding.

The adverse effect therefore of the slave trade on the African household, community and society at large was inestimable. Whole social and political structures were devastatingly broken.

CHAPTER FIVE

ARRIVAL IN THE AMERICAS AND WORKING IN PLANTATIONS

Overwhelming majority of the African slaves taken to the Americas, besides being strong and healthy, were well cultured with an immense sense of self-worth. The first slaves taken to America arrived at James Town, Virginia; the first permanent English settlement in August 1619 by Dutch traders. However enslaved Africans arrived in North America as early as 1500s. Christopher Columbus was thought to have taken the first Africans in the late 1400s on his expeditions to Hispaniola, which is modern day Dominican Republic. It was uncertain whether they were all slaves.

What was not disputed was that before 1619, hundreds of thousands of Africans both free and enslaved, helped with the establishment and survival of colonies in the Americas and the New World. They were also reported to have fought fiercely against European oppressors.

African slaves by definition of that tag, were considered the property of slave masters. They therefore did not enjoy civil, or the criminal legal protections afforded to other citizens of America under the Constitution. They had no say in the number of hours they had to toil in the fields. They worked long hours in severe conditions. Brutal punishment was rife for those considered not working hard enough. Some slaves worked in the slave owners' palatial buildings as house servants. They usually worked from first light (daybreak) to sunset in the evening.

Most slaves worked in plantations in the South which was not as industrialized as the North. The slaves in the North were used in factories to produce manufactured goods. The African slaves performed a host of tasks including picking cotton, harvesting sugar cane, planting and harvesting rice, harvesting tobacco, growing and harvesting coffee and building railroads.

The slave owners' household relied on the plantations for self-sufficiency. Livestock-cattle, sheep; poultry-turkey, geese and especially chicken were reared to provide fresh meat, milk and eggs. Commercially, majority of the plantations devoted all efforts in growing one product, mainly tobacco, cotton or sugar. They were grown in large scales with the slaves responsible for the tedious job of ploughing, sowing and harvesting.

Accommodation for the African slaves were wooden huts with limited furnishing. The huts were grouped together, in most cases in close proximity to the plantations. The house or domestic slaves who included cooks, maids, nannies, drivers and butlers lived in accommodations which were better than those who worked in the fields. They were built fairly close to the main planation houses.

The African slaves worked for almost 250 years in harsh conditions, under brutal supervision and needless to stress, without pay. The slightest hint of insurrection on the fields was met with brutal force often with fatal consequences.

EMANCIPATION

During the American Civil War, on September 22nd, 1862, President Abraham Lincoln issued an Executive Order, The Emancipation Proclamation or Proclamation 95. It changed the legal status under Federal Law of about four million enslaved Africans in the Secessionist Confederate States from slave to free. Abraham Lincoln, the 16th President of the United States is credited with the invaluable role he played in the Emancipation of African slaves.

According to the Proclamation, 'On the First day of January, in the year of Our Lord, one thousand eight hundred and sixty-three, all persons held as slaves within any state or designated part of a state, the people whereof shall then be in rebellion against the United States, shall be then, thenceforward, and forever free; an Executive Government of the United States including the military and navy authority thereof, will recognize and maintain the freedom of such persons and will do no act or acts to regress such persons, or any of them, in any efforts they may make for their actual freedom.'

The Confederates did not want to end slavery for economic reasons. They were also not prepared to end the Civil War. The preliminary Emancipation Proclamation signed by Abraham Lincoln, used the Civil War, fought for the preservation of the Union, in tandem to end slavery. The Confederate States were defeated and therefore Lincoln's main objective of the preservation of the Union was realized.

The turning point was when the Union forces successfully repelled the Southern States from Maryland at Antietam. In one of the bloodiest battles of the Civil War, the Battle of Antietam, as it was called. The dead and the seriously wounded were about 23,000. The success of the Union forces was the opportune time when Lincoln announced the Preliminary Emancipation Proclamation which warned the Southern States to withdraw from the war and join the Union else all the slaves in their states would be declared free. Predictably the Southern States declined to end the war and therefore on the 1st of January 1863, President Abraham Lincoln signed the Preliminary Emancipation Proclamation.

SOME FACTORS ATTRIBUTABLE TO THE EMANCIPATION PROCLAMATION

1. Abraham Lincoln believed that slavery was immoral. He initially thought that containment would eventually make the evil practice die on its own. The rebellion posed by the Confederates

however, compelled him to issue the Emancipation Proclamation.

2. The Southern slaves did not fight in the war, but the Confederates used them to provide essential labour, like digging trenches, cooking and washing for the troops. In order to thwart the practice, Lincoln declared that all slaves were free in the rebellious Southern States.

3. Republicans in the Northern States exerted pressure on the government as the war raged; to turn its attention to preserving the Union by ending slavery in the south.

4. Abraham Lincoln, in addition to suggestions or pleas to recruit the slaves into the Union army, was already of the opinion that the African slaves could be useful in the war effort. Crucially, the inclusion of the slaves outnumbered the Confederate troops, thereby helping to win the war.

5. Abraham Lincoln considered the idea that once the slaves were freed, they could be resettled close by in Central America or even back in Africa. Lincoln's conviction was that such a plan would benefit both races.

THE CONSEQUENCES OF EMANCIPATION

The Proclamation indicated that once the Southern States were defeated, slaves would be free from bondage and live as free people. The Confederates who were envisaging international support became isolated as no country was prepared to confront the

Union whose objective was freedom for the slaves. The slaves who had suffered under the Confederates in the South were given the chance to join the Union army. Black regiments were formed, and they soon showed their mettle. The bravery of the over 180,000 slaves who fought for the Union, showed that they would hold their own against any group. An example of the military prowess of the African slaves was shown in the area of modern-day Haiti and the Dominican Republic.

Toussaint L'Ouverture (1743-1803), a former slave was a French Haitian General who was best known for leading the Haitian Revolution. He first fought for the Spanish against the French, then for France against Spain and Britain. He was the leader of the only successful slave revolt in the Caribbean. He commanded an army of former African slaves and defeated the then formidable forces of the French, the English and the Spanish when those nations attempted to reimpose slavery.

Toussaint L'Ouverture ultimately took control of the whole of Hispaniola, which is the modern-day Haiti and the Dominican Republic combined. He earned the nicknames, Napoleon Noir and the Black Spartacus. In 1802, Napoleon sent his brother-in-law, General Leclerc with an expedition of 20,000 soldiers with secret orders to retake control of the colony. When France under Napoleon reconquered Haiti, L'Ouverture was tricked into a meeting and was arrested. He was sent to Fort-De-Joux in the Jura mountains of France where he faced intense interrogation. He died of pneumonia and starvation on April 7th, 1803, after being held captive for eight months.

SECOND EXAMPLE OF THE BRAVERY OF THE AFRICAN SLAVES- The Maroons were runaway African slaves who formed their own communities. They forced the British General of Jamaica, Edward Trelawny to sign a peace agreement. The agreement stipulated that the Maroons would return other runaway slaves who tried to join them.

One of the main effects of the Emancipation Proclamation was that southerners found out that they were not only fighting against the might of the federal government but also the right to own slaves. The slaves who crossed over to the Union side provided valuable information about the tactics and secret locations of the southern army.

The Emancipation Proclamation paved the way for the total freedom of slaves. The end of the Civil War in 1865 saw the ratification of the 13th Amendment by Congress and officially abolished slavery in the United States and places under her jurisdiction. Arguably this prompted the formation of the Ku Klux Klan on December 24th, 1865. It was formed by a group including veteran Generals of the Confederates. They formed the first branch as a social club in Pulaski. The organization extended into almost every Southern state by 1870.

The organization was against the Republican party's Reconstruction-Era policies, the objectives of which was establishing political and economic equality for Black Americans. The Ku Klux Klan waged an intense secret campaign of intimidation and violence against white and black Republicans alike. Congress passed legislation to curtail the KKK attacks. However, the organization realized their primary objective, the re-establishment of white supremacy. This occurred after Democratic victories in state legislatures across the South in the 1870s.

The 14th Amendment which was passed in 1868 granted citizenship to, "All persons born or naturalized in the United States." The 15th Amendment of the constitution passed in February 1870 prohibited discrimination of the right to vote based on race. Nevertheless, it was not until 1965 that a law allowing African Americans to vote and preventing racial discrimination in voting was passed. The law was signed by Lyndon Johnson on August 6th, 1965. Congress amended the act's general provision, providing a nationwide protection of voting rights.

Notable consequences of the Emancipation Proclamation included Britain and France which had already abolished slavery in their respective countries being dissuaded from recognizing the Confederacy. It was a moral obligation on their part. The focus of the Civil War no longer remained a war to preserve the Union, but an undertaking to free the slaves. The slaves seized the opportunity to fight for their cause after joining the Union army. The 13th, 14th and 15th Amendments passed respectively in 1865, 1868 and 1870 ensured freedom, citizenship, and the right to vote for the African slaves. The period from 1865 to 1877 marked the Reconstruction Era in US history. The period in which the country grappled with the complexities of reintegration into the Union, the states which had seceded and determining the status of African Americans.

The Emancipation Proclamation made President Lincoln, one of the most respected presidents in American history.

CHAPTER SIX

LYNCHING IN AMERICA

President Lincoln brought about freedom and in many cases threw a lifeline to former slaves but lynching by white mobs became a violent act meant to spread fear among blacks. It was also a form of control. Whites who were found or suspected of helping blacks were also in many cases lynched. Those among the white population who opposed lynching fell victims to this inhuman and arbitrary practice: Each lynching was a local act without court sanction or legal jurisdiction. Some whites were lynched for domestic crimes. Some families even took their children along to watch the lynching of blacks.

In the 19th Century, racial tension in the US was high especially during the aftermath of the abolition of slavery in 1865. In the Southern States especially, American whites blamed their woes on the newly freed slaves living in their areas. Between 1882 to 1968 recorded lynching in the whole of America was 4743. Blacks lynched accounted for 72.7% (3446) and whites, 1297. The total number of lynchings was arguably much higher since not all incidents were officially recorded.

The three factors behind lynching were homicide, domestic crimes and rape. Some whites felt that lynching was necessary to protect white women although the incidence of rape was not the main factor.

The end of the Civil War and the abolition of slav- ery in 1865 gave blacks the freedom they desper- ately yearned. Many whites felt that blacks were getting away with too much freedom and therefore they needed to be controlled. Between 1882 and 1968, Mississippi recorded the highest lynching of 581; Georgia and Texas were second and third respectively with 531 and 493. The Southern States were responsible for 79% of the lynching.

In the west where blacks were the victims of lynching, the factors were either homicide or theft of cattle. Not all the states practised lynching. Alaska, Rhode Island, New Hampshire, Massachusetts, and Connecticut were the few states which did not practise lynching between 1882 to 1968. States like Arizona, Idaho, Maine, Nevada, South Dakota, Vermont, and Wisconsin practised lynching, but there was no record of blacks being lynched.

In the Western States, California, Colorado, Indiana, Iowa, Kansas, Michigan, Minnesota, Montana,

Nebraska, New Mexico, North Dakota, Oregon, Utah, Washington, and Wyoming; lynched more whites than blacks for political reasons.

Among the lynching investigated by the NAACP (National Association for the Advancement of Coloured People), was the May 1918 lynching of one Mary Turner. An abusive plantation owner, Hampton Smith was shot and killed. Mary denied that her husband was involved in Hampton Smith's killing and vehemently spoke against her husband's murder. She threatened to have members of the mob arrested. On that fateful day-May 19th, 1918, a mob of several hundred brought the pregnant Mary Turner to Folsam Bridge which separates Brookes and Lowndes counties in Georgia.

The mob tied her ankles, hung her upside down from a tree, doused her in gasoline and motor oil and set her alight. Mary Turner was still alive when a member of the mob slit her abdomen open with a knife. The unborn baby was stomped and crushed as it fell to the ground. Mary's body was then riddled with hundreds of bullets.

Secondly in the same month of May 1918, in Tennessee an investigation carried out by Walter White, Assistant Secretary for the NAACP, involved a reasonably well to do negro, Jesse McIlherron. He bitterly resented the insults by white men. He was always armed and was reported to be teared even by the sheriff. On February 8th, he had a dispute with three young white men who insulted him. There were threats which led to McIlherron firing six shots, killing two of the men.

He sought sanctuary in the home of a negro clergyman who helped him escape. The clergyman was shot and killed. When McIlherron was captured, a throng of men, women and children assembled in the town of Estill Springs. He was chained to a hickory tree while the masses jeered and howled. A fire was set a few feet away. Bars of iron were heated, and the mob put them close to him, initially without touching him. The torturing intensified as McIlheron grabbed one bar which was jerked from his grasp. Consequently, the inside of his hand was prised out. The torturing lasted twenty minutes.

During the torture with his flesh slowly roasting, McIlherron somehow held his nerve and cursed those who were burning him alive. Until his last breath he mocked his tormentors. Lynching of blacks was at its zenith after the Civil War and during the Era of Reconstruction. Lynching declined in the 1930s. The Reconstruction Era 1865 to 1877 was the period when attempts were made to redress the iniquities of slavery and the associated political, social and economic legacy. Consideration also turned to the problems which arose from the read-mission to the Union of the eleven states which had seceded at the outbreak of war.

The Original Economic Migrant

His country was already wealthy,
but sought expansion and international dominance.
He needed raw materials for factories:
in earnest he scrambled for Africa.

He fought the natives and colonised countries:
and resisted like-minded colonialists.
He coerced natives to learn his language
and adopt some of his civilised ways.

Under the pretext of civilising the natives
the quest for international influence prevailed.
He shipped raw materials in quantities:
in return manufactured goods for the ruled.

He did some good for the natives
but relentless in looking after himself.
He introduced Christianity to them
to absolve him from the bad done.

The colonies fought and gained independence
but at his behest are their economies,
the star of Africa, many other treasures:
all seemingly trapped in permanence.

CHAPTER SEVEN

FREED SLAVES AND LAND OWNERSHIP

The abolition of slavery brought into reality the forlorn hope of the former African slaves. However new challenges made life an uphill task for the freed slaves after the Civil War. They struggled to achieve what independence meant. However, with invaluable assistance from Congressman Thaddeus Stevens and others in the Reconstruction Movement, many became educated and even held political positions.

More than four million slaves were freed after the Civil War. Owning a land was crucial in the pursuit of economic freedom and (total) independence. Congressman Stevens's proposal of giving each freed slave, "Forty acres of land and a mule, "was to ensure survival and independence. It was evident according to others that the former slaves might have to fight for their freedom again if they were not given land.

Stevens suggested that the only remedy was to "make them independent of their old masters, so they may not be compelled to work for them on unfair terms."

Stevens and his associates were however in the minority. The Freedmen's Bureau even compelled former slaves to work for meagre wages on plantations owned by white southerners. In the south, despite the Proclamation of Emancipation, many southerners endeavoured to prevent the former slaves from gaining their independence. Consequently, many freed slaves continued to work on plantations. In 1879, some freed slaves realized their dream by being able to purchase land and gain true independence.

According to Wikipedia, by 1910 records show that more Black Americans owned land than ever before in the history of the United States. Over 14 million acres of land were owned by about 210,000 Black Americans.

Historians therefore refer to that period as the height of black land ownership. Since then, however black land ownership has steadily declined.

Some of the restrictions in the lives of freed slaves were in the process of owning and keeping land. Common factors attributable to land loss among freed slaves and their descendants were notably,

1. Lack of necessary paperwork and document; the inability to produce these items resulted in unequal access to programs and services which would have helped them with both obtaining land and ensuring that it remained within the family.

2   Countless newly freed slaves did not have the necessary document such as birth certificates which would have proven their identity. The freed slaves were able to obtain documentation and were required to register for citizenship. However, this documentation was not regarded by the authori-

ties as proof of identity, therefore many slaves were given the same last names of their masters.

3. Another factor was that many freed slaves and their earlier descendants scarcely had access to legal services. It meant that they could not have written wills which would have effectively passed down landownership and the proper titles. If land was not specifically passed on to a certain person or group of people, the property would go to all the next heirs. Therefore, deceit and the sale of land without the knowledge of others were inevitable.

4. The absence or relevant documentation to under-score the identity of freed slaves was deviously used by some whites to impede them from land acquisition.

In 1862, Congress passed the Morill Act of 1862. It was also referred to as the Land Act, meant to offer land grants to whites -only colleges which held programs in agricultural and mechanical courses. In addition, Congress also passed The Homestead Act of 1862 which legalized land in the west. The extra benefit of legalization was the offer of subsidies to facilitate the acquisition of the land. These benefits were however reserved for only whites. Black Americans were not able to benefit from the rights to landownership nor government support.

When slavery was abolished in 1865, Black Americans began to demand land. This led to Field Order 15, issued through what was dubbed 'Savannah Colloquy.' The order gave approximately 400,000 acres of land which lay on the coastline of Georgia and South Carolina to about 40,000 freed slaves. In addition, mules which were used during the war effort but then idle were offered to Black Americans to use in farming. This was known as "40 acres and a mule."

The golden offer to stave off starvation and usher in economic independence was dashed when white rice plantation owners claimed ownership of the land. When Abraham Lincoln was assassinated, in April 1865, his successor Vice President Andrew Johnson over-turned the Special Field Order 15. The new Presidential Order stipulated that black landowners return their land to the white rice plantation farmers. This was strongly opposed by the black owners. The land went back to Confederate planters who were the previous owners.

In 1866, Congress passed the Homestead Act of 1866. The act was meant to make land available in states like Alabama, Arkansas, Florida, Louisiana, Texas and Mississippi for all Americans including blacks. The thrust of this act was to give blacks the opportunity to buy land in these states. Black Americans duly took advantage.

This positive factor was however disappointingly tem-pered by the steep decline in social and political for-tunes for blacks, especially in the Southern States. In 1867, The Federation of Southern Cooperatives was created to offer financial assistance to black farmers to promote the quest for landownership and improve their agricultural practices. In 1890, a second Morill Act was passed giving blacks grants to colleges to partic-ipate in art and agricultural courses. This gave rise to the formation of the first Cooperative Union in Arkansas in the United States in order for Black Americans fight for and protect their rights.

CHAPTER EIGHT

SEGREGATION AND DESEGREGATION

Racial segregation in the United States focused on the separation of the races in the usage of facilities, services and opportunities such as education, housing, medical care, employment and transportation. The term therefore referred to the legally (including social interaction) enforced separation of African Americans and European Americans. The main purpose besides preventing contact between the races was to put white people above blacks.

The Jim Crow laws created separate facilities in the whole of the Southern States for blacks and whites. Segregation by law was called De Jure Segregation. The other type of segregation was called De Facto Segregation; or segregation by the fact that it existed. Jim Crow was a fictional theatre character performed by white actor Thomas Dartmouth Rice ('Jump Jim Crow,'). It was a racist depiction of African Americans and their culture. Thomas Rice based the character on a folk trickster named Jim Crow who had long been popular among the African slaves. He performed his song and dance shows with his face painted black.

Starting from 1832, it portrayed the contemporary ideas of culture held by whites about blacks. Jim Crow a fictional character died out but in the late 19th Century, the term represented a cluster of anti-black laws. In their simplest terms, the laws used to prevent close contact between whites and blacks after the end of the Civil War. Those who broke the laws were punished- fines and prison terms were imposed. What also emanated from the laws was that some whites arbitrarily took the 'laws' into their own hands and subjected blacks to untold brutal punishment. Some blacks also fell victim to lynching.

The Jim Clow laws began in 1877 when the Supreme Court ruled that states could not prevent segregation on common modes of transportation such as trains, street cars and river boats. The specific parts of the Civil Rights Act 1875 were changed by the Supreme Court in 1883 to underscore a "separate but equal" plan. Consequently, states passed laws laying down the requirements for "separate but equal" accommodations for blacks on public modes of transportation. Blacks also had separate schools, churches, cemeteries, ward of conveniences and prisons. However, facilities for blacks were of a lower standard compared to whites.

During the Second World War, segregation remained in the military. Blacks were engaged in less important positions like grave digging and cooking. They were served their meals in separate queues from the white servicemen. Initially blacks were not allowed to participate in combat.

However, as the war progressed, that changed and the increasing numbers who were placed in front-line positions acquitted themselves to the admiration of the white military hegemony.

The aftermath of the Second World War brought American segregation policies under intense scrutiny. Having created a committee to investigate the practice, President Harry Truman issued an Executive Order in 1948 eliminating racial discrimination in all the three branches of the military.

The ensuing years unfolded a series of Supreme Court victories for Civil Rights. Black people broke down racial barriers and with renewed confidence successfully challenged segregation. The sustained collective effort by the blacks, assisted by the conscientious members in white American society at large culminated in the passing of the Civil Rights Act in 1964, which effectively abolished the Jim Crow laws. The law prohibited discrimination in any type of public accommodation. The following year- 1965, ushered in the Voting Rights Act which protected black people's right to vote by barring discriminatory voting laws.

GERMAN PRISONERS OF WAR AND SEGREGATION IN AMERICA-In the Times Magazine 25.07.20 issue, in a feature on Susan Rice, National Security Adviser under President Obama, her father, Emmett Rice was reported to have served in the Second World War in the army Air Force at Tuskegee, Alabama. Mr. Rice, an economist was in the renowned First Black Pilot Unit. When he was serving at a base in Kentucky, he was denied access to the white officers' mess. It was reported in the magazine, "he burnt with indignation after seeing white German prisoners of war eating in restaurants where black Americans wearing the uniform of their country were banned."

DESEGREGATION

Desegregation is the process of ending the separation of two groups, notably in the United States, it refers to race. Desegregation was a cherished objective of the Civil Rights Movement. Prior to and after the Supreme Court's decision in Brown V Board of Education. The movement focused in particular the desegregation of the school system and the military where blacks were admirably making their mark. Invariably, racial integration in American society at large was an associated goal.

In Swann V Charlotte-Mecklenburg Board of Education (1971), the Supreme Court ruled unanimously that forced-busing of students might be ordered to achieve racial desegregation. However, over time, court-enforced school desegregation, waned.

A significant decline in manufacturing in the Northern Cities, a shift of jobs to the suburbs, the South and even abroad, led to an increase in migration of all races to the suburbs. In addition, there was a major shift in population from the North to the Southwest, Pacific Northwest and the South. Those left behind in the Northern and Midwestern Cities were very poor blacks and other minorities.

A report by Jonathan Kozol stated that in the early 21st Century, schools in the United States had become as segregated as they were in the late 1960s. The Civil Rights project confirmed that desegregation of US public schools peaked in 1988. The year 2005 saw the proportion of black students at majority-white schools at a lower level than any year since 1968.

Court-enforced desegregation was considered by some critics as unnecessary or self-defeating. The continued movement of many middle class and wealthy whites from the cities to the suburbs in the 1970s were attributable by first, the need to avoid certain desegregated school systems and secondly, the suburbanization caused by the movement of jobs to the suburbs. Federal support for the expansion of highways and the changes in the economy, were related factors.

In Louisiana it was reported that some white parents were apprehensive to drop their children off because of mobs around segregated schools. The onus therefore fell on black students to change the historic culture of schools. Sociologist David J. Armor in his 1995 book, 'Forced Justice: School Desegregation and The Law,' stated that the efforts to change the racial composition of schools had not contributed substantially to the academic achievement of minorities. Carl L. Bankston and Stephen J. Caldas, in their respective books, 'A Troubled Dream: 'The Promise and Failure of School Desegregation in Louisiana (2002) and 'Forced To Fail: The Paradox of School Desegregation (2005) contended that continuing racial inequality in the larger American society had foiled attempts to force schools to desegregate. They maintained that racial inequality which had resulted in popular associations between school achievement levels of American schools were generally determined by class and racial composition. This resulted in even parents without racial prejudice seeking middle class or better residential neighbourhoods with the best schools for their children.

THE MILITARY- during the American Civil War, blacks enlisted in large numbers. They were mostly enslaved blacks from the South. There were also Northern blacks in the Union army and the navy. In segregated units known as the United States Coloured troops, under the command of white officers. About 18,000 blacks also joined the Union many as sailors. The Union army numbered between 2.5m and 2.75m. Casualties on both the Confederate and Union sides during the war was estimated at 620,000.

In 1776-1777, twelve black American marines served in the American Revolutionary War. However, from 1798-1942, the USMC (United States Marine Corp) adopted a racial discriminatory policy by depriving African Americans the opportunity to serve as marines. Recruitment therefore for 140 years relied primarily on European Americans, Hispanic Americans and a few Asian Americans. In June 1942, the exclusion came to an end and African Americans were finally recruited.

In 1947, one Philip Randolph, a labour movement leader, supported by fellow black campaigners formed a committee against Jim Crow in the military service and training. It was later renamed, The League for Non-Violent Civil Disobedience Against Military Segregation.

In June 1948, black leaders successfully convinced President Harry Truman to confront discrimination in the armed forces. Among many important points advanced was that African Americans had served in the military since the forming of the United States in 1776. President Truman signed Executive Order 9981, which abolished racial discrimination, "On the basis of race, colour, religion or national origin," in the United States forces. The Executive Order led to the end of segregation in the services during the Korean War (1950-1953).

The desegregation of the US Armed Forces was a major moral boosting victory for Civil Rights. A number of whites in the military resisted the order and racism continued in the armed forces but Executive Order 9981 was the first major blow to dislodge segregation. Predictably African American activists sensed that change was within reach.

CHAPTER NINE

CIVIL RIGHTS ACTS 1866, 1875, 1957 AND 1964: AND VOTING RIGHTS ACT 1965

The appropriate change came in the form of a number of Civil Rights' legislature. The first was the Civil Rights Act 1866 (April 9th), coming after the Abolition of Slavery in 1865, was the first US Federal law to define citizenship and confirm that all citizens are equally protected by the law. It was mainly intended to protect the civil rights of persons of African descent born or brought to the United States.

The Civil Rights Act of 1875 was a US Federal law enacted during the Post-Civil War Reconstruction Era which guaranteed African Americans equal access to public accommodations and public transportation. Part of the law stated, "All persons within the jurisdiction of the US shall be entitled to the full and equal enjoyment of the accommodations, advantages, facilities, and privileges of inns, public conveyances on land or water, theatres and other places of public amusement; subject only to the limitations established by law, and applicable alike to citizens of every race condition of servitude. The act was originally drafted by Senator Charles Sumner in 1870; but was not passed until shortly after his death in 1875. The law was not effectively enforced, partly because President Grant had favoured different measures to help him sup- press election-related violence against blacks and Republicans in the South.

The Civil Rights Act of 1957 was the first Federal Civil Rights legislation passed by the US Congress since the Civil Rights Act of 1875. The Bill was passed by 85th US Congress and signed into law by President Dwight Eisenhower on September 9th, 1957. The final vote in the House of Representatives was 286-126, in the House Republican Conference 167-19 and in the House Democratic Caucus 119-107, with 22 members voting present or abstaining. In the Senate on the final date, the vote was 72-18, in the Senate Conference 43-0 and in the Senate Democratic Caucus 29- 18, with 5 members voting present or abstaining.

The Civil Rights Act of 1964, is the most prominent-modern Civil Rights legislation of the United States since the Reconstruction Era 1865-1877. It is a comprehen- sive legislation which is intended to end discrimination based on colour, religion or national origin, in public establishments which have a connection to interstate commerce or is supported by the state.

The Act was proposed by President J.F. Kennedy. It survived a strong opposition from Southern members of Congress and was eventually signed by President Kennedy's successor, Lyndon B. Johnson. President Kennedy was assassinated on November 22nd, 1963, in Dallas. Congress later expanded the act and passed additional civil rights legislation notably the Voting Rights Act 1965.

The Civil Rights Act of 1964 also created an Equal Employment Opportunity Commission with the authority to file lawsuits on behalf of aggrieved workers.

PRESIDENT JOHN F. KENNEDY- There were countless Americans, black and white involved in the Civil Rights Movement. First among the many prominent ones was President John F. Kennedy. On June 11th, 1963, the United States President gave his Civil Rights address calling for the legislation which later became the Civil Rights Act of 1964. The speech was broadcast on both TV and radio. He addressed civil rights as a moral issue: He underscored the disadvantages faced by African Americans.

The speech came not long after the first two African Americans were about to start their university education at the University of Alabama. Prior to that, the students, Vivien Malone and James Hood were denied entry by the then Governor, George Wallace. The President ordered the deployment of the National Guard troops who protected the students as they entered the university.

He called on Americans to consider the struggle for racial equality as an important part of the national interest. "Those who do nothing are inviting shame as well as reality." He went on and implored Americans of all backgrounds to participate in the kind of civic activism which highlights the difficult work of democracy. He argued, "A great change is at hand and our task; our obligation, is to make that revolution, that change, peaceful and constructive for all."

He also reminded Americans, "One hundred years have passed since President Lincoln freed the slaves, yet their heirs, their grandsons, are not fully free. They are not yet freed from the bonds of injustice. They are not yet freed from social and economic oppression. And this nation, for all its hopes and all its boasts, will not be fully free until all its citizens are free."

He also stated, "We preach freedom around the world, and we mean it, and we cherish our freedom here at home, but are we to say to the world, and much more importantly, to each other that this is the land of the free, except for the negroes; that we have no second-class citizens except negroes; that we have no class or caste system, no ghettoes, no master race except with respect of negroes?"

Another part of President Kennedy's speech was, "This our country. It has become one country because all of us and all the people who came here had an equal chance to develop their talents. We cannot say to ten percent of the population that you can't have that right; that your children cannot have the chance to develop whatever talents they have; that the only way that they are going to get their rights is to go in the street and demonstrate. I think we owe them, and we owe ourselves a better country than that. Therefore, I am asking for your help in making it easier for us to move ahead and to provide the kind of equality of treatment which we would want ourselves: To get a chance for every child to be educated to the limit of their talents."

Another poignant part of the speech was, "We have a right to expect that the negro community will be responsible, will uphold the law, but they have a right to expect that the law will be fair, that the Constitution will be colour blind as Justice Halan said at the turn of the century."

In the whole speech, President John F. Kennedy's empathy and humanity resonated. He promised and it was evident that he sought to pass comprehensive Civil Rights legislation to dislodge segregation at a quicker pace.

DR MARTIN LUTHER KING JNR- President John F. Kennedy and Dr Martin Luther King were not reported to be close allies, but they strongly shared a common moral cause- Civil Rights. It was reported that during the early stages of his administration, President Kennedy did not want to be seen as too eager to press for such initiatives as equal housing and voting protection for minorities; even though he saw these changes as inevitable.

This 'reluctant hesitation' on the part of President Kennedy, in my opinion was borne by pressure from aides, because in October 1960, prior to the presidential election, Senator Kennedy rang Mrs. Coretta King and sympathized with her over her husband's imprisonment. Dr King was in jail because of peaceful demonstration and unrelated traffic charges. Many of Senator Kennedy's aides were reported to be opposed to the call as they considered that it could cost them votes in the South.

Dr King was released from jail not long after that call. He admitted, "Now it is true that Senator Kennedy did take a specific step," in his release. The positive move by the future president motivated African Americans. Many historians stated that it helped direct some crucial votes in the Northern States from Richard Nixon to Senator Kennedy in the narrow victory.

The positive contents of President Kennedy's June 11th, 1963, Civil Rights speech indicate that for political reasons advocated by some of his aides, he would not have been 'reluctantly hesitant' in pushing fairly quickly for equal housing and voting protection for minorities.

Dr Martin Luther King born in January 1929, was a Baptist Minister, the spokesperson, and the leading Civil Rights activist from 1955 until his assassination by a white American, James Earl Ray in 1968. He came to prominence in 1955 when he led the 1955 Montgomery Bus Boycott. He later became the First President of the Southern Christian Leadership Conference (SCLC). He advocated non-violence and civil disobedience in achieving some of the key victories in the Civil Rights Movement.

Boosted by his Christian beliefs, he was also inspired by the non-violent activism of the Indian leader, Mahatma Gandhi. Dr King was quoted, "Hate is too much a burden to bear."

In 1962, he was unsuccessful in the struggle against segregation in Albany, Georgia. He helped organize the non-violent protests in Birmingham, Alabama in 1963. In the same year, he led the March on Washington, where he delivered the sterling and famous, "I Have A Dream,' speech. In 1964, he won the Nobel Peace Prize for combating racial inequality through non-violent resistance.

In the years preceding his assassination, he tackled other important factors like poverty, capitalism, and the Vietnam War. He became a target for the FBI (Federal Bureau of Investigation) director, L. Edgar Hoover who considered him a radical. FBI agents investigated him for possible Communist alliances, recorded his extra marital liaisons and informed government officials. In 1964, the FBI agents deviously sent Dr King a threatening anonymous letter. He interpreted that as an attempt to make him commit suicide.

Dr King's next project was a national occupation of Washington D.C to be dubbed, 'Poor People's Campaign.' Sadly, it did not materialize as he was assassinated on April 4th,1968 in Memphis, Tennessee. Allegations were rife that his assassin, James Earl Ray, the convicted killer, acted with the assistance of government agents. His death triggered widespread riots in many American cities.

Dr Martin Luther King Jnr was posthumously awarded the Presidential Medal of Freedom and Congressional

Gold Medal. 'Dr Martin Luther King Jnr Day, a national holiday was enacted at the Federal level by legislation signed by President Ronald Reagan in 1986. Hundreds of streets across the US have been renamed in Dr King's honour. The Martin Luther King Jnr Memorial on the National Mall in Washington D.C. was dedicated in 2011.

ROSA PARKS- Rosa Parks who was regarded as the Mother of Civil Rights and Dr Martin Luther King were inspirational leaders who contributed invaluably to the cause of the Civil Rights movement. In 1955, the defiance of Rosa Parks leading to the famous Montgomery Bus Boycott launched the emergence of 26-year-old Dr King in the Civil Rights and in general the American political scene, according to popular opinion.

Rosa Parks, like countless African Americans and indeed white Americans, was deeply disturbed by the murder of Emmett Till, a 14-year-old black teenager. He was accused of flirting with a white woman, whose husband was one of the white men accused of his murder. None of the accused was found guilty. Coincidentally Till's murder happened just four days before Rosa Park's defiance on the bus and her arrest.

Rosa Park was born on February 1913 and died on October 25th, 2005, at the age of 92. She received national recognition because of her refusal on December 1st, 1955, to give her seat in the 'coloured Section' to a white passenger who could not get a seat in the all-white section. This, as already stated led to the Montgomery Bus Boycott in 1955. The United States Congress called her the 'First Lady of Civil Rights' and 'The Mother of the Freedom Movement.'

She was arrested for her "disobedience;" fired from her job as a seamstress at a local departmental store and received death threats for years. She became an international figure of resistance to racial segregation. She organized and teamed up with Civil Rights leaders including Edgar Nixon, President of the local NAACP (National Association of Advancement of Coloured People) and Dr King who had just become the new Baptist Minister of Montgomery in 1955.

Rosa Parks recalled going to elementary school in Pine Level where school buses took white students to their new school and black students had to walk to theirs. She stated, "I'd see the bus pass every day but to me, that was a way of life. We had no choice but to accept what was the custom. The bus was among the first ways I realized there was a black world and a white world."

CLAUDETTE COLVIN- One of the unsung heroines of the American Civil Rights movement is Claudette Colvin now 81 years old. Nine months before Rosa Park's celebrated stance, 15 years old Claudette refused to give up her seat for a white passenger on a crowded segregated bus.

Claudette, born in Montgomery, Alabama is rightly described as a pioneer of civil rights. In a CNN interview on February 22nd, 2021, the retired nurse spoke about not being afraid taking the courageous stance at just 15 years old. She however conceded that she got scared when thrown into jail.

The incident happened on March 2nd, 1955. When her case was heard at the Montgomery Circuit Court on May 6th, 1955, the charges- disturbing the peace and violating the segregation laws were dropped. However, a conviction for assaulting a police officer was upheld.

In May 2018 Congressman Joe Crowley honoured Claudette Colvin for her lifetime commitment to public service with a Congressional Certificate and an American flag. She was awarded the MLK JR. Medal of Freedom. She was the subject of a National Book Award novel, "Claudette Colvin: Twice Toward Justice." In Montgomery, March 2nd, is marked as 'Claudette Colvin Day,'

JOHN LEWIS- John Lewis was quoted, "Rosa Parks inspired me to find a way to get in the way, to get in trouble good trouble, necessary trouble." During the intense struggle of the Civil Rights Movement, John Lewis served as chairman of the Students' Non-violent Coordinating Committee and worked with Rosa Parks.

John Lewis, the African American Democratic Congressman, died at 80 years old on July 17th, 2020, from pancreatic cancer. He was the last - surviving leading figures of the Civil Rights movement called, "The Big Six." The rest were Dr King, Philip Randolph, Roy Wilkins, Whitney Young and James Farmer. John Lewis at 23, joined Dr King and the rest in leading the 1963 'March on Washington for Jobs and Freedom.' The young activist spoke to the crowd before Dr King delivered the poignant and all- powerful, 'I Have a Dream,' speech.

In 1965, at 25, he was one of the main activists who led 600 peaceful protesters across the Esward Pettus Bridge in Selma Alabama. It was a 54- mile march to the state capital, for equal voting rights for African Americans.

The Governor of Alabama, George Wallace, who in his inauguration speech advocated, "Segregation forever," vowed "I'm not gonna have a bunch of n***ers walking along a highway in this state as long as I'm Governor."

The historic confrontation saw burly state troopers with gas masks supported by a group of white armed men and urged on by a crowd of white people waving the Confederate flags. When the protesters refused an order to disperse; but kneeling to pray, the troop- ers attacked firing rounds of tear gas and using their deadly batons. John Lewis with tear gas in his eyes and choking was clubbed viciously on the head and suffered a fractured skull and concussion. Other protesters were also badly beaten up and trampled on by police horses. In all, 17 protesters were admitted into hospital.

Despite his horrific injuries, John Lewis refused to go to hospital; rather he joined other demonstrators at a church and gave a speech with his hair and clothes stained in blood. He criticized the apparent indifference of the Federal Government in Washington. John later relented and was admitted into hospital for two days. The state-sponsored crack down watched by millions on TV was so brutal that public opinion accelerated the passage of the Federal Voting Rights Act that year (1965).

John Lewis was a key figure in the establishment of the Student Non- Violent Coordinating Committee (SNCC). He later served as his chairman from 1963-1966.

He was elected to the House of Representatives for Georgia's Congressional District in 1987, served 33 years until his death in July 2020. He revealed that besides Rosa Park, Dr King's activism during the Montgomery Bus Boycott, inspired him. John Lewis was also inspired by Dr King's pragmatism in the application of biblical values to the lives of African Americans in the South. He was deeply affected by the assassination of his mentor in 1968.

In Nashville John Lewis organized student sit-in demonstrations at segregated lunch counters in departmental stores. He was once beaten up by a group of young white men who cheered when the police arrived and arrested him for "Disorderly conduct." Referring to his first arrest as a 'baptism,' John later wrote, "Now I had crossed over, I had stepped through the door into total, unquestioning commitments." He was arrested 45 times during his lifetime for non-violent protests.

John Lewis was one of the original 13 'Freedom Riders,' a group set up by the Congress of Racial Equality (CORE). Interstate bus travel regulated by Federal Law; prohibited segregation. The sole objective of CORE was to enforce this Federal law when travelling through the Southern States in 1961. The whole 'Freedom Riding Group was attacked in Anniston, Alabama. Buses were attacked and even one was firebombed. In a bid to stop the violence, James Farmer, the leader of CORE tried to end the rides. However, Lewis and colleagues from Nashville including Diane Nash and Marion Barry took over. Lewis eventually spent 40 days in jail. Robert Kennedy, the then Attorney General appealed for a "cooling off," period and an end to these rides.

During the 2008 President Obama inauguration, he met the police chief of Rock Hill; and told the New Yorker, "Imagine that, I was beaten near to death at the Rock

Hill Greyhound Bus Terminal during the 'Freedom Rides' in 1961. Now the police chief is black." He was arrested five times in Washington as a Congressman, twice outside the South African Embassy protesting against apartheid, twice outside the Sudanese Embassy protesting against the genocide in Darfur and at the age of 73, at a rally for Immigration Reform. In 2016, he was a key figure at a sit-in at the House of Representatives to demand changes to gun laws. John Lewis voted against the first Iraq War and boycotted the inauguration of George W. Bush. He regarded his election illegitimate: As he did of President Trump's inauguration in 2016 because of Russia meddling.

He stated after the death of George Floyd that the 'Black Lives Matter Movement,' gave him hope, He added, "It was very moving to see hundreds of thousands of people from all over America and around the world take to the streets to speak out to get into what I call 'good trouble,' "He told CBS (Columbia Broadcasting System) in June 2020, "This feels and looks different. It is so much more massive and all-inclusive, there will be no turning back."

John Lewis always urged other activists to make, "Good trouble in pursuit of social justice. He was regarded as a 'giant' in the Civil Rights Movement. He was well respected within both Democratic and Republican parties: And American society at large. Michael Rubio, the Republican Senator described him as, "A historic American hero." In 2007, he was awarded the Dole Leadership prize from the Robert J. Dole Institute of politics at the University of Kansas. He was awarded the Presidential Medal Of Freedom on February 16th, 2011, by President Barack Obama.

John Lewis said that after the new President took the oath of office, Obama signed a piece of paper for Lewis with the writing, "Because of you John." Barack Obama.

PRESIDENT WOODROW WILSON-President Woodrow Wilson was born on December 28th, 1856 and died on February 3rd, 1924. He was a Democrat, the 28th President of the United States. Abraham Lincoln, a Republican was the 16th President while John Kennedy, a Democrat, was the 35th to occupy the highest office of the land.

Both Lincoln and Kennedy demonstrated the utmost empathy and compassion to the black cause.

The presidency of Woodrow Wilson was from 1913-1921. His record on race relations, as far as African Americans are concerned was disappointingly woeful. Historians assert that he promoted discriminatory job recruitment policies and racial segregation. During his tenure in office, he segregated the American Civil Service after it had been integrated for decades. Wilson allowed Jim Crow laws to be implemented in Washington D.C. enabling the Secretary of the Treasury and the Paymaster General to segregate their departments. During his first term in office, the House passed a law-making racial intermarriage a felony in the District of Columbia. It was a notable example of Wilson's legacy which African Americans feared; after voting for him in 1912.

In a biography by John Milton Cooper Jnr, the biographer stated about Wilson, "Violence, lynching and virulent racism grieved him." On lynching he, "deplored the passion, disorder, and the sullied international image of white Americans rather than injury, horror and death of black Americans." He was even reported to have been, "appalled that the French army allowed blacks to serve next to whites and worried about Communism creeping into the US among black veterans returning from World War One."

An Executive Order signed on July 26th, 1948, prohibited discrimination against military personnel because of race, colour, religion or national origin. This was a situation which the white military hegemony had tried to address in 1943 after sustained black protests.

In 2013, another biography on Wilson this time by Scott Berg revealed, "For all his talk of even-handedness, Wilson did not consider the races fundamentally, and he had no intention of equalizing them under the law." Berg narrated a confrontation by an African American leader called, William Monroe Trotter, who stated after meeting the president, "Only two years ago, you were heralded as perhaps the second Lincoln, and now African American leaders who supported you are hounded as false leaders and traitors to the race. What a change segregation has wrought." Trotter also implied that blacks would defect from the Democratic Party. Wilson was reported to have lost his temper and stated, "Your tone sir, offends me. You have spoiled the whole cause for which you came."

William Trotter (1872- 1934) was the editor of the Boston Guardian which he founded in 1901. He had congratulated the victorious Woodrow Wilson immediately after the New Jersey Gubertorial (Governorship) election in 1910. Trotter's endorsement of the Democrat was a departure from the traditional support for Republican candidates. Christine Lunardin, a doctoral candidate in the Department of History, Princeton University, stated, "Two generations of neglect on the part of the Republican Party prompted many of the more aggressive and vocal blacks to express their discontent with politicians willing to maintain the status quo,"

The progressive brand of politics which appeared to offer "the alternative which blacks sought, address- ing it as a spectrum of issues ranging from social welfare programs to tariff and monetary reforms." Despite his Southern background, Wilson appeared to espouse real promise by virtue of his long association with Princeton, "first as a Professor of Jurisprudence and Political Economy; and then as President of the University." Additionally, his success or period as a progressive Governor was the lure for blacks. It underscored the feeling that he was a judicious and objective administrator irrespective of the fact that none of the legislation enacted in New Jersey between 1911 and 1913, concerned problems affecting blacks.

During the Presidential campaign, Wilson made an appeal for black votes, promising fair and equal treatment for all. Trotter and other leaders of the black population took the bait and offered unflinching support for Woodrow Wilson. However, amid intensification in the Federal bureaucracy, Trotter who was reported to be, "increasingly disturbed, yet still optimistic", sought and was granted two personal meetings with Wilson." The meeting took place in November 1913 and November 1914. The transcripts of the meetings revealed and confirmed, "the difficulties encountered by blacks in their dealings with the Wilson administration; and Wilson himself, as well as the complexities surrounding and influencing events," Christine Lunardini stated.

DURING THE MEETING- TROTTER— "Mr. President, we are here to renew and protest against the segregation of coloured employees in the departments of our national government. We (had) appealed to you to undo this race segregation in accord with your duty as President and with your pre-election pledges to coloured American voters. We stated that such segregation was a public humiliation and degradation, and entirely unmerited and far-reaching in its injurious effects." President Wilson's - "The white people of the country as well as I, wish to see the coloured people progress and admire the progress they have already made, and want to see them continue on independent lines. There is however a great prejudice against coloured people.

It will take one hundred years to eradicate this prejudice, and we must deal with it as practical men. Segregation is not humiliating but a benefit, and ought to be regarded by you gentlemen. If your organization goes out and tells the coloured people of the country that it is a humiliation, they will so regard it. But if you do not tell them so, and regard it rather as a benefit, they will regard it the same. The only harm that will come will be if you cause them to think it as a humiliation."

WILLIAM TROTTER COUNTERED-" It is not in accord with the known facts to claim that segregation started because of race friction of white and coloured (Federal) clerks. The indisputable fact of the situation will not permit of the claim that the segregation is due to the friction. It is untenable in view of the established facts, to maintain that the segregation is simply to avoid race friction, for simple reason that for fifty years white and coloured clerks have been working together in peace and harmony and friendliness, doing so even through two (President Glover Cleveland) Democratic administrations. Soon after your inauguration began, segregation was drastically introduced in the Treasury and the Postal Departments by your appointees."

PRESIDENT WOODROW WILSON- "If this organization is ever to have another hearing before me, it must have another spokesman. Your manner offends me...your tone, with its background of passions."

WILLIAM TROTTER RETORTED- "But I have no passion in me, Mr. President, you are entirely mistaken, you misinterpret my earnestness for passion."

The President was offended by Trotter's "manner and tone," during their meeting. He therefore banned the spokesperson of the African American delegation from the White House for the remainder of his term in office.

In a leading article, 'A Complex President,' on June 26th, 2020, The Times newspaper reported, "Wilson's name is going to be removed from the Princeton School of Public Policy because of his unconstructive Southern views on segregation and because although he was sympathetic to Catholic and Jewish entry, Wilson acted to bar black students from Princeton." Wilson was then President of Princeton before he became the 28th President of America.

There were many factors to ameliorate the conditions of the freed African after the 13th Amendment. Two key factors were the chance to vote and receive education. The 14th Amendment granted citizenship while the 15th Amendment in 1870, "Declares that the right to vote cannot be denied to any citizen of the United States because of race, colour or previous condition of servitude." In 1965, ninety-five years after the 15th Amendment, the Voting Rights Act (1965) was signed by Democratic President Lyndon B. Johnson, "to overcome legal barriers at the state and local areas that prevented African Americans from exercising their right to vote as guaranteed under the 15th Amendment to the US constitution." The Voting Rights Act is considered one of the most far-reaching pieces of Civil Rights legislation in the United States.

Despite almost a century after the 15th Amendment, in some areas African Americans were still denied, through a number of rules or deceptions concerning the right to vote. A typical ridiculous trick was to ask an African American prospective voter to state the exact number of jellybeans in a jar before being allowed   to vote. Of course, from all accounts not one African American was known to have succeeded. The right to vote was therefore deviously denied millions of African Americans.

CHAPTER TEN

JUNETEENTH ALSO KNOWN AS EMANCIPATION DAY

Juneteenth is short for June Nineteenth. It marks the day- June 19th, 1865- when Federal troops arrived in Galveston, Texas to take control of the state and ensuring all African slaves were freed. The troops' intervention happened two-and-a-half years after the signing of the Emancipation Proclamation. This was first celebrated as Freedom Day for formerly enslaved Africans. It is now celebrated annually throughout the United States. Celebrations, initially in 1866 involved the churches. It gathered momentum, spread to the South and became commercialized in the 1920s and 1930s, mainly involving food festivals. The struggle for post-war Civil-Rights in the 1960s put Juneteenth in the shadows; but its popularity re-emerged in the 1970s focusing on African American freedom and arts. The beginning of the 21st Century saw the cel- ebrations in most major cities in the US. There is an on-going campaign led by African Americans, espe- cially Congresswoman Sheila Jackson for the US con- gress to recognize Juneteenth as a national holiday. According to the Congress Research Service, Hawaii and the two Dakotas are the only states which do not recognize Juneteenth.

Modern observance primarily involved public reading of the Emancipation Proclamation, singing negro spiri-tual songs like, 'Swing Low Sweet Chariot,' and 'Lift Every Voice and Sing.' Literary works by celebrated African American writers like Ralph Ellison and Maya Angelou are read. The celebrations also include rodeos, street fairs, cook- outs, family reunions, park parties, historical reenactments and of course, Miss Juneteenth con-tests. The Mascogos, descendants of black Seminoles, who escaped from US slavery in 1852 and settled in Coahuila, Mexico, do also celebrate Juneteenth.

THE TULSA, OKLAHOMA RACE MASSACRE: MAY 31-JUNE 1ST, 1921. In May 31st to June 1st, 1921, over eighteen hours, a throng of white thugs aided and given weapons by city officials attacked black residents, businesses, churches, libraries and schools, needlessly killing three hundred African Americans and thousands were left homeless. Those responsible included members of the United States National Guard. The attackers' weapons included guns, explosive incendiary devices, some of which were dropped from planes. The Tulsa Race Riot, is also called, 'The Tulsa Massacre,' 'The Greenwood Massacre' or 'The Black Wall Street Massacre.' It remains one of the worst incidents of racial violence in US history.

On May 30th, 1921, a 19-year-old black shoe shiner, called Dick Rowland entered an elevator at the Drexel Building, an office building on South Main Street. Immediately Rowland stepped in, a 17-year-old elevator operator, called Sarah Page, screamed. Rowland fled the scene, the police were called and the following morning, the black teenager was arrested. Rumours about what happened became rife among the city's white community. A front-page story in the Tulsa Tribune that afternoon reported that police had arrested Rowland for sexually assaulting the white elevator operator.

During the evening an angry white mob congregated outside the courthouse, demanded that Rowland was handed over by Sheriff Willard McCullough, who bravely declined. The Sheriff's men then barricaded the top floor to protect Rowland. Around 21:00hrs, about 25 armed black men, including many World War One veterans went to the courthouse offering to help guard Rowland. The Sheriff turned down their offer and ordered them to leave. Meanwhile, members of the white mob tried unsuccessfully to break into the National Guard armoury.

Fearing a possible lynching, about 75 armed black men returned to the courthouse just after 22:00hrs. They were confronted by 1,500 white men some also armed. Shots were fired and the outnumbered black men made a hasty retreat to Greenwood. The ensuring hours saw acts of violence by the mob against blacks including those unarmed. A false belief that black Tulsans were receiving succour from nearby cities with large black populations, heightened further, the racial tension. The dawn of June 1st, 1921, saw thousands of white armed men pour into the black prosperous Greenwood District. Looting, burning homes, businesses, schools, churches, and libraries; covering an area of 35 city blocks.

Firefighters who went to help put out fires, later reported that rioters threatened them with guns and forced them to leave.

A later estimate by the Red Cross listed 1,256 houses burnt, 215 others looted but not torched. Two newspapers, a hospital and hotels were among the black owned properties destroyed or damaged by fire. The National Guard arrived, and Governor J.B.A. Robertson declared martial law shortly before 12:00hrs but the riots had already ended. The National Guard assisted in putting off the fires. However, by June 2nd, 6,000 blacks had been held prisoner by the National Guard for a reported eight days at the local fair grounds.

Hours after the massacre, all charges against Dick Rowland were dropped. The police concluded that

Rowland might have stumbled into Page or unintentionally stepped on her foot as he entered the elevator. He was kept safely under guard during the riot and the next morning left Tulsa and never returned. Prevailing racial tension and envy by some whites about the success of blacks were main factors in the massacre. It was estimated that the monetary cost to the blacks was $200m in today's money.

CHAPTER ELEVEN

FOUR HUNDRED YEARS
OF INHUMANITY

The Oklahoma Race Massacre is just one of innumerable and senseless attacks on black people in America for four centuries and still counting. The first African slaves arrived in America in 1619 as already stated.

Figures differ; historians quote between twelve to fifteen million slaves in total taken from Africa to the Americas and the Caribbean. Hundreds of thousands died before and during the middle passage to the Americas. A figure of 1.8m was estimated as those who could not survive the treacherous journey. Of those who did not survive were those who had died on the slave ships and those who were considered too sick to survive the journey. These two groups were thrown overboard, and the common practice was that insurance papers were completed to claim compensation. Another 'fatal' group was made up of slaves who rightly envisaged even worse brutality on arrival on land. In shackles, chains et al, they jumped en masse and drowned.

Survivors endured untold hardships from 'market' places as 'commodities' and on plantations working as 'properties' of rich, powerful, and influential white slave masters. Even twelve American presidents owned slaves: Eight of this number actually owned slaves while in office. On the vast plantations, any hint of revolt or insurrection was met with unbridled brutal force ending in fatalities.

Abolition of slavery, granting of citizenship and the right to vote in the forms of the 13th, 14th, and 15th Amendments of the American Constitution respectively, were invaluable interventions in the fortunes of the African slaves in about 250 years of toil, heart- ache and (total) desolation. The 15th Amendment was passed in Congress during the Reconstruction Era when the Progressive Wing of the Republican Party dominated the decade after the Civil War. When the Reconstruction collapsed with the withdrawal of Federal troops from the Confederate states in the South in 1877, the white supremacist faction of the Democratic Party emerged supreme. Voting rights of black men were abrogated in courts and racial discrimination in voting in state and local laws. Their rights were restricted by poll taxes, literacy tests, intimidation, and fraud. Another impediment was the infamous 'Grandfather Clause' which was deviously exploited to disenfranchise African Americans. It was not until the passage of the Civil Rights Act of 1965 when it was possible for African Americans to exercise their Constitutional Right to vote. On August 6th, 1965, President Lyndon Johnson signed the law preventing racial discrimination in voting. Congress amended the Act's general provision of Voting Rights.

The African American suffered lynching in the hands of white mobs, many at times encouraged by local media and elected officials. Sometimes responsible law enforcement officers turned a blind eye to the inhuman acts of the arbitrary mobs. Genuinely, at times other law enforcement officers would have enforced order but often the size of the mob and the hatred emanating from them inhibited intervention. An equally important point to emphasize was that the mobs were known to lynch fellow whites who sympathized or tried to aid the besieged and hapless African American population. It must be noted also that some white law enforcement officers put their lives on the line to defend or shield innocent blacks. A humane and a notable example was the brave stance of Sheriff Willard McCulloug and his team (shielding the innocent black teenager) during the Oklahoma Race Massacre in 1921.

The next hurdles on the path of the African American were segregation and the struggle for Civil Rights. They had their toll but could not hinder the continued quest for nothing but racial equality and justice in American society. The African American for 400 years has struggled but thankfully cleared (marginally in some cases) many a hurdle. However, what has remained painfully intractable, is the treatment in the courts, some national institutions and in the hands of some law enforcement officers across the whole of the United States.

In decades, the American public and the outside world have seen countless cases of police brutality towards African Americans. There have been needless fatalities including young people but deplorably prosecutions are scant. It must be noted that majority of police officers acquit themselves professionally and fairly. The criticism levelled against them by blacks and some white Americans, is that their failure to eradicate or nip in the bud the nefarious activities in their ranks, puts all of them in harm's way.

GEORGE FLOYD MAY 25, 2020- And then there was George Floyd. Prior to that fateful day some of the black fatalities include Breonna Taylor 26, Ataliana Jefferson 28, Auro Rosser 40, Stephen Clark 22, Botham Jean 26, Philando Castille 32 and Freddie Gray aged 23.

AMY COOPER V CHRISTIAN COOPER- On the 25th of May 2020, Amy Cooper, a 41-year-old white woman called police and falsely claimed that Christian Cooper (no relation), a respected black South African comic editor, was threatening her life. The incident happened in Central Park, New York when Christian, a bird watcher asked Amy to put her cocker span- iel on a leash. A video of the incident went viral. It showed Amy saying, "I am going to tell them (police) there is an African American." Amy, head of Insurance Investment Solutions at Franklin Templeton apolo- gized and was placed on administrative leave by her employers. However Christian Cooper was reported to have said that he did not want her to lose her job.

Amy stated that her life had been "devasted" as she had to face the consequences of the false claim that a black man was threatening her.

GEORGE FLOYD- On Monday 25th of May 2020, an employee of a grocery shop in Minneapolis followed protocol and called police after suspecting that a fake $20 bill had been 'tendered' by a customer. Floyd, whom it was alleged used the $20 bill was still outside when police arrived. The employee stated after the incident that he remembered Floyd as someone who was always polite and added, "Floyd may not have even known that the bill was counterfeit." The owner of the grocery shop, Mike Abumany Yaleh stated that he didn't realise that Floyd had died until the following morning. He added, "We were all outraged." He went on, "Minorities are not being treated equally in this country and this is an issue that has to be addressed and fixed by our leaders in the community."

The tragic incident was captured on video by a 17-year-old Darnella Frazier on a smart phone. When the police first arrested him, George Floyd was reported to have told them, "I am not a bad guy." The officers were, Derek Chauvin, J. Alexander, Thomas Lane and Tou Thao. When police officer Derek Chauvin had his knee on his neck, Floyd beseeched, "Please, please, I can't breathe." He also said, "My stomach hurts, my neck hurts, everything hurts. I need some water or something, please, please, I can't breathe." Transcript released later revealed that he told the police officer, "I can't breathe" more than twenty times, but Officer Chauvin arrogantly and callously failed to heed his mournful plea. Moments before his tragic death, the transcript also revealed that he cried for his dead mother and his children, "Momma, I love you, tell my kids, I love them. I'm dead."

The 82-page of body -camera transcripts revealed that one of the concerned and anxious onlookers questioned if Floyd had a pulse, "He's not even breathing right now bro, you think that's cool?" The first contact unfolded thus- When Lane, with his gun drawn, initially approached Floyd who was in a car with other people, he repeatedly apologized, "I am sorry, I amsorry." Seeing the drawn gun, he said, "God dang man, man I got shot. I got shot the same way officer, before." He went on, "Please officer, don't shoot me, please man."

Officer Lane then asked one of the occupants why Floyd, "was getting all squirrelly and not showing us his hands and just being all weird like that?" Hill the occupant, replied, "Because he's been shot before." He concluded, "He got a thing going on, I'm telling you, about the police."

George Floyd, a strapping six-footer, a "gentle giant" was handcuffed. He was of no threat and helpless on the ground. The behaviour of the four policemen especially Derek Chauvin was an act of blatant arrogance and an unimaginable nefariousness. Officer Chauvin, at one point said to the helpless and hapless Floyd, "Relax," but he had his knee on Floyd's neck for 8 minutes 46 seconds until he breathed his last breath.

No matter how one tries, it is excruciatingly difficult to imagine how Floyd, despite his heartfelt pleas for "mercy," was actually feeling. The ultimate manifestation was unfolded in the words, "I'm dead." Yes, individually, mankind was numbed with disbelief and the world collectively was impotent to save a helpless and an innocent life.

What was it all about? A counterfeit $20 bill. It is no secret that from time immemorial, some politicians and businesspeople especially in the western world with inside knowledge of impending government policies and key company decisions respectively, make thousands or even millions unscathed in the twinkle of an eye. Prior to the lockdown this year in England, I overheard a father promise his young son £20 (not dollars) if he would hoover the inside and wash the outside of the family car. The young man's reply, "Is that all?" Yes indeed, considering that £20 is more than $20. So, for a mere $20 fake bill and for 8 minutes and 46 seconds- a grueling life-suffocating span- a human being lost his life with the whole world watching unable to come to the rescue.

On June 6th, 2020, An American Conservative commentator, Glenn Beck stated, "I don't care what George Floyd did. The officer should have not treated him like that and killed him: But we still must ask: Is he a hero?" It must be noted that George Floyd had a prison record, also drug and theft convictions. Should he have been murdered in broad daylight because of his history? Certainly not! A black female right winger, Candice Owen wrote, "The fact that he has been held up as a martyr sickens me." Do I have to comment on this? Hardly, it is all there for both black and white people to see. What more, President Trump was reported to have retweeted the comments.

In 2018, according to the Washington Post website, the New York Attorney General filed a lawsuit against Trump and his three children, Donald Jnr, Ivanka and Eric, alleging "persistent illegal conduct," at the President's personal charity. It stated that the Trump Organization had repeatedly misused funds of the nonprofit establishment to pay off business creditors to decorate one of Trump's golf clubs and to stage a multi-million dollars give away at the 2016 campaign events. The Guardian website stated that the President admitted to personally misusing the money but according to the New York Attorney General, Trump previously denied any wrongdoing. The New York Judge also signed off an agreement to close the Trump Foundation and distribute $1.7m to not-to-profit organizations. The New York Supreme court fined the President's organization $2m. This is the ultimate depth of hypocrisy. Any more comments? Well, I can only state that poor George Floyd lost his life for allegedly tendering a fake $20 bill in a grocery shop.

What a cruel and sad world which regrettably, many human beings in all races and societies face daily?

CHAPTER TWELVE

PUBLIC HOSTILITY AND BLACK FATALITIES IN THE HANDS OF LAW ENFORCEMENT OFFICERS

The African survived slavery with all the iniquities associated with it; including the resistance of the Confederates which prolonged the gruesome practice for another agonizing twenty years before abolition. Arbitrary lynching by some sections of the white population had its toll. The atrocities in recent decades have been meted out by some (a few but a lethal force) officials of law enforcement. The pain, the incessant struggle and the fight for social justice have been part and parcel for the African's life in America for four centuries and counting.

On August 28th, 1955, 19-year-old Carolyn Bryant Donham (now 84 years old), claimed that a 14-year-old African American, who had arrived in Mississippi from Chicago on a short summer vacation, had offended her (wolf-whistling) in the family shop. A few days later, Roy Bryant, Carolyn's husband and his half-brother, dragged Emmett Till from his uncle's house, beat him up senselessly, shot him in the head and dumped him in the Mississippi. The acquittal of the two killers by an all-white jury, yet again highlighted the long history of horrific persecution of African Americans in the United States.

'The Blood of Emmett Till,' is a book written by a white gentleman, Timothy B. Tyson, a Duke University Professor, six decades after the murder. The author wrote that Carolyn stated that her long-ago allegations that Emmett grabbed her and was menacing and sexually crude, "that part is not true." Witnesses admitted that the only 'offence' was the wolf-whistling. It must be noted, Emmet was five years younger than Carolyn. Some years after, it was reported that all the members of the nine-men white jury reported that they knew that the defenders were guilty, yet they acquitted them. Professor Tyson, in an interview with NBS (National Broadcasting Service), stated that it took him seven years to research and a year to write the book.

In October 1942, two 14-year-old black boys were lynched on Christopher Columbus Day. Charlie Lang and Ernest Gren had pleaded guilty to ambushing a 13-year-old white girl and trying to attack her. They were found hanging on a bridge. This was followed a few days after by another lynching of another African American.

On June 17th, 2015, a 21-year-old white man, Dylann Roof shot and killed nine African American men and women during a bible study meeting. It was a racially motivated attack in the historic Emmanuel Methodist Church in Charleston, South Carolina. On January 11th, 2017, the unrepentant white supremacist was sentenced to death by a jury. He was reported to have "chuckled to himself" as he confessed the killing to FBI investigators.

On February 23rd, 2020, an unarmed 25-year-old African American jogger, Ahmaud Arbery was shot dead near Brunswick in Glynn County, Georgia. Father and son, 64-year-old Gregory and 34-year-old Travis McMichael who were armed pursued Ahmaud in a pickup truck while he was jogging on Holmes Road. They claimed that Arbery fitted the description of a black person suspected of involvement in a series of local break-ins. A third person, William 'Roddie' Bryan Jnr followed Arbery in a second vehicle and used it to block his path. He took the video of the confronta- tion by the McMichaels. The younger McMichael was alleged to have fired a gun thrice at point blank range at Arbery who fell. His father watched from the back of his truck. Both are in prison. Bryan Jnr was jailed on May 21st, 2020, in Brunswick, Georgia.

In an interview with CNN (Cable News Network) Mr. Bryan stated that he had been praying for the Arbery family. He went on, "If there wasn't a tape, then we wouldn't know what happened. I hope that it, in the end, brings justice and peace to the family." It took two months for the suspects to be arrested, which outraged many white Americans, not to mention the African American population. Brunswick District Attorney, Jackie Johnson, was reported to have prevented police from arresting the McMichaels as Gregory had worked in her office. Gregory had worked as an investigator for twenty-four years. He retired in May 2019. In 2014, he faced suspension after it was learnt that he had worked for years without the relevant firearms and deadly force training. District Attorney Jackie Johnson contacted the state's training director about Gregory McMichael after the disclosure. Eventually Gregory was granted a waiver for the important training and he worked on for five years. It was the leaked video which was the turning point of the Arbery case. District Attorney Jackie Johnson recused herself from the case.

It is deplorable to see or read about members of the public taking the law into their own hands, however it is indefensible to witness or learn of the bias or overt racism by some members of the judiciary and law enforcement towards black people or for that matter any other human being. It must be noted that in some poor areas ordinary white working-class Americans are also treated unfairly though fatalities do not proportionally match that of blacks.

African Americans account for about 14% of the total American population of about 330 million. On June 10th, 2020, the indenpendent.co.uk quoted a 34-year-old black writer, Alex Miller. He stated that black people represent 47% of overturned convictions. Murder cases with black people wrongly convicted were 22% more likely to occur than with white people.

POLICE BRUTALITY- In recent years a spate of incidents of police brutality against especially blacks have come to light because of the availability and common usage of smart phones. The list containing circumstances leading to black fatalities pre-dating May 25, 2020 (George Floyd) is heart- breaking.

2012- On the night of February 26th, 2012, Trayvon Martin, a 17-year-old African American was shot and killed by an adult and much bigger white man. In 2013, Zimmerman who claimed self-defence, was acquitted of Martin's murder. Consequently, the slogan' Black Lives Matter,' was used for the first time leading to the formation of the movement in that year. Three black women, Alicia Garza, Patrisse Cullors and Opal Tometi are the founding members. The movement is now a global organization-The Black Lives Matter Foundation.

2014- On July 17, 2014, Eric Garner at the age of 43, died in Staten Island, New York after police officer, Daniel Panteled was alleged to have put him in a choke hold which had been banned by the NYPD in 1993. During the restraint which included four other police officers, Garner was reported to have pleaded, "I can't breathe," eleven times. Garner was suspected of selling loose untaxed cigarettes.

In December 2014, a Grand Jury decided not to indict the former officer, This decision sparked off protests and rallies: By December 28th, 2014, more than fifty demonstrations had been held across the United States. Garner's daughter, Erica, Rev Al Sharpton and a host of others protested against police brutality. On December 30th, 2017, Erica at the age of 27, died in Brooklyn of complications from a heart attack. Eventually in August 2019, five years after the incident, Officer Panteled was fired from the police.

The New York city's watch dog agency records reveal the officer was the subject of seven misconduct complaints in the years before the fatal incident.

On August 9th, 2014, an 18-year-old African American Michael Brown Jnr was shot six times and killed by 28-year-old white policeman, Darren Wilson, in Ferguson, Missouri. Protestors believed that Brown was surrendering to the police, but the police officer claimed that after a brief chase, the teenager stopped and charged towards him. Michael Brown's friend who was with him during the incident refuted the policeman's account. She stated that Brown turned round with his hands raised.

In March 2015, the US Department of Justice, having carried out its own investigation cleared officer Darren Wilson of civil rights violations in the fatal shooting of the teenager, Michael Brown Jnr.

On November 22nd, 2014, 12-year-old Tamir Rice was killed by 26-year-old white policeman Timothy Loehmann. A caller had called police that a man was pointing "a pistol" randomly in a park in the city of Cleveland's Public Works Department. The caller ended the call, "its (pistol) probably fake." Yes, indeed it was found to be a toy pistol. Officer Loehmann who was with 46 years old fellow officer Frank Garmback, later stated that instead of showing his hand, it appeared that Tamir Rice was trying to draw, "I knew it was a gun and I knew it was coming out." He shot twice hitting Rice in the torso. The youngster died the following day.

Evidence presented to a Grand Jury in late 2015 concluded that Rice was drawing what appeared to be an actual firearm from his waist as the police arrived. Loehmann was not indicted. It was later revealed that Loehmann, in his previous job as a police officer in the Cleveland suburb of Independence, was considered an emotionally unstable recruit unfit for duty. He failed to reveal this in his job application; and the police department failed to review his previous personnel file before hiring him. In 2017, after an investigation, he was fired for withholding that information. A lawsuit brought by Rice's family was subsequently settled for $6m.

Loehmann's colleague, Garmback was put on a 10-day suspension. 2015- On July 13th, 2015, 28 years old African American, Sandra Bland died in a police cell three days after being arrested for a minor traffic offence. She was found hanged in a cell in Waller County, Texas. Her death was ruled a suicide. The decision gave rise to protests and allegation of racial violence against her.

The availability and common usage of smart phones over the last decade or so have empowered more witnesses to take videos and bring to light, numerous evidence of police brutality. Hitherto majority of these atrocities would have gone unnoticed. In 2015 and 2016, some of the fatalities involved Walter Scott,

Freddie Gray, Samuel Du Bose, Alton Sterling, Philando Castille and Terence Crutcher. The only case in which a policeman was prosecuted was the case involving Walter Scott.

AUGUST 2019- Elijah McClan, a 23years old African American, a massage therapist had gone to a convenience shop and was walking home in Aurora, Colorado on 24th August 2019, when somebody called 911. The person described to police that the individ- ual (McClan) "looked sketchy" and was wearing a ski mask and waving his arms. Three police officers arrived and after a struggle to handcuff McClan, they got him to the ground and applied a carotid hold. This hold causes unconsciousness because it restricts blood flow to the brain.

Paramedics arrived on the scene and after fifteen minutes, they injected him with ketamine. Ketamine is a powerful sedative which could cause among other side-effects, abnormal heart rhythms, slow or high heart rate, memory loss, delirium, dizziness, and generally psychomotor retardation: Slowing down of mental and physical activity; including speech, thinking and mobility.

Having been injected with ketamine, McClain went into cardiac arrest on route to hospital. He died six days after the incident. The three white police officers, Woodyard, Rosenblatt and Roedema were placed on administrative leave. However according to reports they have all been reinstated.

A few days after the release of the autopsy report, Dave Young, the Adams County District Attorney, announced that there would not be any criminal charges, as there was not enough evidence that the officers broke the law when they used force on McClain. The Interim Chief of the Aurora Police Department, Vanessa Wilson, amid protests by the McClain family for police reforms; announced a ban on carotid holds.

On June 25th, 2020, Colorado's Governor, Jared Polis signed an Executive Order which appointed the State Attorney General, Phil Weiser to re-examine the case and file charges if the facts demanded prosecution.

RAYSHARD BROOKS-The repercussions of the gruesome and senseless murder of George Floyd were still unfolding when on June 12th, 2020, Rashard Brooks, 27 years old African American, a father of three was shot and killed by Garrett Rolfe, a white police officer. The Atlanta police chief resigned immediately, and officer Rolfe was fired. Brooks' death was declared homicide. The Georgia Bureau of Investigation stated that officers were called to a Wendy's Drive-Thru restaurant in South Atlanta at about 22:30 hrs. Brooks had fallen asleep in his car which was blocking other customers in the queue. The first officer, Devin Brosnan, having knocked on the car window a few times, opened the door and reminded Brooks- "Hey man, you're parked in the middle of the drive-thru line here."

Brooks eventually woke up and was asked to pull over into a parking spot. When the car was parked, Brooks was asked how much he had drunk. "Not much, about one drink," he replied. He later revealed to the police that he had had a drink at his daughter's birthday. Officer Brosnan, having checked Brooks' licence, used his radio and called for assistance. Officer Rolfe arrived, interviewed Brooks, a sobriety test was done starting just after 23:00hrs lasting about seven minutes. During a 41-minute interview, the video showed that Brooks appeared relaxed and complied with the instructions of the officers. Rolfe told Brooks, "I think you've had too much to drink to be driving," when the breath test was done. He then instructed him, "Put your hands behind your back."

A struggle ensued when officer Rolfe attempted to put the handcuffs on Brooks. During the struggle Brooks managed and got himself free and took one of the police tasers and ran off. Rolfe pursued him with another taser but soon took out his handgun. Brooks was seen in the video turning around and pointing the taser at officer Rolfe and firing it. The officer hit Brooks twice in the back. He was about 5.5 meter (18 yds) from the officers. A third police bullet was reported to have hit a witness's car.

The prosecutors stated that officer Rolfe kicked Brooks as he lay on the ground. Brosnan was accused of standing on Brooks's shoulder. After the shooting, both officers were accused of not providing medical attention for two minutes. The ambulance arrived a few minutes after, and Brooks was taken to hospital. He later died after surgery, having suffered organ injuries and blood loss.

BREONNA TAYLOR- On March 13th, 2020, 26 years old African American emergency medical technician, Breonna Taylor was fatally shot when three police officers were executing a no-knock search warrant for drugs.

The police officers who were from the Louisville Metro police department Kentucky, were Jonathan Mattingly, Brett Hankison and Myers Cosgrove. Taylor was not involved in drugs but her ex-boyfriend Jamarcus Glover was reported to be a dealer. She was with her new boyfriend, Kenneth Walker when the police entered the apartment.

When Walker heard the pounding of the door, he claimed that he thought it was Broenna's ex-boyfriend. He did not know it was the police. Licensed to carry a gun, Walker then fired a gun which hit officer Mattingly in the femoral artery of his upper thigh. The Sergeant returned fire with six shots. The two other officers also opened fire bringing the total number of shots to at least 22. Breonna was struck eight times and died on the scene.

A Grand Jury Indicted Walker on a charge of attempted murder of a police officer. The charge was dismissed in May 2020 at the request of the Commonwealth's Attorney, Tom Wine. In June, Louisville's police chief, Robert Schroeder announced that Brett Hankison had been sacked. The chief stated that Hankison "blindly" shot ten rounds into Breonna's apartment through "a patio door and window which were covered with material that completely prevented you from verifying that any person was in an immediate threat or more importantly any innocent persons present."

Sgt. Mattingly and officer Myers Cosgrove who also fired some shots, were placed on "administrative reas-signment." The whole case is being investigated by the Justice Department and the FBI as well as Kentucky state officials. The city has passed a law banning "no-knock" warrants.

The Taylor family filed a lawsuit against the city of Louisville. On September 15th, 2020, it was reported that

Breonna's family had received a $12 million settlement. In the same month Kenneth filed a civil lawsuit against the city's police department. His attorneys argued that he is immune from being arrested and charged again due to the Kentucky "stand your ground" law. On October 30th, Sgt Mattingly fired a counter lawsuit against Kenneth complaining that he committed battery, assault and intentional emotional distress. In the complaint, his attorney stated that Kenneth Walker "willingly or maliciously" fired at the official. The attorney continued, "Sgt Mattingly was shot and nearly killed by Kenneth Walker. He is entitled to and should use the legal process to seek remedy for the injury that Walker has cost him."

Police brutality especially against African Americans was rife, talked about; but until the recording of Rodney King's beating and humiliation by four white officers of the LAPD in 1991, there were no pieces of concrete evidence to back what victims and witnesses alike reported of as police brutality. Former Los Angeles police officer, African American, Bernard Parks described the video, "It was the singular most important piece of evidence." The case underscored widespread racism in some American police departments. It emerged that it was common practice for police officers to brag about beating up black suspects and describing them in racially derogatory terms. The importance of the video taken by 17 years old Darnella Frazier in the George Floyd's case is inestimable. In Rodney's case (March 3rd, 1991), twenty-nine years old George Halliday a bystander used a Sony video 8 handy cam to film the police brutality.

Rodney King who was 26 years old had stopped his car after an eight-mile pursuit by police through the streets of Los Angeles, California. Rodney King suffered brain-damage, however the four police officers were acquitted the following year. The incident triggered the LA Race Riots in 1992. The rioting went on for five days with sixty-four people losing their lives. Ten were shot by law enforcement officers and the forty-four died in other homicide and incidents associated with the riots. The damage to the city was put at $1 billion. Three days into the riots, Rodney King went on TV and called for calm-"Just get along." Years later he said that he wanted the statement to be his legacy.

In 1992 in an interview with the Los Angeles Times, he admitted coming to terms with his legacy, but dealing with the past had not been easy. He was quoted," I sometimes feel like I'm caught in a vice. Some people feel like I'm some kind of hero. Others hate me. They say I deserved it. Other people I can hear them mocking me for when I called for an end to the destruction, like I am a fool for believing in peace." King met Mr. Halliday (the video man) by chance in 1993 and told him, "You saved my life." They then shook hands.

King died at the age of 47 on June 17th, 2012. His death was ruled accidental drowning after his fiancee had discovered his body at the bottom of a swimming pool. On July 29th, 2020, (auction) bidding for Mr. Halliday's video camera was reported to start from $225,000.

There are a considerable number of other African American fatalities which has not come into public recognition. The fatalities culminated in the murder of George Floyd and the killing of Rayhard Brooks. Both cases especially George Floyd's made global headlines.

Despite the tragic case of George Floyd, the global attention and repulsion it received; in certain places some law enforcement officers still act with impunity. On Sunday August 23rd, 2020, at 17:11hrs, in Kenosha, Wisconsin, law enforcement officers were called to deal with a domestic incident. A video taken by 22 years old Raysen White showed three officers following 29 years old Jacob Blake half-way around his car. He was closely followed by 31 years old white officer who was pointing his gun at him. The officer could be heard saying, "Drop the knife, drop the night," although Blake could be seen clearly adjusting the hem of his white vest. The person who took the video, "did not see a knife in Blake's hands." The state Governor, Tony Evers stated after Blake had been shot at close range seven times, that he had not seen any information to suggest that Blake had a knife or another weapon. He promised to move forward with reforms to curb law enforcement misconduct.

Returning to our muttons, it was officer Rusten Sheskey who was seen pulling Blake's vest as he was open- ing the driver's side of his vehicle. The officer fired the seven shots into Blake's back as he was about to enter his car. This atrocity happened with Blake's three children aged 3,5 and 8 years old sitting at the back of the car. Police later stated that Detective Criminal Investigating Agents, "recovered a knife from the driver's side floorboard of Mr. Blake's car. He was reported to have told investigators that he had a knife.

Kenosha News reported that Blake, a security guard and community volunteer was "trying to break up a fight between two women." His partner, Laquisha Booker confirmed to the local media that their three very young children were at the back of the car when their father was shot seven times in the back. She was quoted, "That man literally grabbed him by his shirt and looked the other way and was just shooting him with kids in the back screaming."

Court records revealed that the County Court prosecutors charged Blake on July 6th, 2020, with sexual assault, trespassing and disorderly conduct in connection with a case of domestic abuse. It is not known whether this had a bearing on the domestic dispute on that fateful Sunday August 23rd, 2020. However, because of the charge, a Blake family member revealed that in hospital, Blake was "shackled" to his bed and a police officer stood guard close by. This is extremely disturbing. The victim of police brutality is paralysed and under heavy sedation after a very difficult operation. It is inhuman as it is unbelievable and may I chip in senseless!

Concerns were raised by his family and lawyer. His father told CNN (Cable Network News) "Why do they have that cold steel on my son's ankle? He couldn't get up if he wanted to." Blake's uncle, Justin Blake lamented, "This is an insult into injury. He is paralysed and can't walk and they have him cuffed to the bed." The shooting caused serious injuries to Blake's spinal cord, stomach, kidney, liver, colon and intestine. The shackles were removed on August 28th, 2020 - five days after the incident. The officer guarding his room was removed after Blakes lawyer agreed to a court hearing on the charges and "the arrest warranted was vacated," according to the August 29th,2020 issue of The Times Newspaper.

The case is yet to go to court, but what is certain is nobody in his right mind, in the presence of his young children would take a mere knife to attack three-armed law enforcement officers. Had Blake tried, he would not have stood a chance "in hell." Many in the black community know and have said that the yelling, "Drop the knife, drop the knife," well in advance before Blake opened his car, was a ploy by officer Sheskey to claim later that he feared for his life, hence his unprovoked action. Yes indeed, on September 25th,2020, CNN reported that Sheskey told investigators that it wasn't just his life he was defending when he fired his weapon seven times; but also, he was afraid Blake was attempting to kidnap a child in the back seat of his vehicle. His lawyer Brendan Matthews stated that Sheskey heard a woman say, "He's got my kid. He's got my keys." If he believed so and all the officers believed that Blake had a knife, could they not have held back within reasonable distance and still pointed their guns at him? If it was a kidnapping attempt, were they not in a position to immobilise the car about to speed off? Did the child (children) at the back of the car appear afraid because of an imminent kidnapping? 'Discretion is the better part of valour,' as the saying goes. Discretion is a crucial ingredient in any profession especially an important role like law enforcement: And may I hesitate to add, psychiatry.

Law enforcement officers, as responsible adults in my opinion, are capable of exercising prudence in a variety of challenging situations. Why therefore do a minority of them woefully fail to use their judgment to stave off serious injuries and fatalities to some members of the public they serve? Discretion and prejudice are not bed fellows. One must prevail; as reason and anger, the other human traits cannot co-exist. When prejudice stifles sound judgment or discretion, the results sadly are serious injuries and fatalities, not forgetting that it makes the law enforcement officer'sjob even more difficult. Even in the Blake case, to grudgingly accept that officer Sheskey feared 'child kidnapping,' was shooting Blake seven times to kill him, proportionate to the envisaged outcome of a kidnapping episode? Extreme caution and duty of care should be exercised at all times.

I believe overwhelming majority in the American population and the world-over, familiar with this case are praying (May God Forbid) these innocent Blake children do not suffer the after effects-trauma of this dreadful and easily avoidable incident. In all the media coverage, I did not see or read about any focus on the situation of the young Blake children. They knew their father as an able-bodied person. His paralysis now, remains a constant reminder of that fateful incident on that August Sunday of all days.

Officer Rusten Sheskey once told Kenosha News about his job, "What I like most is that you're dealing with people on perhaps the worst day of their lives and you can try and help them as much as you can and make the day a little bit better. And that for the most part, people trust us to do that for them. And it's a huge responsibility and is really trying to help the people. We may not be able to make a situation right or better, but we can maybe make it a little easier for them to handle during that time.

We're in a public service job, a customer service job, and the public is our customer. I think that especially with the officers we have here, everybody strives to make sure the public feels served and happy with the services they receive. A lot of the officers go way out of their way to make sure that that's I think the KDP embraces that."

Yes indeed, but deplorably officer Sheskey's entire behaviour on that fateful Sunday, as far as the Blake family is concerned, ran counter to the statement quoted above. Sheskey mentioned "we" meaning all members of the KPD. If a secret poll were to be conducted, almost all his fair-minded professional colleagues, would mark 'highly disapprove' of his action. His indefensible behaviour made their already diffi- cult job, more intractable. An African American elder stated that the last time they had "a police shooting was six years ago." Sir Robert Peel stated, "The police are the public, and the public are the police." Officer Sheskey rightly stated, "The public is our customer." If that is the way to treat a customer, then a considerable period back to the classroom is acutely long overdue: If miraculously not being tagged, 'unsuitable,' Let us for a moment forget the plight of the Blake family. One is at pains to think how a responsible public officer can behave in such a way to damage his/her own future in a moment of gross misjudgment or as somebody put it, "madness." It also plunges his family and dear ones into the depths of desolation. In the annals of history, who wants his/her family's name to be synonymous with the Kenosha Riots of 2020?

In 2015, Sheskey was sued for $50,000 after allegedly making an illegal left-hand turn in a police car, hitting a teenage girl driving a jeep. Rusten Sheskey, has seven years' experience as a law enforcement officer. The rioting and looting which ensued after the incident, saw as reported, 30 businesses torched, and other properties damaged. I have yet to read about the overall financial cost to the city of Kenosha. On account of the George Floyd murder, the September 16th,2020 issue of the Daily Mail reported that the vandalism, looting and the Black Lives Matter protests across 140 American cities, would cost insurance companies $2B.

TRAUMA-I need to return to the subject of trauma. Wikipedia defines trauma as "often the result of an overwhelming amount of stress that exceeds one's ability to cope or integrate the emotions involved with that experience." The experience of the Jacob Blake's three young children - 3,5 and 8- is one of the most traumatic imaginable for any child, black, white, brown, red or whatever skin colour, to endure. The children-society.org.uk website states, "Trauma and feeling of stress are psychological and physical responses to a one-off prolonged and/or repeated exposure to one or more distressing or life-threatening events.

Many children and young people are resilient and often symptoms of trauma diminish with time-but where a situation is exceptionally threatening, this is less likely."

Traumatic experience could generate strong mental and physical reactions. These undoubtedly remain with a child years after the event. On the part of the young Blakes, their father's paralysis is painfully a con- stant (and visible) reminder of his changed condition.

Factors which emanate from traumatic experiences include victimhood- thinking, passivity, passive-aggres-siveness and the false-self.

VICTIMHOOD-THINKING- According to Wikipedia, "A victimhood mentality may manifest itself in a range or different behaviours or ways of thinking and talking. Identifying others as the cause of undesired situation and denying a personal responsibility for one's own life or circumstances exhibiting heightened attention (hyper vigilance) when in the presence of others."

PASSIVITY- When a child is neglected, it is likely that he/she may show passivity in adulthood. Passivity is acceptance of what happens without active response or resistance. Or allowing others to do things to you without complaining or fighting back.

PASSIVE- AGGRESSIVENESS- Wikipedia defines, "is characterised by a pattern of passive hostility and an avoidance of direct communication. Inaction, where some action is socially customary is a typical passive-aggressive strategy. Such behaviour is sometimes protested by associates, evoking exasperation or confusion. It may be an expression of difficulty in dealing with one's own negative emotions."

FALSE-SELF- is our self -image to cope with emotional trauma of early childhood. It is also a load of habit- ual thinking patterns and emotional routines that are stored in the brain and nervous system.

The fatal repercussion of Jacob Blake's incident was that on August 26th, 2020, a 17 -year- old white teenager, Kylie Rittenhouse allegedly shot and killed two demonstrators and wounded a third. He was reported to be a 'Law Enforcement and Blue Lives Matter' supporter from Antioch, Illinois. The teenager was reported to have spent time as a safety cadet. In the August 28th,2020 issue of the Daily Mirror, he was pictured at the front row of President Donald Trump's rally in Des Moines, Iowa in January 2020. It was alleged that he fled to the family home in Antioch after the incident. He handed himself over and was arrested. On the night of the shooting, Rittenhouse was quoted as saying, "People are being injured. It's our job to protect. And that's why I have my rifle."

A video revealed that Rittenhouse's third victim, according to the mailonline, was armed with a hand-gun. The teenager's attorney, Lin Wood, claimed that the 17 years old was "attacked" with "lethal force," and that he acted in self-defence as he shot the opposing protestors. It was also reported that one of the victims was hit five times. On September 9th, 2020, President Trump refused to condemn Rittenhouse's action. He rather stated that he acted in self- defence. Trump attacked the demonstrators but did not say anything about police brutality attributable to the demonstrations, looting, destruction of property, the deaths of two demonstrators and a third being wounded.

If this fatal incident did not happen, in about five years' time Kylie Rittenhouse would have become a law enforcement officer. It is not difficult to envisage what a person like that with entrenched views would do when dealing with an African American or any of the members of a minority group. He would not only carry them out, but likely to pollute the minds of a few officers who otherwise would be discharging their duties professionally without any blemish.

On July 28th, 2017, in address to law enforcement officers President Trump appeared to instigate the officers to be violent when dealing with people suspected of committing a crime. He was quoted, "Please, don't be too nice." It appeared that he was referring to the gang MS-13. However, the undeniable impression was that the President's comments were in general about police handling of suspected criminals. He was quoted on the ABC News go.com website, "When you see these thugs being thrown into the back of a paddy wagon, you just seen them thrown in rough. I said, 'please don't be too nice."

In 1989, Donald Trump, then just a businessman, paid for full-page advertisements in four New York City newspapers including the New York Times, calling for the reinstatement of the death penalty. This was in response to the arrest of four black and brown teenagers accused of the brutal rape of a white female jogger in Central Park, New York. Trump paid $85,000 for the advert, 'Bring back the death penalty, bring back our police,' two weeks after the attack, before any of the teenagers faced trial. There was no DNA evidence connecting the boys (between 14 and 16 years old) to the attack. In 2002, a prisoner called Mathias Reyes confessed to the Central Park rape.

Consequently 'The Central Park Five' became 'The Exonerated Five.' One of them Yusef Salaam who was 15, (now 46 years old) spent seven years in prison. Two years after being released, he was still encountering difficulties in adjusting to normal life. He declared, "I would tell anybody about what happened to me and how Trump rushed to judge us." This was sheer naked prejudice. Utterly wicked and shameful. In 2019, when President Trump was reminded in the White House about his role regarding 'The Central Park Five,' he refused to apologise. He stated, "You have people on both sides of that, they admitted their guilt."

In 1999, A West African immigrant, Guinean Amadou Diallo was fatally shot by four New York police officers who were all subsequently found not guilty. Diallo, from Chicago, was working as a street vendor with the ambition of educating himself and acquiring a career.

On February 4th, 1999, Diallo was returning to the building he lived in when four plain clothes police officers, who were part of the Street Crime Unit, approached him and fired 41 shots. He was hit 19 times. What happened to the remaining 22 shots? This was nefarious, utterly unprofessional, extremely dangerous and woefully reckless. The four police officers were, Sean Carroll, Richard Murphy, Edward McMellon and Kenneth Boss. The tragedy-the officers claimed that he fitted the "general description" of a serial rapist, according to the New York Times. It must be emphasised, "general description," and that was enough for these very public servants to take the life of an innocent black man. His precious life did not matter to these four white officers who were acting as judge and jury. The officers claimed that they thought he had a gun. It was later found that he had just a mere wallet. According to Wikipedia, their claim relating to the crime a year earlier, "was never confirmed by objective evidence."

The Street Crime Unit came under intense scrutiny after the Diallo killing. It became the focus of a Federal Civil Rights investigation and a class lawsuit alleging that the unit engaged in racial profiling. In 2000, a Federal investigation from the Department of Justice under Attorney General Janet Reno established the fact that the Street Crime Unit engaged in racial profiling. According to the Associated Press, investigators found out that nearly 90% of people who were stopped and frisked were black and Latino. In April 2002, NYPD Commissioner Raymond Kelly announced that the unit's remaining detectives would be deployed to other units within the NYPD.

On March 30th, 2020, a 41 years old black man died from asphyxiation after being restrained by police officers. According to the skynews.com website, 41 years old Prude was seen in hospital on March 23rd, 2020, for mental health evaluation after expressing suicidal ideations. The following morning at about 03:00hrs, his brother Joe Prude rang police for help saying that his brother had run out of his (Joe's) house in Rochester, New York. The footage on TV revealed that Daniel had taken off his clothes. He complied when the police instructed him to get on the ground and put his hands behind his back. He sat on the ground naked and shouted to be freed. He then spat on the ground which compelled the officers to put a spit hood over his head. The police later explained that they were concerned about being infected with coronavirus. Mr. Prude writhed on the ground and demanded to have one of the officer's gun. According to Sky, the officers slammed his head to the ground and restrained him. Mr. Prude was heard sobbing and asking for help. He continued to cry until he went silent.

The officers became concerned when they noticed fluid coming out of Mr. Prude. He was attended by paramedics but died in hospital on March 30th, 2020. The medical examiner ruled his death as a homicide caused by "complications of asphyxia in the setting of physical restraint." The report listed "excited delirium" and "acute intoxication by or PLP," as contributing factors. Joe Prude stated during a press conference, "I placed a phone call for my brother to get help, not for my brother to get lynched." He questioned, "How did you see him and not directly say, 'the man is defenceless, buck naked on the ground? He's cuffed up already.

Come on." Joe ended, "How many more bros gotta die for society to understand that this needs to stop?"

There are a considerable number of other African American fatalities which has not come into public recognition. The fatalities culminated in the murder of George Floyd, as already stated in these pages.

The gruesome manner in which George Floyd lost his life in the hands of the police does appear to have stopped the irrational deaths of African Americans in the hands of a minority of law enforcement officers. The latest incident happened on April 11th, 2021, in Brooklyn Centre, Minnesota. Daunte Wright, a 20-year-old African American wanted by the police was stopped by traffic police. He managed to wriggle free as he was being handcuffed. Wright went into his car, but he was shot by Kimberly Ann Potter, an officer with twenty-six years' experience. The African American drove on and was reported to have hit another vehicle and was pronounced dead. Officer Potter claimed that she mistook her gun (black) for a taser (brown). There is a difference in weight as well.

The Independent Newspaper reported the demonstration by a white officer of the "huge difference" between a gun and a taser. In a TikTok video, which went viral, the white police officer described how difficult it is to confuse the two items in a police arsenal. The video reported to have been posted from the account of a man "named Brian B. had about 6m views and 1.4m likes before the account was taken down after it became viral and triggered an extensive online conversation."

Brian B. with a 12 -year experience as a police officer was quoted, "I'm not going to put my life on the line to try and fix your stupidity and deal with restoring the peace with my public that I serve just because of your stupid actions." He added, "Ninety-nine percent of our job is communication. You don't have to be quick to pull out a gun or a taser on somebody and think everybody is a threat."

The now former officer Potter has been charged with second-degree manslaughter of the 20-year-old Wright. She was released from Hennepin County jail after posting a $100,000 bond. Potter's boss Tim Gannon who resigned along with her after the tragic incident claimed that she accidentally fired her gun instead of deploying the taser.

On April 13th, 2021, USA Today News reported that police officer Rusten Sheskey, who shot African American Jacob Blake seven times in the back in August 2020, had "returned to regular duty and won't face any administrative discipline." The announcement was made in January by District Attorney Michael Graveley that officer Sheskey would not face any criminal charges in the August 23rd, 2020, incident which has left Jacob Blake paralysed from the waist down. Chief Daniel Miskinis was reported to have issued a press release on Twitter stating that Sheskey had "also been cleared of breaking any internal policies and has been back on duty after months of administrative leave since March 31st." Chief Miskinis was quoted, "Although this incident has been reviewed on multiple levels, I know that some people will not be pleased with the outcome." He added, "However, given the facts, the only lawful and appropriate decision was made."

Patrick Salvi Jnr. Blake's Attorney described the revelation that Sheskey had returned to full duty without discipline, "very surprising." Salvi enquired, "How can anyone say this is a desired result for a police encounter?" He described it "a very sad state of affairs" if Kenosha police truly believed that Sheskey acted in accordance with policy and training. He ended, "but that is not true, and we'll prove it in our lawsuit." In the United States police officers are rarely held accountable, therefore it seems a minority within their ranks will continue to act with impunity.

According to the www.sun.co.uk of the 765 people killed by police in 2020, 28% of them were black "despite comprising 13% of the US population." In an interview on CNN on April 17th, 2021, African American Dr Rashawn Ray, Professor of Sociology at the University of Maryland, Centre Park, stated among other significant points that in the last five years, the American taxpayer has incurred $20B (yes billion) compensation to victims of police brutality. Seemingly the American taxpayer is willing to foot these huge (and avoidable expense) figures rather than invest in marginalised and vulnerable African Americans, denied reparation for almost 250 years of forced free labour of their African ancestors. Investing in this disadvantaged group to be productive in society, would be a wise move rather than risk a minority within this group to unfortunately resort to disruptive actions in society whenever they see the opportunity during crises.

CHAPTER THIRTEEN

GEORGE FLOYD CHANGED THE WORLD

In one of the interviews with the Floyd family, his six years old daughter, Gianna Floyd said, "Dad changed the world." In an interview with 'Good Morning America,' she stated mournfully, "I miss him." Yes, indeed he changed the world. It took just 8 minutes and 46 seconds. He was reported to have been a doting father. His five children include another daughter of 22, and an adult son. There are two grandchildren.

George Floyd's murder evoked (white and black) American anger which grew intensely and instantly the Black Lives Matter became a global movement. Racial minorities the world over, citing injustices from time immemorial, vented their pent-up anger and frustration. The demonstrations which ensued drew strong support from white populations especially the younger generation. Even among the older generation, there were some who hitherto were passive, ignorant or even dismissive of systemic racism against non-whites in their populations. The George Floyd incident was the catalyst. They saw the light and a considerable number openly admitted and were rueful about their biases, tacit or blatant.

In my second book, 'Our Generation' anthology of poems, one of my pieces is, 'A Day to Change the World.' Twenty-four hours in comparison is eternity. Mortal as he was and all mankind is, George Floyd took a mere 8 minutes and 46 seconds to tap global conscience and changed the world.

MY POEM

A DAY TO CHANGE THE WORLD
Give me a day to change the world.
A world of prejudice and hatred.
A world of strife and war.
A world devoid of fairness, full of injustices.

Just a day for the oppressors to trade
places with the oppressed.
The victor to feel the pain of the vanquished. The
master to shoulder the yoke of the enslaved.
Just a day with the turnkey behind bars
and the prisoner on the outside.
The Prince to be a pauper and pauper, Prince. A
Catholic, a Protestant and Protestant, Catholic.

Just a day for black to be white and white, black.
Night to be day and day, night.
The North to be South and South, North.
Winter a day in June and Summer in January.

'Normalcy' restored, I would dream of
a world rid of prejudices, hatred,
denial, want, cruelty, conflict and war.
A world of plentiful, freedom, our Maker's Utopia.

In fact, there have been countless reverberations of injustices, with slavery as a back-drop in many countries over many decades. On this occasion, these reverberations should hold, dislodge or uproot injustice with justice for all races. According to the Forbes website, between 2013 and 2019, American police killed over 7,500 people. Ninety-nine percent of those deaths resulted in no charges against the police. Of those killed nearly 25% were black even though the percentage of blacks in the US population is almost 14%. In 1990 alone over 1,000 civilians were killed by police. Forty-eight police officers were killed doing their job. Forbes added that though violent and property crimes are down, the police have killed more people so far in 2020 when compared to previous years.

Inhuman acts towards minorities especially blacks by some members of the police are not exclusive to the United States as already stated in these pages. In apartheid South Africa, state sponsored police brutality towards black South Africans was part and parcel of daily lives on African soil. In 1960 Sharpeville Massacre, 70 blacks were killed, 180 injured and among the 250 casualties, there were 29 children many were shot in the back as they fled.

On March 21st, 1960, at the police station in the township of Sharpeville in Transvaal (part of modern Gauteng), a crowd of 5,000 to 7,000 demonstrated against the (racist) pass laws. The South African pass laws were integral to the dreaded Apartheid system of government. It separated the South African Indian, coloured and black African citizens according to race. Between 1948 -1994, according to Radio Free South Africa, 21,000 died because of political violence. Fourteen thousand of the fatalities happened during the six-year transition from 1988-1994 when democracy was achieved.

Black South African, Steve Biko born on December 18th, 1946, was expelled from high school for political activism. He enrolled in the Liberal Institution, St Francis College where he graduated in 1966. When he entered university of Natal Medical School, he joined the multi-racial National Union of South African Students (NUSAS), a moderate organization which advocated for the rights of blacks. He soon became disenchanted with the union because he believed that society should be restructured around the culture of the black majority. In 1968, he therefore co-founded the all-black South African Students' Organization (SASO). He became the first president the following year.

SASO was based on the philosophy of black con-sciousness which encouraged blacks to recognize their inherent dignity and self-worth. In the 1970s, the black consciousness movement gained massive sup- port in other university campuses and the urban black communities throughout South Africa. In 1972, Steve

Biko became one of the founding members of Black People's Convention, affiliated to the black conscious-ness groups. In 1973, Biko was banned by the Apartheid authorities who had been feeling extremely uneasy about his activism. Other members of SASO were also proscribed. The associations, movements and public statements were therefore restricted.

Biko, aware of the focus on him stealthily formed the Zimele Trust Fund in 1975 to help political prisoners and their families. The following two years, he was arrested four times; held for months on each occasion with- out trial. In August 1977, he and a fellow activist were arrested at a roadblock and ended up in Port Elizabeth jail. On September 11th, Biko was found naked and shackled outside a hospital in Pretoria, 740 miles (1,190 km) away. He died the following day of a massive hem-orrhage. However, the South African Minister of Police announced that he died after a seven-day hunger strike. This blatant lie provoked anger of black South Africans (and indeed majority of fair-minded whites), who took to the streets. Some students were killed by police in the nation-wide protests,

During the deliberations by The Truth and Reconciliation Commission, chaired by Archbishop Desmond Tutu, four apartheid-era police officers admitted killing Steve Biko. He was only 30 years old.

On July 22nd, 2017, Rashan Charles, a 20 -year -old Black British man died after being chased and restrained by Metropolitan police officer in Dalston, East London. It was reported that prior to the arrest he had swallowed a package containing caffeine and paracetamol. According to the BBC, an inquest ruled that Charles's death was accidental. Rashan's uncle Rod Charles stated, "Rashan Charles's death was avoidable and in the absence of effective action by those governing our police services, more avoidable deaths in the UK will occur. Rod Charles is a retired Metropolitan Chief Inspector of Police. He added, "I know that there will be circumstances when police officers and other law enforcement must use the highest levels of force and sometimes it will culminate in death but there have been too many cases where people died and none of them merited the highest levels of force.

There were Sean Rigg, Roger Sylvester, Edison da Costa, Rashan Charles...I could go on."

On mental health, retired Chief Inspector Rod Charles agreed with the IOPC (Independent Office of Police Conduct) assessment that the crisis in mental health care provision, had made the problem worse, though it failed to account for the circumstances of many of the deaths. He was quoted," The responsibility of care and management of people suffering poor mental health should sit with health care specialists. However, for decades these have been on to police, who do not have the depth or breadth of specialist training needed for this caring role."

On October 5th, 1985, an African-Caribbean lady, 49 years old Cynthia Jarrett died of heart failure after four policemen raided her home at the Broadwater Farm Estates. The police stated that they were looking for stolen property but found none. Approximately five hours before her death, her son Floyd was stopped about a mile from the Farm by police over his vehicle tax disc. He was taken to the Tottenham Police Station and charged with theft and assault. (He was later acquitted of both charges). The raid was executed hours after Floyd was arrested'.

On October 6th, 1985, a day after Mrs. Jarrett's death, her family met the Metropolitan police, discussed her death and demanded an inquiry. The family appealed to the community with 1,000 flats housing over 3,000 people to refrain from any form of public disorder over her death.

However, a riot occurred that night. Five hundred police with shields, helmets and truncheons battled rioters including the youth. The police were pelted with bottles and petrol bombs. Cars were overturned and set alight. Shops and some buildings were also set alight. Looting was rife.

At about 22:15hrs, 40 years old Police Constable Blakelock was reported to have been stabbed in the neck. He died later in hospital. Midnight saw fifty-eight policemen and twenty-four others taken to hospital.

Nineteen years after P.C. Blakelock's death 44 years old Nicholas Jacobs of Hackney was charged with his murder. He was 25 years old during the riots. On April 4th, 2014, an Old Bailey jury cleared Mr. Jacobs by a majority verdict. Speaking on April 16th,2014 to BBC Newsnight, Mr. Jacobs stated that he would "be out-side the courts petitioning" if he were in the position of PC Blackelock's family. Among other things, he stated, "without a doubt nobody has a right to take another person's life."

In March 1987, three men, Winston Silcott, Engin Raghip and Mark Braithwaite were charged with PC Blakelock's murder and sentenced to life imprisonment, irrespective of the absence of witnesses and no forensic evidence. 'The Tottenham Three Are Innocent,' campaign requested vehemently for a retrial. On November 25th, 1991, all three were cleared by the Court of Appeal when an ESDA test revealed that police notes of interrogations (the only evidence) had been tampered with. Braithwaite and Raghip were released after four years in prison. Silcott remained in jail for a 1984 murder of one Tony Smith in Tottenham. He was convicted in February 1986. The trail judge recommended a minimum 14 years' imprisonment. He was released on licence in October 2003, having served 18 years.

The endemic racial injustice and therefore tension in the country especially in the capital raised its ugly head yet again during the Brixton Riot in 1985. The riots in September were sparked by the accidental shooting of a black woman, Dorothy 'Cherry' Groce, by a Metropolitan police officer. The police were after her 21 years old son in connection with robbery and a suspected firearms offence. The police believed that he was hiding in his mother's house. Two days of rioting ended with the death of photojournalist, David Hodge; 43 civilians and 10 police officers were injured. Fires were set off; a building was destroyed, 55 cars were burnt, and 58 burglaries were committed. Looting again was rife.

In March 2014, the police apologized for the wrong-ful shooting of Mrs. Groce. An inquest held in July the same year concluded that eight separate police failures were attributable to her death. The then new Commissioner of Police, Sir Bernard Hogan-Howe later, "apologized unreservedly for our failings" to the Groce family.

FRANCE- Racial injustice and therefore tension, is not confined to only the US and UK. In France, Non-Governmental (NGO) Action by Christians for the Abolition of Torture revealed that each year, 10 to 15 people lose their lives through action by the police. Most of the victims are young black men and other young men of North African origin living in poor neighbourhoods. The anthropologist, Didier Fassin established the "gulf between the police and residents of disadvantaged neighbours; 80% of police officers are from rural areas or provincial towns where the socio-ethnic make- up is radically different."

According to the Defenceur Des Droits (Defender of Rights, Responsible for Protecting Citizens from Official Discrimination) "Young men perceived as Arabs or black, are 20 times more likely to have their identi- ties checked. Abusive identity checks feel like a permanent injustice and are often what sets off unrest." Protests in France against police brutality led to the Interior Minister, Christophe Casataner, announcing on June 8th, 2020, the banning of chokehold by police during an arrest.

In 2016, the UN Committee Against Torture expressed its concern regarding "allegations of excessive use of force by the police and the Gendarmerie, which has in some instances led to serious injuries or death." A few examples of blacks and members of the Arab community who died through the action of the French police.

ADAMA TRAORE- The 24 years old born on July 19th, 1992, died on July 19th, 2016, after he was arrested and restrained by French police. The Malian French national, in the company of his brother was stopped by police for an ID check. He did not have his with him, so he took to his heels. He was later found hiding in a house and was taken into custody. One of the three police officers who arrested Traore admitted that he and his colleagues pinned him down using their body weight. He however denied that their action caused his death. Initially an autopsy by the French state stated that Traore's medical condition combined with an alleged use of alcohol and narcotics resulted in the cardiac arrest. Other conflicting medical reports were reported. However, a second autopsy demanded by the family concluded that he died from suffocation, mostly likely by the policemen's weight as they pinned him down.

Assa Traore, the sister of Adama shouted to a crowd of more than 20,000 protesters, "We are here because the justice system is complicit in police violence." She was quoted by the Daily Parisien, "A judge is covering up the Gendarmes who are responsible for my brother's death." Arie Alimi, a lawyer covering police violence stated, "Everybody agreed Adama Traore died from asphyxiation."

LAMINE DIENG- On June 17th, 2007, Lamine Dieng a 25-year-old French- Senegalese died after suffocat- ing in a police van. The French police had his hands in handcuffs and his feet were tied.
BOUNA TRAORE AND ZYED BENNA- These two teenagers, fifteen and seventeen respectively, were elocuted in the police suburb of Clichy-Sous-Bois. The boys were chased by police as they were on their way home after watching a football match. The police were accused of not helping the boys, despite the knowledge that the boys were in danger when they were seen approaching the EDF power facility. The police were adamant that

they were blameless. A third teenager, Muhittin Altun, escaped with burns.

The deaths sparked three weeks of protests, clashes with the security forces in poor city suburbs across France. Vehicles and public buildings were burned. Thousands of rioters were arrested. This led to the first state of emergency in twenty years. In 2012, after years of arguments through the courts, France's highest court overturned a ruling which dropped the "failure to help" charge against the police officers. If found guilty, the two police officers would have faced up to five years in prison. The defence like the prosecution, however called for an acquittal.

Other members of French's minority population to have died in police custody were Abou Bakari Tandai, 38-year-old Malian Ali Ziri, a 69-year-old Algerian Abdelhakim Ajami, a 22-year-old Tunisia and Mohammed Boukrourou, a 41-year-old Moroccan.

MICHEL ZECLER- On November 21st, 2020, the French news website Loopsider published a video about the violent arrest of a black music producer, Michel Zecler in the 17th District of Paris. The video is reported to last 12 minutes. The video images also obtained by the Associated Press both from security camera inside the studio and filmed by neighbours outside, show the three officers pursuing Zecler into his music studio where they are seen repeatedly punching him and beating him with a truncheon.

He suffered injuries to his head, forearms and his leg. The officers went out and called reinforcement and even threw a tear gas into the studio to force nine more people inside; out. According to El Ali, Zecler's lawyer, "Outside they are still beaten up and thrown to the ground and that's when a police officer sees they are being filmed." The violence then stops. Zecler was then arrested.

On Thursday November 26th, 2020, the Paris Prosecutor's office dropped the police officers' fabricated charges against Zecler. The Prosecutor rather opened an investigation "for acts of violence for a person in position of authority," and "false allegation." Zecler's offence was that he was not wearing a (Covid-19) mask which was mandatory outdoors in Paris. The police claimed that he appeared "nervous" and a "strong drug smell" came from him. They also alleged that he was "dangerous" towards them.

The French Interior Minister ordered the suspension of the officers involved. President Macron stated that the incident was "shameful to France." Michel Zecler told the Associated Press that he felt "good" that "the truth is out." He added, "I want to understand why I have been assaulted by police who were wearing a police uniform. I want justice actually, because I believe in justice of my country."

AUSTRALIA- In Australia, police brutality against the indigenous aboriginal people is also endemic. In 1991, a Royal Commission made 339 recommendations to reduce the worryingly number of deaths in police custody. The New York Times reported on November 11th, 2019, "400 indigenous people have died while in police custody since 1991." No police officers were charged for murder.

The paper reported that in 2007 a police officer was acquitted of manslaughter after the death of a man on Palm Island, off Australia's northeastern coast. The death led to months of riots. Yasmine Musharbash, a senior lecturer in Anthropology at The Australian National University was quoted, "People have always been frightened about being in the cells." She added, "Now you have mothers saying to their children to stay the hell away from police."

KUMANJAVI WALKER- On Saturday night, the 19-year-old Aboriginal died after he was shot two or three times at the Central Australian town of Yuendumu 300km from Alice Springs. Two police officers went to a house in the northern territory to arrest Walker for breaches of a suspended sentence. The death sparked anger and protests in communities and cities across Australia. Authorities initially stated that the teenager had lunged at police with a weapon. They however changed that and charged 28-year-old Constable Zachary Rolfe with one count of murder and opened an investigation. The decision was received with widespread cheers. The Guardian quoted Thalia Anthony, Associate Professor of Law, "A charge of murder against a police officer in relation to a death in custody of an indigenous person is almost unprecedented."

Walker did not receive "critical emergency care" for his injuries in the police station. Concerned family members who were waiting outside the police station "were not notified until hours after his death."

EATHAN CRUDE- On April 18th, 2015, 19-year-old Cruse in handcuffs was severely beaten in his parents' house by armed officers from the joint counter terrorism squad. The officers used disproportionate force in the arrest during a dawn raid in Melbourne. Cruse was awarded $400,000 in damages for the "cowardly and brutal attack."

DAVID DUNGAY JNR- In December 2015, four days after Christmas, prison officers stormed the cell of 26 years old Dungay Jnr after he refused to stop eat- ing a packet of biscuits. According to the Guardian Australian News, he was "restrained and adminis- tered a sedative Midazolam and died." David was the youngest of four children of Leetona Dungay. David was serving an eight-year prison sentence for "assault, aggravated attempted sexual intercourse and party to robbery." He was just three months away from release when he died. His big brother Ernie Dungay was quoted, "Is there the death penalty in Australia? Because that is what happened to my little brother,"

In July 2018, Western Australian's Police Commissioner Chris Dawson, formally apologized for the treatment of the Aboriginal People at the hands of police. He con- ceded the "significant role" the police played in the dispossession of Australia's First National People. The Police Commissioner highlighted the "forceful removal of aboriginal and Torre Strait Islander children from their families and communities, the displacement of moth- ers and their children, sisters, fathers and brothers, the loss of family and the resulting destruction of culture have had grave impacts."

The 1991 Royal Commission regarding aboriginal deaths in custody (RCIADIC) established that the aboriginal population was grossly overrepresented in custody. The Commissioner stated that aboriginal people were "in gross disproportionate numbers, com- pared with non-aboriginal people in both police and prison custody and it is this fact that provides the immediate explanation for the disturbing number of aboriginal deaths in custody."

In January 2018, it was reported that though Aboriginal and Torres Strait Islander adults make up around 2% of the national population, they make up 27% of the national prison population. The Jesuit Social Services stated, "The over representation of Aboriginal and Torres Strait Islander Peoples in the Criminal Justice System is a national disgrace."

BRAZIL- It was reported that in the first four months of 2020, Rio police, admitted killing 606 people. Police violence went up despite the recent covid19 lockdown which even resulted in a sudden drop in robberies and other criminal activities. The police kill almost six people daily, a 43% increase in comparison to the month of April 2019. It is estimated that the 9,000 people killed by the Rio police in the last decade, more than 75% were black.

On May 18th, 2020, three police officers allegedly in pursuit of suspects, went into a house in the Salgueiro Favela. In occupation were six unarmed cousins who had assembled to play. The police opened fire and hit 14 years old Joao Pedro Matos Pinto in the back. A relative drove the victim to the police helicopter used in the raid. The police took him away. Having endured over seventeen agonizing hours not knowing the whereabouts and of the condition of the teen- ager, the family eventually found Joao's body at the Coroner's office.

Three days after, the police were involved in another shooting, they claimed that they were responding to "gunfire from unidentified suspects." On that occasion, those caught in the incident were teachers, students and other volunteers outside a school in the Providencia Favela. They were distributing food packages to families left destitute and hungry by the economic downturn brought about by Covid-19. 19-years-old student, Rodrigo Cerqueira, who was killed; was described by his teacher as a "wonderful boy."

On these two occasions May 18th and 21st, the police did not make any arrests neither was there any injury to any of the officers. The Brazil police, as in many countries around the world, often cite self-defence as the reason for the civilian fatalities. It is acknowledged in Brazil that at times it is true because of the threat posed by dangerous gangs. However, in many cases it is also established that it is not because of armed gangs.

On April 17th, 2020, Brazil's Supreme Court Justice Edson Fachin ruled that Rio De Janeiro police should leave crime scenes intact and desist from taking bodies to the hospital which was a ploy to destroy vital criminal evidence. The ruling dictated that forensic experts should include photographs in their reports.

THE GEORGE FLOYD EFFECT

The repercussions of the death of George Floyd in the hands of the US law enforcement officer, in the company of three others on May 25th, 2020, have been far-reaching. The gruesome incident reignited the perennial debate of the black man's pain in bondage from the early seventeenth century, through abolition in the nineteenth century and the continued inhumane treatment and the indefensible racial injustices into the 21st Century.

Global citizens took to the streets and protested their indignation that the abolition of the vile trade did not entirely sooth the pain of the black man. Governments of different political persuasions and national institutions have all failed to bring about racial equality. When the masses protested, the companies, big and small, prestigious and not so renowned, unequivocally got the message. Vaults were opened and archives, yellowed with age were turned over to find the link to the human trade.

Slavery brought immense wealth to individual fami- lies; and has underpinned the economy of the United States, UK and some European nations.

High at the top of the list to declare a direct link to slavery, are of course the financial institutions: And they do not come any bigger than the Bank of England. The bank issued a statement published on June 19th, 2020. The heading, 'Statement in Relation to the Bank's Historical Links to the Slave Trade.' It reads," There can be no doubt that the eighteenth and nineteenth century slave trade was an unacceptable part of British history. As an institution, the Bank of England was never itself directly involved in the slave trade but is aware of some inexcusable connections involving former governors and directors and apologizes for them. The bank has commenced a thorough review of its collection of images of former governors and directors to ensure none with any such involvement in the slave trade remains on display anywhere in the bank. The bank is committed to improving diversity and is actively engaging with staff, particularly with our BAME colleagues, to help us identify and shape concrete steps that can be taken now to progress the bank's efforts to be as inclusive as possible."

The guardian.com/business website published on June 18th, 2020, that Barclays, HSBC and Lloyds are among the UK banks which had links to slavery. Many directors received compensation after slavery was abolished in 1833. Jasper Jolly wrote, "The slave trade was abolished in the British Empire in 1807 but it was not until 1833 that the Slavery Abolition Act finally banned the ownership of other human beings. However, 46,000 former slave owners continued to benefit financially as the subsequent Slave Compensation Act provided £20m in payments- a sum worth billions in 2020 terms. Despite the name of the act, the former slaves were not compensated."

Jasper Jolly added that the University of London's Legacies of British Slave Ownership project reveals that 10% to 20% of the rich people in Britain "can be identified as having had significant links to slavery." The huge amount the British government borrowed to pay off slave owners was finally repaid fully in 2015. Companies with links to slavery in the past include...

ROYAL BANK OF SCOTLAND- It was founded in Edinburgh in 1727. Hundreds of banks it later acquired had links to the slave trade. A report funded by the bank in 2009 revealed that directors of RBS predecessors "had owned slaves as well as giving loans and other support to plantation owners." The British government has 62% state in the bank. A spokesperson was quoted, "We have a strong multicultural network across the bank and have recently set up a taskforce led by our BAME (Black, Asian and minority ethnic) colleagues who will look at what more we can do as a bank. This includes looking at making contributions to BAME groups."

BARCLAYS BANK- a spokesperson stated, "The history of Barclays, like other institutions, is being examined following recent events. We can't change what's gone before us, only how we go forward. We are committed as a bank to do more to further foster our culture of inclusiveness, equality and diversity, for our colleagues, and the customers and clients we serve."

HSBC- was founded in 1865 to finance trade between European and Asian countries. It merged with the Midland Bank, UK in 1992. It had links with the London Joint Stock bank whose first manager, George Pollard was reported to have received £2,416 (more than £230,000 in today's money) in compensation for giving up 134 slaves in Nevis. A spokeswoman stated," HSBC has operated across the globe for over 150 years and is fully committed to driving a diverse and inclusive culture. We are committed to learning from the past and, in particular, anything that would be inconsistent with our values today. HSBC has zero tolerance towards racial discrimination, or any other type of discrimination."

LLOYDS BANKING GROUP-This group enjoyed a rapid expansion in the 1860s, a far cry from its first 100 years of operation from one office in Birmingham. John White Carter, a director of one of the acquired companies, received compensation for five estates which had 80 slaves at the time of abolition. The UCL database reveals that eight former companies associated with Lloyds have links to "claimants or beneficiaries" of compensation. A Lloyds spokeswoman stated, "A lot has changed during the 300 - year history of our brands and while we have much within our heritage to be proud of, we can't be proud of it all. We stand against racism, slavery and discrimination in all its forms and truly believe that by reflecting, understanding, promoting and valuing the diversity of our colleagues, we will deliver better results. We can do better, and we will do it together."

LLOYD'S OF LONDON-According to the UCL database, Lloyd's of London started in a coffee house more than 330 years ago. In the 1730s it emerged as the lead- ing insurance group in the world. The group played a vital role in the building of the British Empire. Lloyds of London was unquestionably involved in the slave trade. Simon Fraser, a founder subscriber member of Lloyd's was paid in today's money an equivalent of £400,000 for giving up a plantation in Dominica with at least 162 enslaved Africans. The descendants of slaves sought reparation from Lloyd's in 2004. The group con- ceded that the slave trade was "an appalling and shameful period of English history, as well as our own, and we condemn the indefensible wrongdoing that occurred during this period." The group plans to fund organizations which support BAME groups and "invest in positive programs to attract, retain and develop black and minority ethnic talent."

ARBUTHNOT LATHAM- The joint founders of this private bank, Alfred Latham and James Alves Arbuthnot, were linked to the slave trade. Latham received compensa- tion after the abolition of slavery in 1833. It was founded in the same year. "The bank grew into a major funder of Britain's colonial exploits, including Cecil Rhode's gold fields in South Africa." A spokesman of the bank is quoted, "Arbuthnot Latham stands against racism and discrimination in all forms and is committed to diversity across the bank."

GREEN KING-The pub chain which is reputed to run no fewer than 3,300 pubs, restaurants and hotels was founded in 1799 by 19-year-old Benjamin Green. Green later became the owner of sugar cane planta- tions in the West Indies. He was against abolitionists of the vile trade in humans. He received in compensation about £500,000 in today's money for three plantations in the West Indies. Nick Mackenzie, Green King's chief executive lamented, "It is inexcusable that one of our founders profited from slavery and argued against its abolition in the 1800s." The company plans to offer financial reparations.

Other revelations caused by the George Floyd effect, by British establishments include the National Trust. The September 22nd, 2020, issue of the Daily Mirror, under the heading, 'Trust Has 93 Homes from Exploitation," revealed in a column, "The National Trust says 93 of the properties it runs have links to historical slavery and colonialism. Displays will now be reviewed to tell the full story to visitors."

The report examined links to plantation owners and those paid compensation for slaves freed through abolition. Properties tainted with colonialism include Winston Churchill's home, Chartwell in Kent, and writer, Rudyard Kipling's home, Bateman's in Sussex. DrTanya Cooper, a spokesperson stated," This report is the fullest account to date of the links between places in the care of the National Trust and colonialism and slavery." She added that it was not exhaustive and that more research would be done.

On the same September 22nd, 2020, Vanessa Allen, under the heading, 'National Trust's 100 Sites Have Links to Slavery,' stated, "The Trust has insisted that it does not want to censor history, but that it has a duty to ensure its supporters and visitors know about the origins of some of its properties." Vanessa named a Tory councillor in Somerset, Lucy Trimnell who opposed the disclosure; she "cannot support the naming and shaming of innocent families who left those properties to the custodianship of the National Trust." She threatened to cancel her family's membership.

"The National Trust which has 5.6 million members and 500 historic sites around the UK, said it commissioned the report last September. The audit details properties' links to slave traders but also to families whose plantations used slave labour, and who were paid compensation after the slave trade was abolished. It said 29 Trust properties had links to successful compensation claims, including Glastonbury Tor in Somerset and Blickling Hall in Norfolk," Vanessa Allen explained. 'From Chartwell to Lundy, National Trust lays bare its historic links to slavery,' this was the headline in the Guardian on the same day in September. Mark Brown, the Arts Correspondent quoted Dr Tanya Cooper, the Trust's Curatorial and Collections Director, "We are not doing anything more than present the historical facts and data. Not everyone feels comfortable talking about this." She added that it was important for "people to draw their own conclusions and make their minds up about things." Mark Brown's report ended with a final quote from Dr Cooper in a response to a leaked survey about the outrage and rumoured exodus of members. "We haven't noticed a massive drop-off in membership. We just haven't seen that most of our members join because they care about history, and beauty and heritage, and they are interested in this work. They want us to do it responsibly."

The Times, on the same day had the heading, 'Trust Flags Colonial Sins of Its Stately Homes; to Herald Its Contribution to Proceeds from Slavery and Colonial Exploitation.' "Dozens of the country's most renowned stately homes are tainted by slavery and colonial exploitation, according to the National Trust," David Sanderson stated. He quoted senior Trust figures regarding, "a significant number of the collections, houses, gardens and parklands in our care were created or remodelled as expression of the taste and wealth, as well as the privilege, that derived from colonial connections and in some cases from the trade in enslaved people."

A Trust report on September 22nd, 2020, shed light on Stone, Buckinghamshire, "where records refer to the sale of slaves that may be linked to First Viscount Cabham: Ham House in South West London is linked to a founder of the Royal African Company which shipped 200,000 slaves." David Sanderson concluded, "Those involved in the trade and financing of slavery, the report says, included the Hebberts of Hare Hill and the Rutsons of Nunnington Hall. The inquiry did not cover National Trust properties in Scotland," the Times ended.

On February 24th,2013 Sanchez Manning of the Independent Newspaper wrote, "The true scale of Britain's involvement in the slave trade has been laid bare in documents revealing how the country's wealthiest received the modern equivalent of billions of pounds in compensation after slavery was abolished." Sanchez Manning cited," The biggest single payout went to James Blair (no relation to Orwell), an MP who had homes in Marylebone, Central London and Scotland. He was awarded £83,530, the equivalent of £65m today for 1,598 slaves he owned on the plantation he had inherited in British Guyana." Manning drew a comparison, "John Gladstone the father of 19th, Century Prime Minister, William Gladstone, "received £106,769 (modern equivalent £83m) for the 2,508 slaves he owned across nine plantations." Manning also stated, "The British government paid out £20m to compensate 3,000 families that owned slaves for the loss of their 'property' when slave ownership was abolished in British colonies in 1833."

"In the countryside, profits from West Indian plantations built some of the most beautiful state homes and rolling estates of England," Tristram Hunt, Museum Director and former Labour MP wrote in the June 12th, 2020, issue of the Daily Mirror. He continued, "Harewood House- the West Yorkshire seat of the Lascelles family- owes its magnificence to the 27,000 acres of sugar cane fields held across Barbados, Jamaica and Tobago, as well as a particularly inhumane fleet of slaving vessels anchored off the coast of Anomabu, Ghana." Hunt explained further," More than that, the wealth that came from sugar and slavery gave Britain the funds for the industrial revolution. Our pioneering history of industrialisation- in coal, cotton and shipbuilding was heavily indebted to the riches that followed from the enslavement and sale of Africans. The beauty and elegance of Edinburgh, London, Glasgow and Bath were secured by slave investments. We need to acknowledge that history. At the Victoria and Albert Museum, we have traced the origins of some of our collections to slave money and highlighted this terrible contrast between beautiful objects and the bloody funds behind them."

The systematic racism, numerous losses of black lives in the hands of police culminating in the daylight lynching of George Floyd, not only evoked national outrage, grief and pain, but jolted the conscience of corporate America. Succession of companies, retailers and numerous brands have pledged financial support to black causes. They include...

1. AIRBNB-The company announced a donation of $500,000 to be split between the NAACP (National Association for the Advancement of Coloured People) and the Black Lives Matter Movement.

2. ALLBIRDS- The sneaker company made a "rapid response contribution" to the Black Lives Movement and the NAACP legal defence and educational fund.

3. AMAZON- This global company donated $10m to be spread across ACLU Foundation, Brennan Centre for Justice, Equal Justice Initiative, Lawyers' Committee for Civil Rights Under Law, NAACP, National Bar Association, National Museum for African American History and Culture, National Urban League, The Thurgood Marshall College Fund and Year Up.

4. APPLE- CEO Tim Cook announced," Donations of an unspecific amount" to be made by the company to organizations including, Equal Justice Initiative, "a non-profit organization committed to challenging racial injustice."

5. BAD ROBOT- J.J. Abrams's Production Company pledged $10m over the next five years to organizations with "anti-racist agendas that close the gaps, lift the poor and build a just America for all. An initial $200,000 investments will go to the Black Lives Matter Movement, Community Coalition, Equal Justice Initiative and Know Your Rights Camp."

6. BANK OF AMERICA- Pledged $1 billion over four years of additional support to help local communities, address economic and racial inequality accelerated by the global corona virus pandemic.

7. BILLIE- The -Direct-To -Consumer Razor Company donated $100,000 to be shared by the Black Lives Matter Movement and NAACP. The company stated," We stand as one. We stand with the memory of those lives lost through systemic injustice and racism. We are donating $100,000 across BLM and the NAACP, a step toward hopefully making our country the safe place it should have always been."

8. HOME DEPOT- CEO Craig Menear announced a $1m donation to the Lawyers' Committee for Civil Rights Under Law. Menear also stated that the company would work for change internally.

Other companies donating to black causes are Bombas, Brooklinen, Brooks Running, Cisco stated, "the other pandemic: the killing of Black Americans." Walmart has pledged $100m over five years to create a new centre for racial equality. Target announced, a $10m commitment to advance social justice through supporting partners like National Urban League and the African American Leadership Forum. Other supporters of black causes include DE.A. Games, Square Enix, UbisoftEtsy, H & M Clothing, Everlane, Tom Shoes, Spanx, Levis, Gap Brands (Athleta, Old Navy and Gap).

Among the countless global stars of TV, radio, businesspeople and sports people, is Michael Jordan who donated, $100,000 "to groups fighting for racial equality and social justice." The Jordan brand is spreading the amount "over the next ten years."

In the March 13th,2021 issue of the Daily Mirror, US Editor, Christopher Bucktin wrote, "George Floyd's family have reached a £19.4m settlement over his death. Minneapolis council approved the sum after relatives filed a suit against the US city and four police officers involved." He added that the amount included "£360,000 to enhance the district where the father of five died last May aged 46."

RONALD GREENE- Before George Floyd, there were many other victims of police brutality, known by law enforcement and some members of the public, but not gaining national publicity. Other incidents captured on police body cameras remained concealed from the public. However, one incident involving 49 years old unarmed African American barber, Ronald Greene was leaked in the latter part of May 2021. Associated Press obtained and published part of the footage of the police body camera after it had been kept a secret for two years.

Some members of the Louisiana state police claimed that during a high-speed chase on May 10th, 2019, outside Monroe, Louisiana, the African American crashed his car against a tree and died on his way to hospital. When the police reported the cause of death to doctors in the hospital, one of the doctors was reported to have stated," It does not add up." The police later conceded that Greene had died during a struggle. Instead of rendering aid, the troopers were alleged to have left Greene unattended, face down, for nine minutes. The footage of the police camera revealed how the unarmed Greene was tasered, punched several times in the side of his body as he lay defenceless on the floor. He was dragged on the floor by his feet while handcuffed and shackled. At one stage an officer put his foot on Greene's body as he shone a torchlight on his face. The area these troopers patrol is reported to be 40% African American.

During the confrontation, Ronald Greene's mournful pleas fell on deaf ears. He was heard on the footage, "okay, okay I'm sorry." He even responded politely to one command, "Yes sir." He was heard pleading, "I'm scared officer, I'm scared, I'm your brother, I'm scared." Ronald, a Christian, at one point, at the impact of a vicious blow, yelped in pain, "Jesus!" One officer was heard in the footage boasting how he beat the hell out of Ronald and at one point thought he was "dead." Some of these rouge officers do not think black lives matter because they are cocooned by 'Qualified Immunity.' A picture of the dead Ronald shown by CNN after an interview with his mother and sister, showed no fewer than four serious indentations on his head probably caused by a police baton. What a sad and at times unchristian world we live in. Zero morality!

Ronald Greene's mother and sister were reported to have wailed "like they were at a funeral" after meeting Governor John Bel Edwards and watching part of the footage. The behaviour of these police officers, I believe not only shamed their own families, majority of good and professional police officers, especially in the US, it brought to the fore, two factors. Wickedness and madness intertwined to equal psychopatic behaviour. It rests firmly in the depths of moral depravity. Shameful!!! Sir Robert Peel is wailing in his grave with the Greene family and other families black and white who have lost loved ones through police brutality.

According to Wikipedia, one of the troopers involved in the Greene incident, Dakota DeMoss was given letters of reprimand and counselling for violating the department's rules about courtesy and recordings. He was later arrested for using excessive force while hand-cuffing a motorist in a separate incident. A second trooper, Chris Hollingsworth, died in a single-vehicle car accident hours after learning that he would be fired in his role in Greene's death. A third trooper, Kory York, was suspended for 50 hours for dragging Greene and improperly turning off his body camera. He is reported to have returned to duty.

A federal wrongful death and a federal civil rights investigation are in the pipeline.

CHAPTER FOURTEEN

THE ROLE OF A POLICE OR LAW ENFORCEMENT OFFICER

The Uniformed Bully

It was evening, a winter Sunday.
He swaggered towards my car
followed by two of his pals.
I was about to enter my car.

"You look like a drug dealer,"
he said in derisive arrogance.
"Open your car for a search,"
he ordered in contemptuous screech.

Is it a crime to be out at seven?
Was it a crime to have used the cash machine?
Is it a crime to own an "E" Reg. Rover?
Is it a crime to look different?

My mind was a jungle of thoughts as I obliged.
He led the two provokingly past me.
They searched my car frantically
but found nothing to feed their hatred.

"Did you come to England by plane or boat?"
"Are you thick in the head?"
the bully and stooges in uniform intimidated
as they shamelessly discredited their profession.

The role of a police officer as defined in the internet -'A police officer serves to maintain law and order in local areas by protecting members of the public and their property, preventing crime, reducing the fear of crime and improving the quality of life for all citizens.' According to Wikipedia, "A law enforcement officer is a public employee whose duties primarily involve the enforcement of laws. Modern legal codes use the term 'Peace Officer' (or in some jurisdictions, law enforcement officer) to include every person vested by the legislating state with law enforcement authority."

I have intentionally not included the word 'power,' which arguably is often misplaced and misused in the execution of duty. Morally, no human being has 'power' over another human being, even one's own child. The appropriate word in my opinion is 'authority' invested in a person donning a legally approved uniform, cap (if required) and a badge. All personnel in law enforcement roles should behave or perform judiciously and conscientiously.

PHILIPPINES-In the Philippines although it is not written in the job description of the police that they could kill with impunity, according to Amnesty International, in the 'War on Drugs', more than 7,000 people were killed between July 2016 and January 2017. The victims were fellow Philippinos, the same colour of skin as the police officers. Amnesty International attributed the excessive number of deaths to the direct instructions of Rodrigo Duterte. Amnesty reported that the Philippines President ordered the police forces, "to kill anyone they believe to be connected to the drugs trade when he assumed office in June 2016."

TRUMP Vs PHILIPPINES' DUTERTE: POLICE BRUTALITY- On August 24th, 2017, Charlize Alcaraz of Affinity Magazine US wrote "The month of August has undoubtedly witnessed a profound division of humanity motivated by abuse of power. On a global stance, both western and eastern politics have become more compa- rable regarding Trump's response to the tragedy in

Charlottesville and Duterte's stance on police brutality after the killing of 17 years old Kian Delos in the midst of the Philippines' war on drugs." The report confirmed, "According to an official transcript of the phone call produced by the Philippine Department of Foreign Affairs, "Trump initiated a conversation by making quick comparisons between him and the Philippines' head of state."

On July 26th, 2020, in the Observer, under the head- ing 'Portland's Summer of Reckoning,' reporter Chris McGreal wrote, "Clashes between protesters and Federal officers sent in by Donald Trump are playing out nightly on American TV screens. But behind the street battles lie decades of racial injustice that scar this liberal city and complicate simple narratives." Chris McGreal stated that only 6% of Portland's 650,000 res- idents are African Americans but they accounted for 30% of shooting by police over the past three years. Black people are also many times more likely to be arrested or stopped by the police.

In 2010, a young black man was killed by police in Portland. Aaron Campbell's family feared he might be suicidal after the death of his brother earlier in the day. They duly called the police. According to the report the officers who checked on him, "quickly established he was not a threat to himself or anyone else." The offi- cers involved sent a text message to allay any fears. However, a second police unit arrived as Campbell came out of a building. They shot him with a non-lethal "bean bag" round. When Campbell naturally reacted by reaching to the part of the injury, officers claimed that he was going for a gun. They shot him dead, but Campbell was found unarmed.

The Civil Rights leader, Jessie Jackson referred to the killing as "an execution." A letter by the Grand Jury to the District Attorney stated, "This was very difficult for us as a Grand Jury, as our sympathies lie with the Campbell family and the mood of the community. As a group, we are outraged." Earlier the Grand Jury had ruled that the officer who shot Campbell "acted within the law but that did not mean he was innocent."

Utter nonsense! Unbelievable. The City's police department's racist reputation prompted President Obama's administration to demand reforms and placed it under Federal Court oversight in 2014. Although it side-stepped the issue of race, in doing so critics suspected that it was a move to save the Democratic leadership from embarrassment.

The role of police or law enforcement officers in any country, includes pursuing, arresting and detaining any individual suspected of breaking the law of a specific country or state within a federal system of government.

Until the person is found guilty, in the court of law, not a kangaroo court (lynching), that person remains legally 'suspected' but innocent until proven guilty.

It is not stated anywhere or implied that a police officer or a law enforcement officer has the right to take the life of a suspect. Yes! a 'suspect,' because the person has not been to court and found guilty of the crime he was alleged or suspected to have committed. Even if anybody is found guilty of any crime, it is not the duty of the police to exact punishment. The one and only exception is when a police or law enforcement offi-cer(s) genuinely believes, without any form of preju-dice, faces a dire situation where he is in mortal danger or members of the public are of grave risk of being killed.

An apt example of this important fact was underlined by Rod Charles, the retired black Metropolitan Chief Inspector of police's statement on British TV, "I know that there will be circumstances when police officers and other law enforcement must use the highest levels of force; and sometimes it will culminate in death." He however painfully lamented, "But there have been too many cases, where people died and none of them merited the highest levels of force." He then named four of the black victims and ended, "I could go on."

Examples can be noted in any country even where genuine police officers, in the pursuit of their duty to enforce the law and protect the public, have lost their lives. In the UK in 2017, P.C. Keith Palmer was knifed and killed in a terror attack at Westminster. In 2012, 23 years old Nicola Hughes and 32 years old Fiona Bone were murdered in Greater Manchester. On November 18th, 2005, P.C. Sharon Beshenivsky 38, was shot dead at the scene of a robbery in Bradford. She was the seventh policewoman killed in UK while on duty. Another high-profile incident costing the death of P.C. Yvonne Fletcher, was during the Libyan Embassy siege in April 1984.

The death of 28 years old P.C. Harper on August 15th, 2019, is a recent example of how difficult the police officer's job is. P.C. Harper with his colleague, P.C. Andrew Shaw (now retired), answered a call regarding a stolen quadbike in Berkshire. In a brave attempt to prevent three young offenders from stealing the quadbike, the brave and dutiful policeman had his leg accidentally caught in a strap and was dragged for a mile behind a car being driven by the oldest culprit who was 19 years old. The remaining two were both 18. The young driver was reported to have "swerved violently at speeds of up to 60 miles per hour." P.C. Harper's colleague P.C. Shaw, "found him dying on the roadside." P.C. Harper's widow was put into, "a lost and endless world of numb despair." They were married barely a month before the incident on July 18th, 2019. Only a flint-hearted per- son will fail to empathize and show sympathy for P.C. Harper's widow, his mother, and all loved ones.

In August 8th, 2020, issue of the Daily Mirror, under the caption, 'Hero P.C. Back on Feet.' It was reported, "Courageous P.C. Claire Bond spent sixteen months learning to walk again after being run over, dragged along the ground and crushed against a fence by a drug dealer."

In September 2018 P.C. Bond responded to a call that a car had crashed near a 10km race. The drug dealer was trying to get away from police.

However, P.C. Bond sensed that if she did not stop him, he could drive into a crowd injuring many people. The P. C's selfless act in pursuit of her public duty, averted a potential tragedy. The mother of four, the younger two being 14 and 9, endured a five-hour operation to save a shattered leg.

Thankfully, she is now back on duty. P.C. Bond's bravery was recognized with the 'Emergency Services Award' at the 'Pride of Birmingham Awards' in partnership with TSB.

No wife, mother, father, children and any other loved ones of a police officer would accept that he or she could go to work and not return or suffer serious injuries while performing this important public duty. The bravely, dedication and endearing humanity of majority of police or law enforcement officers are sadly and unfortunately overshadowed by the senseless and reckless behaviours by a few within their ranks.

The offending minority within the police personnel, sadly and too often in cases highlighted in the media, carry their naked biases and bigotry with them to work. We all know the consequences whether in the UK, US, France and other countries where minorities have been for far too long been at the mercy of police and law enforcement officers. A loved one would not accept a police officer not returning home: equally and naturally a black mother would not accept that her son would not return to her bosom, after being arrested by police for an alleged criminal offence.

Police and law enforcement officers are ordinary citizens (including plain clothes detectives) until they don their uniforms, caps and put on their badges. Professionally the prejudices and bigotry which admittedly are endemic in sections of the general public, should be actively suppressed. No doubt some officers in their professional capacity, appreciably manage to contain these human traits very well. Some politicians lack the moral and political courage to rid society of this endemic and pernicious problem. Perhaps one is asking for too much as some politicians-past and present are on record of expressing racial views to create divisions and sow mistrust in society. The 'Rivers of Blood' speech by MP Enoch Powell on April 20th, 1968, during a Conservative Association meeting in Birmingham, is a typical example. He was sacked by the Prime Minister, Edward Heath.

In 1978 during an interview on TV, 'World in Action,' the future Prime Minister, Tory MP Margaret Thatcher claimed that the British people feared being "swamped" by immigration from the Commonwealth and Pakistan. The BAME (Black, Asian, Minority Ethnic Group) was probably under 10% of the total population. Even the last census in 2011 put the percentage at 13%. The Independent stated that in 2010, current Tory Prime Minister Boris Johnson stated, "It is said that the Queen has come to love the Commonwealth partly because it supplies her with regular cheering crowds of flag-waving piccaninnies." This is an extremely derogatory term. It refers to a small black or aboriginal child. US President Trump is known for openly and unashamedly making racist statements yet claiming, "I am the least racist person in this room," during the 2020 Presidential debate with Joe Biden. He was also quoted at other times saying, "I'm the least racist person you have ever met," He was quoted by the Washington Post, during the early part of his presidency as referring to immigrants from Haiti and African nations as coming from "shithole countries."

If some politicians fail to set a good example, the majority of conscientious police officers with the support of the majority of the populace, should be able to proudly uphold the integrity of their profession by distancing themselves from the few but potent (or is it pongy) bad apples within their ranks. On the front page of the Daily Mirror, August 4th, 2020, under the headline, 'Police Stop Me All the Time Last Week They Even Sent A Riot Van,' Jeremy Cross wrote about the desolation of former England black footballer Danny Rose and his resignation, or may I say, lament, "What can I do?" Jeremy Cross quoted Rose, "I got stopped last week which is a regular occurrence whenever I go to Doncaster. Each time it's 'Is this car stolen?', 'Where did you get this car from?', What are you doing here?' and 'Can you prove that you bought this car?' Danny Rose was also quoted, "The last time, when I had just been at my mum's house, I had pulled up at a car park, so the engine was off. The police pulled in and brought a riot van and three police cars. I got my ID out and they breathalyzed me. It's just one of those things to me now. What can I do?"

Often some people in society state that blacks should not complain, "the police are doing their duty." Danny Rose's experience is just one of countless, faced by blacks daily and official statistics abrogate the assertion that, "They are doing their duty." What is most baffling is that Danny Rose, capped by England, until some months ago; played regularly for top Premiership Club, Tottenham Hotspur. How come none of the police officers recognized him and conceded (grudgingly for some) that 'this black boy's monthly salary is more than the yearly (I repeat, yearly) salary of the Prime Minister of the day. He could and indeed can buy a fleet of exorbitant cars on the market, buy a mansion for his mama in Doncaster and still be left with a hefty bank balance to keep his bank manager feeling eternally blessed. Alleluya!

I had a personal experience with a police officer when working as a Branch Manager for a leading Oil Company in S.E. London in the mid - 1970s. Petrol was then between 67p to 70p a gallon (not a litre. A gallon is 4.55ltr). There were often raids by police on premises or companies where immigrants predominantly worked. One afternoon a police officer, on his own came to my branch and demanded that I gave him the list of all people working in my branch. I told him that I had a full-time English lady as cashier, the rest were African, Sri Lankan and Indian students who worked part-time to supplement the cost of their daily living. When I refused to give him the name and addresses of the students he retorted, "You are being stubborn," to which I responded that if he had a search warrant or approval from the oil company's head office, "I would not be in your way." Disgruntled, the police officer left without further exchanges. I promptly reported the incident to head office.

A week after, the same officer emerged from nowhere, yet again on his own. In my office he flashed a letter purported to have been written by me informing the police about drugs. Initially it was a shock, but I quickly sprang into action because as a former schoolteacher I always look out for spelling and of course grammatical mistakes. He acted suspiciously because he did not allow me to handle the letter let alone read it. Luckily, I saw that at the bottom of the letter, the 'writer' had written out my surname as a signature. I then told the police officer, "I don't know your name, but do you spell your name wrongly." He replied, "No." I countered, "Well neither do I, my name is spelt 'AMARTEIFIO BUT AMARTEFIO (first 'I' missing) and moreover I do not smoke let alone inform anybody about drugs." I then stood up in the office and needless to stress he retreated utterly dejected. It was so shameful the English lady felt sorry for me. I assured her that I was "ok" although I was seething with anger.

The officer did not come to the branch again.

I left the petrol retail business after 13 years of service in 1985 after an armed robbery. A gun was pointed at me and the robbers went away with over £6,000 and credit card vouchers already bagged for collection by Securicor. In the late 1990s, I returned to my other profession -as a Registered Mental Nurse. I was working with a leading Psychiatric Hospital again in South East London. Driving on the Farquar Road, Upper Norwood SE19 at about 19:30hrs, I saw a police car in front with two police officers in it. Suddenly the driver applied his brakes. Sensing that, I slowed down and main- tained the distance between the two cars, I was never tempted to overtake their (police) car. I kept my dis- tance and the two cars proceeded towards the West Dulwich Croxted Road roundabout.

Instead of the police going their way, they went round the roundabout and within moments they were behind me and followed me to the middle of a short road by the side of Dulwich College. This short road is normally quiet but for the odd dog- walker or two. I saw the police car's lights flashing and I immediately stopped. They stopped about twenty metre behind and came out with truncheons drawn. I remained in my car and opened the window slightly when the first officer came close, "You were speeding," he said haughtily. I replied, "If you thought that I was speeding why didn't you stop me at Farquar Road where there are many people?" He then stated, "You are arguing," to which I said, "I am not a youngster, this is what some of you do to intimidate young black men whom you then accuse of being aggressive." He then looked at my road tax again and having spoken to somebody on his radio, retreated to their car without another word. I proceeded to work, obviously arriving about half- an-hour late. I was so angry that I could only remember their car registration but not the specific numbers on their uniforms.

The following day I went to the nearest police station and reported the incident to a senior officer whom I admit was polite, reassuring and on the whole receptive. There have been other unnecessary encounters with the police, but the two stated episodes will suffice. I will rather shed light on some positive encounters with the police.

In the 1970s and 1980s drive-outs (petrol theft) in forecourts around the country was common. Majority of police officers responding to the cashiers' callouts were professional and even cordial in their approach. Once a policewoman spent about half an hour in one of the branches I managed, after she had responded to a drive-out. She was very professional but even asked about my background in Ghana. I seized the opportunity and gave chapter and verse about life in Ghana and other countries in Africa. In Ghana for example, the abiding factors in society are the strong middle class of professionals and businessmen, the influence of the church for majority of people, strict parents who espouse Christian values, good behaviour and good education. I was heartened because this police officer was amenable, full of humour to create and maintain rapport. The fifth principle of policing states, "Friendship to all members of the public...and ready exercise of friendly good humour..."

When I was held at gunpoint in 1985 at one of the branches during the robbery, and the alarm was raised, all the police officers who responded in about five minutes were very professional and supportive.

In the field of psychiatry as well overwhelming majority of police officers my colleagues and I encountered, behaved professionally without a hint of bias or disdain.

They are normally called in cases of missing patients or to assist in managing very violent patients.

Unquestionably the police profession is a very difficult one especially in a multiracial country like UK, US or France. This is a profession which needs 100% (no less) support of every member of the public they serve.

Impossible but necessary. Even if a tiny percentage of the population constantly feel aggrieved by the behaviour of a minority of police officers, the problem becomes a blemish. Even genuine human shortcomings from the police could create mistrust.

SIR ROBERT PEEL- He founded the police force in 1829. He was the Conservative Prime Minister from December 10th, 1834, to April 8th, 1835; and again, from August 30th, 1841 to June 29th, 1846. He approved a force of 95 Constables, 88 Sergeants and 20 Inspectors. By 1856, over 200 police forces were established in England and Wales. He was one of the founders of the modern Conservative Party.

In 1822, the concept of policing was taken up by Robert Peel when he became Home Secretary. The Peel's Metropolitan Police Act 1829 set up a full-time, professional and centrally organized Police Force for Greater London area called the Metropolitan Police.

During the early 19th Century, attempts by the government to set up a police force faced strong public opposition. The suspicion was that a large and possibly armed police force could be wrongly and therefore illegally used as an arm of a particular party in government to suppress protest or support unpopular political decisions.

Sir Robert Peel- The Peelian principles, according to Wikipedia, "summarize the ideas that Sir Robert Peel developed to define an ethical police force. The approach expressed in these principles, is commonly known as policing by consent in the UK and other countries such as Canada, Australia, and New Zealand. The definition went on," In this model of policing, police officers are regarded as citizens in uniform. They exercise their powers to police fellow citizens with the implicit consent of those fellow citizens. 'Policing by consent' indicates that the legitimacy of policing in the eyes of the public is based upon a general census of support that follows from transparency about their powers, their integrity in exercising those powers and their accountability for doing so."

THE NINE POLICING PRINCIPLES AND THE THREE CORE IDEAS AS STIPULATED BY THE LAW ENFORCEMENT ACTION PAFRTNERSHIP are as follows.

THE NINE PRINCIPLES.

1. To prevent crime and disorder, as an alternative to their repression by military force and severity of legal punishment.

2. To recognize always that the power of police to fulfill their functions and duties is dependent on public approval of their existence, actions and behaviour, and on their ability to secure and maintain public respect.

3. To recognize always that to secure and maintain the respect and approval of the public means also the securing of the willing cooperation of the public in the task of securing observance of laws.

4. To recognize always that the extent to which the cooperation of the public can be secured diminishes proportionately the necessity of the use of physical force and compulsion for achieving police objectives.

5. To seek and preserve public favour, not by pandering to public opinion, but by constantly demonstrating absolute impartial service to law, in complete independence of policy, and without regard to the justice or injustice of the substance of individual laws, by ready offering of individual service and friendship to all members of the public without regard to their wealth or social standing, by ready exercise of courtesy and friendly good humour, and by ready offering of individual sacrifice in protecting and preserving life.

6. To use physical force only when the exercise of persuasion, advice and warning is found to be insufficient to obtain public cooperation to an extent necessary to secure observance of law or to restore order, and to use only minimum degree of physical force which is necessary on any particular occasion for achieving a police objective.

7. To maintain at all times a relationship with the public that gives rarity to the historic tradition that the police are the public and that the public are the police, the police only being members of the public who are paid to give full-time attention to duties which are incumbent on every citizen in the interests of community welfare and existence.

8. To recognize always the need for strict adherence to police-executive functions, and to refrain from even seeming to usurp the powers of the judiciary of avenging individuals or the State, and of authoritatively judging guilt and punishing the guilty.

9. To recognize always that the test of police efficiency is the absence of crime and disorder, and not the visible evidence of police action in dealing with them.

THE CORE IDFAS.

1. The goal is preventing crime, not catching criminals. If the police stop crime before it happens, we don't have to punish citizens or suppress their rights. An effective police department doesn't have high arrest stats; its community has low crime rates.

2. The key to preventing crime is earning public support. Every community member must share the responsibility of preventing crime, as if they were all volunteer members of the force. They will only accept this responsibility if the community supports and trusts the police.

3. The police earn public support by respecting community principles. Winning public approval requires hard work to build reputation: enforcing the law impartially, hiring officers who represent and understand the community, using force only as a last resort.

The importance of the nine principles of policing was summed up by former Police Commissioner William J. Bratton, who was quoted by Michael Nagle of the New York Times in 2014, "I carry these with me everywhere, my bible." Commissioner Bratton was commissioner of the Boston Police Department (BPD) 1993-1994, Chief of the Los Angeles Police Department (LAPD) 2002-2009, New York Police city Police Commissioner 1994-1996 and again 2014-2016.

It is event that had some police and law enforcement officers carefully and habitually ("I carry these with me everywhere, my bible") adhered to these painstakingly crafted principles and core ideas, countless fatalities including minors and the mentally unwell, would have mercifully been avoided over many decades. The Law Enforcement Action Partnership website stated that the core principles and ideas, "remain as crucial and urgent today as they were centuries ago." There should not be any surprise on this point as psychology teaches us that basic human behaviour is unaffected by time, place or by race. Jesus was betrayed over two thousand years ago. We are in the 21st Century and human beings are still betraying others who have their welfare at heart. Credit therefore goes to Sir Robert Peel and his commissioners who crafted these principles and ideas which will stand the test of time.

In the United States, the Law Enforcement Oath of Honour reads-'On my honor, I will never betray my badge, my integrity, my character, or public trust. I will always have the courage to hold myself and others accountable for our actions. I will always uphold the Constitution, my community and the agency I serve.' Whether in America or the rest of the civilised world, the principles are the same. The key words are honour, integrity, and courage.

Yes indeed! Policing like politics is about human beings not about inanimate objects, therefore great care is paramount. A careful assimilation of the principles and ideas shows that they collectively and almost individually rule out all the police actions leading to the countless (human) fatalities. The only exception regards cases where police and law enforcement officers, mortals as we all are, yield to human fallibility. Sadly, as we all know, when even police officers make genuine mistakes, mistrust abound because of loss of life.

In the tragic case of George Floyd, many of Sir Robert Peel's police principles and core ideas were violated by law enforcement officers complicit and accused of his death. Part of Principle No.2 refers to "public approval," police "actions and behaviour" and "on their ability to secure and maintain public respect." Arguably overwhelming majority of the American public disapproved the behaviour of these law enforcement officers in this

case and others, hence the national and global outrage demonstrated through several weeks of protests.

Part of Principle No.5 refers to "by ready offering of
individual service and friendship to all members of the
public without regard to their wealth or social standing." And "by ready offering of individual sacrifice in
protecting and preserving life." It is no secret that in
most countries around the world, minorities, poor people and the vulnerable disproportionally suffer in the
hands of some police officers. "Protecting and preserving life" - the footage shown endlessly on TV globally,
depict unquestionably an arrant disregard to "protecting and preserving life." A modicum of common-sense
dictates that pressure on any part of the neck inhibits
the flow of blood and oxygen to the human brain. Any
adult, trained or untrained, public official or not; should
know that.

Principle No.6 begins, "To use physical force only when
the exercise of persuasion, advice and warning is
found to be insufficient" and "to use only the minimum
degree of physical force which is necessary on any
particular occasion for achieving police objective."

On this principle, the law enforcement officers awfully
and woefully neglected their public duty.

Principle No.8 states unequivocally, "and to refrain from
even seeming to usurp the powers of the Judiciary or
avenging individual or the state, and authoritatively
judging guilt and punishing the guilty." It was claimed
on TV that George Floyd and former Minneapolis officer, Derek Chauvin once worked together as security
officers in a night club and might have known each
other. It was claimed that there was an altercation

between the two. The Telegraph quoted a work colleague, David Pinney interviewed on CBS News, "They
bumped heads." He added, "It has a lot to do with
Derek being extremely aggressive with some of the
patrons, which was the issue." Was it vengeance?
Whether it was or not, Derek Chauvin and his associates parading as law enforcement officers were judge
and jury over an alleged usage of a mere $20 fake bill.
A suspect remains so, until proven guilty in a court of
law. The action of Chauvin and the other law enforcement officers went against the letter and spirit of
Principle No.8; judiciously and conscientiously crafted
by Sir Robert Peel and his commissioners.

The world-wide political community, until George
Floyd's death had been shamefully, not vocal enough
(some totally silent) over the endemic American problem of police brutality disproportionately towards
blacks especially and other minorities. It has been a
common practice for some heads of state especially
in the west to raise human rights violations in Iran, China
and some other countries but hardly the US. The manner and circumstances surrounding George Floyd's
death awoke the conscience of the global population emanating in protests and in some cases violent
clashes with the police in some countries. Some com-
mentators contend that the silence of some foreign
politicians especially since 2017 was to avoid bullying
reprisals from the Trump regime in the White House. The
reverberations of the gruesome murder of George
Floyd, on this occasion evoked some criticisms from
foreign governments. It must be noted that majority of
the criticisms were couched or assuaged in diplomatic
language. The global populace however would have
none of that. They were vehement in their protests and
in countries also known for police brutality, the anger

was raw. According to NBC News website, at least 40 countries world-wide held protests "echoing support for the hundreds of US protests in response to the May 25th killing of George Floyd." Besides protests in some African states, the protests in especially the UK, France, Brazil and Australia were poignant as previous head-line fatalities of police brutality were revisited.

In Paris, planned demonstration outside the US Embassy and the lawns near the Eiffel Tower were banned. However, several hundred protesters, some holding 'Black Lives Matter' placards, signs and flags assem-bled on place de la Concorde close to the Embassy. In Germany protesters gathered at the Central Alexander-Platz Square in Berlin. In Australia like UK, France and some other European countries, demonstrations were held in several cities. In Brisbane police estimated that 10,000 joined a peaceful protest wearing masks and holding 'Black Lives Matter' placards.

According to Reuters many protesters "wrapped them-selves indigenous flags calling for police mistreatment of indigenous Australians." Even in troubled Syria, a mural of George Floyd was drawn in sympathy.

What is highly disturbing is that some of the police officers perpetuating these inhumane acts, appear to forget that they are discrediting their profession, putting them-selves and especially their (professional) hardworking colleagues in harm's way. On a personal note, what about their loved ones, who without a doubt do not condone such criminal activity. The atrocities of these police officers are etched in history for generations.

Policing is an all-important public service; therefore, overwhelming majority of critics do not even contemplate abolishing the police in cities in the US where mistrust is deep-seated. Urgent reforms should include the embedding of social workers and mental health professionals into the ranks of the police service. Such a move will no doubt alleviate if not eliminate entirely, fatalities including minors and the mentally unwell. On February 1st, 2021, the Guardian reported a harrowing incident under the headline,' Rochester Police Officers Suspended After Girl, Nine, Handcuffed and Pepper-Sprayed.' On Friday January 29th, a nine- year- old black girl was involved in a family disturbance. During the domestic incident, she was reported to have "indicated that she wanted to kill herself and the girl had wanted to kill her mom."

The police had wanted to take her to hospital but the nine-year-old refused. During the struggle with police, she was crying and screaming, "I want my dad." The police managed and got her into the back seat of their car with her hands in handcuffs. In the video, she was seen distraught when a male officer told a colleague, "Just spray her at this point." When indeed the nine years old girl was pepper-sprayed, she screamed and shouted, "wipe my eyes, please." The Guardian reported that one officer then closed the police door. There were seven police officers on the scene. It was reported that a number have been suspended pending an internal investigation.

It was heart-rending for me to watch the short video. I would have found it equally harrowing if the nine-year-old were white. The male officers who handled her, to my observation, were not overtly aggressive. What was most disturbing was that she was handcuffed and yet pepper-sprayed amid her painful screams and plea, "I want my dad." During the later stages a female officer took over and with her reassurances- "I will get you your dad" ......" What is your dad's name?" the young girl appeared a bit more receptive. I have already advocated for mental health officers and social workers to be embedded within the police service as part of police reforms. This harrowing case is a typical testimony. It is not every day a nine-year-old girl threatens "to kill her mom" of all people and also to kill herself. Something needs to be done urgently in the interest of all humanity.

The police are tasked with the role of serving their respective communities, notably protecting andwhen required saving lives, without unduly putting themselves at risk. They unfortunately face attack both verbally and physically. The trend is on the increase both in the US, UK and other countries. If even an attack on the police emanates from the backlash of the vile behaviour of Chauvin and others on May 25th,2020, it would be terribly unfortunate. The racism and bigotry of the minority should not be allowed to tarnish the reputation of the majority of genuine professionals.

Police and law enforcement officers are citizens of the very society they serve. If political policies of a particular government give rise to poor or inadequate housing, some of which breed anti-social behaviour including criminal activity, it is these officers who have to do the mopping up.

Whom do you call when there is criminal activity? One does not call the President, Prime Minister or the Home Secretary. One calls the crime busters-the police. The responding police and law enforcement officers would be aware of the inequalities in society and the behaviour of the hardcore criminal fraternity. They must deal with the situation, professionally without a hint of bias or misplaced sympathy.

During the miners' strike of March 6th, 1984, lasting until March 3rd,1985, thousands of police officers were deployed to keep order. Many suffered injuries, some seriously, during confrontations with strikers. Some surely might have sympathy for the miners because of the closure of the collieries. Other police officers might not have liked the stance of the miners' leader, Arthur Scargill. So, despite the conflict of 'interests' among the group of police officers, they had to hold the professional line. The poll tax riots in March 1990 also pitched the hapless police against fellow citizens. Again, the police suffered casualties so were some of the protestors. Were the police exempt from paying the poll tax? No, they faced paying the same unpopular poll tax (as citizens) but their duty was to uphold the law.

On July 7th, 2020, British athlete Bianca Williams, her husband and their very young baby were stopped by police as they were driving to their home in Maida Vale, West London. The 26 years old was handcuffed while her three-month-old baby was at the back of the car. It was reported that the police questioned the way the car was being driven and also it was on the wrong side of the road. The officers also claimed they indicated for the car to stop but Bianca's husband Santos, made "off at speed."

According to the Guardian the couple were informed that they were being detained for the purpose of a search under Section 1 of the Police and Criminal Evidence Act 1984. The police searched their vehicle but found nothing. The couple and their baby were allowed to go. However, they refuted the police allegation during a TV interview. Bianca, who was concerned about the welfare of her baby when she was handcuffed was reported that it felt like "being black is a crime."

On August 13th, 2020, the Daily Mirror reporter, Trevor Marshallsea, under the headline, 'Top Cop Backs Officers Over Black MP Stopped In a BMW,' revisited an incident which involved Dawn Butler and her black friend in Hackney on August 9th, 2020. Dawn accused the police of racial profiling. They were driving "a nice car." In a video, Dawn did not complain about individual officers but enquired why they were stopped. The police, to their credit admitted making a mistake by incorrectly entering the BMW's number plate into the computer. It therefore "flagged up as being from another region." The reporter stated that the Metropolitan Police's Deputy Commissioner Sir Steve House said that proper channels for MP Dawn Butler's complaint should have been made. The Deputy Commissioner was quoted," Trial by social media is unfair and damaging to officers." Having admitted to the mistake by the police, Sir Steve House was quoted, "I expect officers to have professional curiosity. I would have done the same." Sir Steve House should not forget that these seemingly innocuous mistakes could lead to tragedy. I humbly refer the Deputy Commissioner to the first three Principles of Policing, already spelt out in these pages and part of the third core ideas of policing, which reads, "Winning public approval requires hard work to build reputation: enforcing the laws impartially "Yes 'professional curiosity' is a useful tool (experience) but should be acted on at the right time and in proportion not disproportionately affecting a particular section of the population all the time. One would be interested to read Sir House's comments about Danny Rose's experience in the hands of the police in Doncaster. Majority of people within the black and minority population would consider Sir House's comment highly controversial. 'Professional Curiosity' is boundless in its meaning and connotation.

Let us assume that I know specifically what the 63 years old Deputy Commissioner was inferring. In the field of psychiatry, where I have spent almost five decades, especially when dealing with aggressive and violent patients, one should always rely on his/her professional curiosity. A patient may appear aggressive and because of his history become violent. It is right to make an assessment and envisage imminent danger, however it would be wrong to act on one's conclusion and call the 'Team' to restrain that patient. The 'perception' of the threat posed may just be so. The patient looks aggressive but yet to hurt a fly. Professionally there are a number of strategies to use as tools of distraction.

I do not shop at my local corner shop where the owner has for nineteen successive days, lost goods through theft. If on the twentieth day, out of habit, I decided to shop there and incidentally fit the description of previous offenders; and my actions appear suspicious, the owner would be wasting police time by raising the alarm.

Many blacks face the same racial profiling in America. Professional singer, song writer and composer, Teddy Pendergrass (of Blessed Memory) born in Philadelphia, bought a Rolls Royce at the height of his fame. He complained how the police stopped him all the time because of his car. Since he was successful and a huge global star, the police would have recognized him. Like Danny Rose, it meant nothing, the police still stopped him. In 1982 when Pendergrass slammed his car into a tree; he later spoke about how the police often stopped him. Sadly, he was paralysed from waist down because of the accident. He died at the age of 59.

So how does one acquire professional curiosity? Many factors come to mind, notably background, education, training and experience. No two officers have the same level of professional curiosity, irrespective of the number of years in the role. Police officers are human; one's unconscious bias or outright prejudice could slip into the conclusion. It could lead to the professional tag being dislodged and the curiosity becoming just 'naked' curiosity. The Deputy Commissioner stated, "I would have done the same." This is where sadly Sir Steve House is also wrong. How could he be certain he would have arrived at the same conclusion (mis- take or no mistake) as the officers referred to in MP Dawn Butler's case? If the police in that part of London had been focusing solely on looking at number plates 'from a different region,' the criminal fraternity would have had a free reign. History underlines the fact that often when black people are in possession of nice and expensive cars, (Danny Rose) some police officers (I repeat, the prefix and qualifying word 'some') become unnecessarily suspicious.

This is not a judgment, like doing calculation in mathematics, with the same outcome unless one calculates wrongly by not following the right formula. The formula for working out the perimeter (the total length of the outer boundary) of an area is 2 (Length + Breadth/ Width). If the length of John's garden is 50 feet and 20 feet in width, it would be 50+20=70. One then multiplies 70 by 2= 140 feet. A formula producing an answer in this case is 'concrete' all day long. In my incessant quest to remain numerate, I have yet to find a formula which states, 'Black person + Nice Expensive car = (equate) Theft.' What every human being (including a police officer) is thinking is 'abstract' until it is manifested in behaviour or in action.

On June 14th, 2020, during a counter demonstration by a far-right group at a Waterloo Station in London, 49 years old Patrick Hutchinson, a Black Lives Matter activist, supported by four black colleagues of Ark Security, saved a 55 years old white man with the opposing demonstrators from severe injury during a stampede. Downing Street hailed Mr. Hutchinson, "His instincts in that matter represent the best of us." In an interview, Mr. Hutchinson stated that he and his colleagues "stopped somebody from being killed." He was also quoted, "My fear was he would have ended up being killed. The news and narrative would have switched BLM (Black Lives Matter) killing a white man." The entire media both in the UK and abroad praised this courageous and noble act of Mr. Hutchinson and his four colleagues. It was later revealed in the June 18th, 2020, issue of the Daily Mirror that 55 years old Bryn Male (the rescued white man) is a retired detective in the British Transport Police Robbery Squad in the 1990s.

In the August 15th, 2020, issue of the Daily Mirror, under the headline, 'Cop Accused of Being Nazi Group (National Action) Member Faces Trial,' Tess de la Mare reported that a police officer faced trial "allegedly being a member of a banned Neo-Nazi group and possessing an indecent image of a child." Part of the charge relates to the Terrorist Act 2000. The twenty-two years old Probationary Officer, Benjamin Hannam of Enfield, North London, was accused of lying on his application and vetting form to join the Metropolitan Police. He was charged in July 2020 with being a member of National Action from December 17th,2016 to January 1st,2018 after an investigation by the force's Counter Terrorism Command, Scotland Yard. National Action was outlawed under terror rules in December 2016. According to the website, opendemocracy.net/en/counter radical right, "Law enforcement agencies have been breeding grounds for far- right ideology for decades and is not just an American problem."

On the website, face2faceafrica.com, it was reported that three Wilmington, US police officers had been fired after recording themselves talking about "slaughtering and wiping blacks off the map." All the three officers admitted that the voices in the recorded conversations were theirs but blamed their racist remarks on "stress."

On the internet serving police officers anonymously, for fear of reprisals, report the pernicious race comments by their colleagues. Arguably majority of police and law enforcement officers do not share or harbour these toxic views. If only the majority would come together, expose and condemn these corrosive views, the world would be a better place for all humanity. The above instances of arbitrary misuse of an important public position as a police or law enforcement offi- cer, are just a few of the countless examples why heads of police services in many countries have a difficult job on their hands.

Since May 25th, 2020, there have been two separate incidents of a police officer kneeling on the neck of a black suspect in a bid to make arrest. On August 16th, 2020, an official in Halifax, West Yorkshire UK, had a confrontation with a British Asia man suspected of assault.

Mail-on-line showed a footage on August 18th, 2020, of Ahmed Hassan waving his hands across his throat during the arrest. The officer appeared to make an attempt to hit him during the incident shouting, "Chill out or I'll choke you out, chill out or you're going to sleep, chill out, chill out." What a chilling remark? The officer was removed from frontline operational duties and the victim released under investigation.

The Yorkshire Police subsequently made a voluntary referral to the Independent Police Conduct Authority. Ahmed later contacted the Mail- on-line and quoted among others, "I never thought something like that could happen in the UK. We hear about this in the US but for it to happen in the UK is appalling." This incident and others unreported are a testimony of how extremely difficult policing could become after incidents like that on May 25th, 2020. Police chiefs everywhere, genuine, and professional, can be forgiven these days to sleep with one eye closed but both ears opened. Is it possible? Arguably majority on the frontline may be walking on eggshells in light of recent events.

It is commendable in human interactions but too much extra care and sensitivity could lead to mistakes being made. Some members of the public could also detect this change and deviously exploit it. Police personnel were aware of the pressures in the role before joining. The minority within their ranks should behave professionally, irrespective of their social or political views. The police should approach each case they encounter judiciously and conscientiously without being swayed by other considerations. It may be difficult for some, but it is the only way to win public support across the races.

In an interview of TV Channel 4, on August 13th, 2020, reported on the mailonline by William Cole, the Metropolitan Police Commissioner Dame Cressida Dick, denied that the force was institutionally racist and added that allegations around racism in the Metropolitan Police were not "helpful" labels for the police. Dame Cressida was quoted, "We have zero tolerance of racist behaviour within the Met. Just last week somebody was sacked for racist conduct, and everybody knows that is the case." The Dame went on "We embraced the challenge, if you like, that was set for us twenty years ago by Sir William MacPherson in the Stephen Lawrence Inquiry in which he came with a definition of institutional racism' I was the per- son charged with implementing the recommendations and I'm very proud of what we did. I think we have come a very, very, very long way."

This is laudable and appreciated by all fair-minded black people. However, the problem is so intractable because of a number of factors some of which I have highlighted in these pages that, the Dame's genuine "we have come a very, very, very long way," sadly leaves more, and more and more and an extra more to be done. More grease to Dame Cressida's elbow and those of her conscientious officers, to be able to do the extra 'mores' to combat this endemic problem, a scourge in many societies. All shoulders to the pro- verbial wheel.

The year 2029 will be the 200th Anniversary of the founding of the police force (service). It is only about eight years away. What are the chances of the police redeeming a considerable measure of the goodwill the disaffected minority should have for them? I am optimist, with the appropriate education, willingness on both sides and genuine understanding of the strengths and foibles of all mankind, this important milestone would be celebrated with maybe (I repeat, maybe) blacks and other minorities feeling a bit more comfortable in their relationships with the police and law enforcement officers. The greater responsibility lies with police and law enforcement hegemony. Lest I forget, political parties in tandem have a crucial role to play.

CHAPTER FIFTEEN

SUFFERING OF AFRICANS, STATUES OF SLAVE TRADERS AND OWNERS

The African in America has endured untold suffering from 1619 when the first slaves landed in James Town Colony. This is often referred to as the beginning of slavery in America, although enslaved Africans arrived in North America as early as the 1500s.

It was the silence of the majority to the suffering of the black man, which in some quarters is construed as 'complicity,' leading to the formation of the Black Lives Movement in July 2013. The majority kept quiet for 394 years. The obvious conclusion is that the loss of lives and untold injustices meted out disproportionally to African Americans do not matter. It is therefore crucially justifiable for a group of black women to shake the world off its slumber and declare passionately," Black Lives Matter." Of course, in many organizations especially political parties, you have the radical wings. You have the far left and the far right, globally especially in the US and in Europe. Nobody is asking to ban any party. In fact, Black Lives Matter is not a political party. Admittedly some radical views about policing issues have been raised by some supporters of the infant movement. Some other radical ideas have been ascribed by others to the movement. Any genuine and humane person should focus on the thrust of the slogan, which is the lives of the oppressed, matter: And so indeed any other lives-white, brown, yellow or red.

During the Black Lives Matter protest, some activists focused their attention on statues of the leading figures of the Trans - Atlantic Slave Trade.

EDWARD COLSTON- In Bristol, the statue of the 17th Century slave trader was the first to be removed from its plinth. The bronze statue, which was erected in 1895, was a focal point of utter indignation and the city of Bristol's role in the slave trade. According to the Guardian –June 8th, 2020- petition to remove Colston's statue attracted 11,000 signatures. The petition stated, "While history shouldn't be forgotten, these people who benefited from the enslavement of individuals do not deserve the honour of a statue. This should be reserved for those who bring about positive change and who fight for peace, equality and social unity." The Royal African Company which Colston joined by 1680, transported more than 100,000 slaves from West

Africa to the Americas and the Caribbean between 1672 and 1689. The slaves were crammed into ships to maximize profit.

Edward Colston was described as a merchant and philanthropist. The noun 'philanthropy' is derived from two Greek words-'philos' meaning, 'love' and 'anthropos' meaning 'humankind.' The Readers' Digest Oxford Complete Wordfinder, defines philanthropy, as a love for mankind.

Therefore, the essence of the word is the loving of fellow human beings. Edward Colston, as a slave trader with others was responsible for the deaths of thousands of Africans during the middle passage. If he was really a philanthropist, he would not have been party to the most horrific and nefarious act in human history. Perhaps some humans in Colston's eyes were less human than others: Or to put it starkly, some are not humans at all as the iniquitous acts over four centuries have lamentably shown. The monetary gain which is still being enjoyed in some European countries and the US is not even tainted, but sadly immersed in African blood.

The slaves, including women and children were branded on their chests with the company's initials-RAC. Unhygienic conditions in the ships had their toll on the Africans who suffered dehydration, dysentery and scurvy. More than 20,000 died during the crossings and their bodies thrown overboard. Colston became the Deputy Governor of the African Royal Company in 1689-1690. He was a Tory Member of Parliament. He was regarded as a philanthropist. His name was extensively commemorated on landmarks in the city of Bristol until June 2020. His bronze statue used to stand on Colston Avenue.

When Colston's statue was toppled on Sunday June 7th, 2020, demonstrators jumped on it and the jeering from the large crowd turned into thunderous cheers. They rolled the statue down the street and dumped it into the Bristol harbour. The Mayor of Bristol who is of Afro-Caribbean extraction stated, "I know the removal of the Colston statue will divide opinion however, it's important to listen to those who found the statue to represent an affront to humanity."

In London where there was a bigger crowd also demonstrating, Mayor Sadiq Khan, expressed solidarity with "Londoners of all ages, races and backgrounds who were engaged in peaceful protest." He lamented that the "vital cause" had been undermined by a tiny minority. On the same Sunday in June, the Metropolitan Police Commissioner stated that 27 officers had been injured in a week of protests. Dame Cressida Dick explained that 14 of the police casualties occurred the previous day- Saturday, when "a minority of protest- ers became violet," towards officers outside Downing Street. Dame Cressida added that two police officers were seriously injured.

SIR ROBERT PEEL- The statue of the twice Tory Prime Minister and founder of the Metropolitan Police in 1829, was a target of protestors in Manchester where it stands in Piccadilly Gardens. The reason behind the action of the protestors was that Sir Robert Peel's father was an advocate of slavery.

Hundreds of petitioners called for the removal of the statue. In opposition were also hundreds who demanded it to be kept. However, during the week-end of the protests, Sir Peel's statue in Glasgow was vandalised.

It was reported in the June 10th, 2020, issue of the Daily Mail that 130 councils were in discussion about statues of people who had links to colonialism and the slave trade. The 130 Labour councils reported that they would assess the "appropriateness" of the monuments in the wake of the toppling of Edward Colston's statue in Bristol.

ROBERT MILLIGAN- (1746-1809) Milligan was a well – known Scottish merchant, slaveholder and founder of London's Global Trade Hub, West India Docks. Milligan's monument was the next to fall after that of Colston. His statue was crafted by Richard Westmacott in May 1809. He was a "wealthy merchant" and "a fierce proponent of slavery in Jamaica." He grew up on his family's sugar plantation in Jamaica. He left Jamaica at the age of 33; and lived in Hampstead, London. Under the heading, 'He Transformed London Thanks to Exploitation,' the Mail also described him as a "Man of vision." Milligan had been frustrated by delays and thefts at London wharves. He lobbied Parliament to let him build a wet dock with a high wall. Milligan was the Deputy Chairman of the West Indian Dock Company when the docks' foundation was laid in July 1800. According to Wikipedia, he had strong links with the political stalwarts of the day. The stone-lay- ing foundation was attended by Lord Chancellor Lord Loughborough, Prime Minister William Pitt, The Younger and company chairman, George Hibbert. Milligan was known to have advised the government on how to quell a rebellion by escaped slaves. The Mail con- cluded, "The Milligan statue was put up in 1813 by the directors of the West India Docks Company, with a plaque highlighting his role in developing the area that is now a financial hub."

The West Indian Docks monopolised the importation of products mainly, sugar, rum and coffee from the West Indies for 21 years. His statue which was outside the Museum of London Docklands, commemorated the vital role he played in the construction of the West India Docks. The paper added, "Milligan's legacy is tarnished by his history as a slave owner, trader and his fervent support of the brutal practice." A petition by the Tower Hamlet's Labour Councillor Ehtasham Hague was attributable to the removal of the statue in the wake of the Black Lives Matter protests. Part of the Comment and Analysis on racism in the June 14th, 2020, Observer reads, "The fallout from the sym- bolic toppling of the statue of slaver Edward Colston and his plunge to the bottom of Bristol harbour, was the most effective lesson many of us schooled in British classrooms will have had in the facts of the slave trade. (How many knew that taxpayers only finished paying the debt of compensation to slave -owning families in 2015?). It is only those who would rather not examine the past who demand it be set in stone."

The Canal River Trust stated that the statue was removed to "recognise the wishes of the commu- nity." The Trust had worked with the London Borough of Tower Hamlet, the Museum and partners in Canary Wharf to have it removed. Milligan owned two sugar plantations and 526 slaves in Jamaica.

On-lookers and protesters in a crowd cheered and clapped as a crane was used to remove the monu- ment from its plinth. The Mayor of London, Sadiq Khan was quoted, London had to face "an uncomfortable truth" with its historic links to slavery." While the event in the London Docks was unfolding, thousands of people gathered in at Oxford University College to ask for the removal of a statue of imperialist, Cecil Rhodes.

Other statues with links to slavery include-SIR THOMAS GUY- According to the RBC website, he made his money from the stock market bubble of 1720. Sir Guy who founded Guy's Hospital in 1721, had shares in the South Sea Company when trading commenced in 1711 with slaves sold to the Spanish Colonies. The British firm formed specially to sell slaves to the Spanish colonies had a target of selling 4,800 adult men annually.

SIR THOMAS PICTON- The Daily Mail reported that the Leader of Cardiff Council Huw Thomas called for the marble statue of the "sadistic 19th, Century slave owner" to be removed from the City Hall. The Leader said that Sir Thomas Picton who was killed in the Battle of Waterloo in 1815, was an "afront" to black people in the Welsh capital. Councillor Thomas added, "The growing awareness and understanding of the brutal nature of his governorship of Trinidad and his involvement in slavery makes it difficult to reconcile his presence in City Hall." The Mail reported that Sir Thomas Picton was tried in England for illegally torturing a 14- year- old girl. He was convicted but the conviction was later quashed.

SIR FRANCIS DRAKE- The naval officer and explorer sailed around the world with his cousin, Sir John Hawkins of Plymouth. The latter is considered as England's first slave trader. During their voyages in the 16th, Century they sold slaves to work in plantations in the newly discovered Americas. Sir Francis Drake was a Mayor of Plymouth hence his statue stands in the city's Hoe Park.

HENRY DUNDAS- This former Tory Home Secretary's statue can be found over St Andrews Square, Edinburgh.

In 1792, as Home Secretary, he delayed the abolition of slavery with the belief that it should be gradual. This contributed to the loss of thousands of lives. The Leader of the Edinburgh City Council was quoted that there would be "no sense of loss" if his statue was removed.

WILLIAM BECKFORD- William Beckford also known as Alderman Beckford was one of the leading landowners in the West Indies in the 18th, Century. He was also the head of one of Britain's most powerful families. He derived his enormous wealth from several sugar plantations in Jamaica with about 3,000 African slaves at work. He was twice the Lord Mayor of London with a statue standing in the City's Guildhall.

CECIL RHODES- Cecil Rhodes (July 5th, 1853- March 26th, 1902), according to Wikipedia, the English-born was the son of an Anglican Vicar. He was sent to the then British Colony of Natal in South Africa at the age of 17 because of poor health. He was sickly and asthmatic. He became a British mining magnet and politician in Southern Africa. He became Prime Minister of the Cape Colony from 1890-1896.

Rhodes was a staunch believer of British imperialism. The Southern African territory of Rhodesia (now Zimbabwe) and was founded by Rhodes and his company, British South Africa Company. The territory Rhodesia was named after him in 1895.

The 'Rhodes Must Fall,' a protest movement which began on March 9th, 2015, was initially directed at his statue at University of Cape Town (UCT), which Commemorated Cecil Rhodes. The movement gained global status and resulted in a large movement, decolonised education in South Africa. On April 19th, 2015, after an UCT Council vote the previous night, the statue by Marion Walgate in 1934 was removed. The calls for the removal of the statue had been growing for decades. Afrikaner students made the initial demand for the removal of the statue. Their demand was based on the fact that Rhodes, the arch imperialist wanted to continue with British rule in South Africa. He also considered the Afrikaner population to be inferior to the British.

The movement within the university regarded the statue as a symbol of oppression and white supremacy. In 1930, a distinguished literary personality, Evelyn Waugh was quoted by the Mail's Robert Hardman in the June 10th, 2020, issue, "A very small amount of dynamite should be enough to rid us forever of the High Street front of Oriel." Even in Cecil Rhodes's hometown of Bishop's Stotfold, Hertfordshire, there is a campaign to rename places named after him. Example, museum and arts centre named after him is changing its name.

The movement at the university broaden its horizon to include, "Institutional racism, the lack of racial transformation at the university and access to tertiary education and student accommodation. The students' protests including occupying UCT offices, civil disobedience, and violence. Some of the actions they took included throwing faeces at Rhodes's statue and burning art vehicles and buildings.

The Rhodes Must Fall Movement in England got a shot in the arm. In Oxford where Rhodes's statue has stood above the High Street entrance to his old college, Oriel, for more than a century; on Tuesday night, June 9th, 2020, 1000 people including members of the Black Lives Matter movement demonstrated. The statue was not removed as Edward Colston's was, however Oriel College issued a statement that it would "continue to debate the issues."

It is often quoted that many people including President Bill Clinton and three Australian Prime Ministers- Bob Hawke, Tony Abbot and Malcolm Turnbull- benefited as students from the Rhodes Scholarship. Wasim Sajjad (Pakistan), Dom Mintoff (Malta), John Turner (Canada) and Norman Manley (Jamaica) were the other beneficiaries who became heads of state. The scholarship named after Cecil John Rhodes, attracts more than 80 scholars each year from the US, South Africa, Canada, New Zealand, Australia, India, Kenya, Germany, Hong Kong, Jamaica and Botswana. Thirty-two scholars are chosen and awarded scholarships worth $50,000 each for two-year study at Oxford University. The revelations in Rhodes's will when he died in 1902 led to the creation of the scholarships. The Group, Rhodes Trust which is entrusted with awarding the scholarships was formed when he died in 1902. It took 75 years for the first black South African to be awarded a Rhodes scholarship. In 1907 Alain Locke was the first African American to win a Rhodes Scholarship. According to Wikipedia, over the last four decades, African Americans have won a Rhodes scholarship almost every year. However, the businesstech.co.za/news revealed that after Alain Locke's award, "Thereafter, there were virtually no 'black scholarships' until the 1960s."

On January 24th, 2017, it was reported on the Independent website that "A student activist involved in the campaign to remove a statue of Cecil Rhodes from the university had accepted a £40,000 Rhodes Scholarship. In one of the repercussions of the Rhodes Must Fall campaign, business.co.ZA/news/trending reported that 200 international scholars stated that they took a Rhodes scholarship as a form of reparation, "knowing that Cecil Rhodes did not intend it for us when he wrote his will."

In the past, there was obvious discrimination in the distribution of the scholarships. When Gemma Ware and Thabo Leshilo from the 'Conversation' asked historian, Professor Paul Maylam what Rhodes actually stated in his will, it was revealed, "Rhodes's will specified that only males could be awarded Rhodes scholarships. There was a clause in the will which stated that 'race' should be disregarded, but Rhodes clearly viewed race in terms of the English/Dutch divide." The website quoted Rhodes's view about white supremacy, "Rhodes was an ardent white - supremacist, as revealed, in a couple of these statements- 'I say the natives are like children, they are just emerging from barbarism.' 'Treat the natives as a subject people as long as they continue in a state of barbarism and communal tenure; be the lords over them and let them be a subject race.' "

The will stated that £100,000 should be used to expand the Oriel College's buildings on the High Street to support Oriel fellows, to maintain "the dignity and comfort" of the High Table(!) and to fund the maintenance of the college's infrastructure." According to Wikipedia, Rhodes was worth $8m ($10,467,200 in today's money). The pertinent questions are, how did a sickly 17 years old from Hertfordshire amass so much worth in just 32 years dying at the age of 49.? How many hard-working Africans suffered serious injuries (or death) in the mines to receive penury (wages) to make one individual extremely rich? Health and safety in mines over 100 years ago in Africa hardly compared with conditions in Europe let alone current standards.

The June 14th, 2020, Observer explained that a frank reflection of Empire and the past 400 years of the "national story" should not deny "the contingent narrative of assert-stripping and land -grab justified by beliefs of moral exceptionalism and racial supremacy. There should be a commitment to understand the ways that a blinkered reading of Britain's imperial past continues to drive systematic racial injustice." Prime Minister Boris Johnson was quoted, "We cannot pretend to have a different history." According to Wikipedia, the economic benefits of the slave trade to Britain between the 16th Century and the 19th Century, when about 12 million Africans were taken across to the Americas and the Caribbean, for free labour, is inestimable. Enormous profits creamed from the toil of the slaves working in British Colonies, especially in the Caribbean, were used to support British banks and factories to boost the industrial revolution. The profits were made from exporting manufactured goods to Africa (the irony) and importing slave products such as sugar, rum and coffee. The main British ports which prospered as a result, are Bristol, Liverpool and Glasgow.

Some personalities within the leadership of African kingdoms or empires, especially in West Africa benefited. Some Africans were acutely aware of the negative impact of slavery as stated by Howard W. French in the Guardian's 'The Long Read.' He wrote and I quote, "What is less well known is that in many parts of Africa, such as the Kingdom of Kongo and Benin, Africans fought to end the trade in human beings once they understood its full impact on their own soci- eties. Enslaved people resisted in numerous shipboard revolts, or by simply taking their own lives at sea rather than submit to bondage."

The mass transportation of Africans and the subsequent 'Scramble for Africa,' dealt a devastating blow to Mother Africa. In addition to population loss and massive exploitation of natural resources, mainly by Europeans, wars between kingdoms; and among tribes created a massive political instability. It is 400 years ago but some Europe countries and America are still reaping the economic benefits.

Unsurprisingly some descendants of slave owners can be found in the British House of Lords. In the June 16th,2020 issue of the Observer, under the headline, 'As Statues of Slave Traders Are Torn Down, Their Heirs Sit Untouched In The Lords', Catherine Bennett provided a list.

1. FRANCIS BARING - 6th Baron of Northbrooke, an opponent of Lords' reform is reported as a descendant of Francis Baring, the anti-abolitionist and banker, the 6th, Baron of Northbrook dismissed as exaggerated, the "physical suffering of the negro."

2. Among the names revealed through the University of London database of slave ownership, is the Conservative Peer, Douglas Hogg, Viscount Halisham, is a descendant of Charles McGrel, a merchant compensated £129,464" for 2,489 slaves. In today's money that is equivalent to £100m.

3. The Tory Peer, Carrington who became a Life Peer (Baron Carrington of Upton, County of Nottinghamshire) in 1999 was a descendant of Baron Carrington who received £4,908 compensation for the 'loss' of 268 slaves.

4. The 14th, Lord Halifax of Cameron, a Tory Peer, is a descendant of the 6th, Lord of Cameron who

owned vast plantations in Virginia. The 6th, Lord Halifax was reported in Catherine Bennett's article, to have enjoyed what he called, "bedding down with a negro wench."

5. Seaford of Sussex, on the House of Lords' register, is a descendant of slave owner George Ellis, compensated for more than 1,000 slaves.

Douglas-Pennants used his "exploitation of 1,000 slaves," to fund, "among other things, the Penrhyn Estate in North Wales." His family received £14,683 17s 2d compensation. Richard Pennant, a staunch anti-abolitionist instructed his staff to take care of his assets, "I do not wish the cattle nor the negroes to be overworked." Lord Gage of Firle Place's ancestor, John Gage, received £1,759 8s 11p compensation for 108 slaves.

CHAPTER SIXTEEN

WHAT BLACKS AND OTHER MINORITIES SEEK

Slavery, colonisation (which started from the Scramble for Africa) and widespread exploitation of blacks and other minorities have unfolded over the last four centuries. Generations have protested, died even massacred in what at times represent an intractable pursuit of seeking respect as fellow human beings. The overwhelming plea to be judge by the "content" of one's "character" and not the "colour" of one's "skin" remains unanswered for a majority of black people in a world of prejudice, bigotry and blatant racism.

What do we want? Fairness and equality. It is safe to assert that every member of the BAME (Black, Asian and Minority Ethnic) minority community in any multi-racial country craves fairness and equality when it comes to jobs, education, health, housing, justice and respect as a human being. Members of the BAME community often speak about 'white privilege' of their brothers and sisters.

What is white privilege anyway? According to one Professor Andrew, the term White Privilege was first used by African American writer, W. E. B. Du Bubois in 1935. He was quoted, "Even if you are poor and not doing the best in society, there's still the benefit you get from being white." The theory of white privilege, according to a conservative group, known as 'The White Privilege Conference, 'White folks possess an inherent advantage that is denied to others simply because of their skin colour.' Is that all? How can one disprove this statement? Personally, I can state that it goes against morality and Christian values. Peggy McIntosh, the 86 years old American feminist, anti-racist activist, scholar, speaker and senior research scientist of the Wellesley Centre for Women wrote in an essay in 1988, 'White privilege and male privilege. Personal account of coming to see correspondences through work in women studies.' She defines her understanding of white privilege as unearned advantage based on race which can be observed both systematically and individually, like all unearned privileges in society (such as those related to class, religion, ethnicity, sexual orientation, age or ability). Peggy McIntosh is also the founder of National SEED project on inclusive curriculum (Seeking Education, Equality and Diversity). Wikipedia, having quoted Peggy McIntosh's definition as, "An invisible pack of unearned assets," added, "The concept of white privilege also implies the right to assume the universality of one's own experiences, marking others as different or exceptional while perceiving oneself as normal."

White privilege is boundless advantages enjoyed by a white person because of the colour of his/her skin in a society affected by racial inequality and injustice. The main definition by Wikipedia- "White privilege is the societal privilege that benefits white people over non-white people in some societies, particularly if they are otherwise under the same social, economic and political circumstances, with roots in European colonisation, the Atlantic Slave Trade, and the growth of the second British Empire after 1783, white privilege has developed in circumstances that have broadly sought to protect white racial privileges, various national citizenships and other rights of special benefits."

The Equal Opportunity Act of 2010 which took effect in August 2011 replaced the same Act of 1995. According to the website, gov.uk/guidance/equality- "The equality Act 2010 legally protects people from discrimination in the workplace and in the wider society." The Race Relation Act of 1976 was established by the United Kingdom's Legislature to prevent discrimination on the grounds of race. The categories covered, include discrimination on the grounds of race, colour, nationality, ethnic and national origin, when it comes to employment, education, housing, health and the provision of goods and public functions. The Act also established the Commission for Racial Equality, with the aim to ensure that the rules of the Act are conscientiously upheld.

In the United Kingdom, the promotion of equality, diversity and human rights, underscores the equality of opportunity for all. It offers the individual the opportunity to realise his/her potential unfettered by prejudice and discrimination. Irrespective of where an individual was born, that individual 'parents' background, the colour of that person's skin; he/she has the right to be treated fairly and be protected against racial discrimination and prejudice.

In the United States on May 17th, 2019, the House of Representatives passed a bill-The Equality Act. It amended the Civil Rights Law— "including the Civil Rights Act of 1964, The Fair Housing Act, The Equal Credit Opportunity Act, The Jury Selection and Services Act; and several laws regarding employment with the Federal Government to "explicitly include sexual orientation and gender identity as protected characteristics."

"All men are created equal," in its true meaning without any other explanation, is pivotal to the much heralded and famous American Declaration of Independence, one of the most important document in the coun- try's history. Equality is rightly explained as "Everyone having the same fundamental rights, irrespective of circumstance."

RACE RELATIONS IN FRANCE- The French constitution in 1958: France is an indivisible, secular, democratic and social Republic, guaranteeing that all citizens regardless of their origin or religion, are treated as equals before the law and respecting all religious beliefs. According to Wikipedia, French political tradition does not use the term "Racial Minority" written or in discussion, because of all the rights which the French Revolution embod- ies: There are two important concepts which are, "The notion of the state and the notion of man." The French political tradition therefore considers these rights as, "A universal and natural (or inalienable) benefit of being humans."

Unlike other states which give migrants specific rights such as the right to receive an education in their spe- cific language, the French only recognises "rights in the context of citizenship and human characterisa- tion." In tune with their colonial policy of assimilation (the British was indirect rule). The French state strongly insists that foreign-born nationals, who have acquired French nationality, "be considered French and not by ethnic self- identity." In 1990, the French Commission on Human Rights, published its annual report regarding the state of racism in France. In 2016, the commission reported that 33% of the French believe that races do not exist while 80% believe that some races are more superior to others.

THE AFRICAN SLAVE- The first French slave expedition started in 1594. The middle of the 17th, Century saw the Caribbean Islands of Martinique, Guadeloupe, Saint-Dominique (Haiti), Saint Martin and Saint Barthelemy occupied by the French. The movement of African slaves to French colonies however had been legalised in 1626. The trade in slaves was made legal by Louis XIII in 1642. The Senegal Company was founded in 1673. It was responsible for the provision of slaves to the Island of Saint Dominique. In all, 17 French ports were involved in the slave trade, amassing over 3,300 slave expeditions. Nantes was the main slave port responsible for about 42% of France's slave trade. Other notable ports were La Rochelle, Marselle, Honfleur, Lorient, Le Havre, Bordeaux and Saint-Mario.

In 1865, Louis XIV set up the code noir (Black Code). It was a set of rules written by Jean-Baptiste Colbert. The rules were based on the principle that the African slave had no judicial rights whatsoever and was the property of his master. Notable examples of the rules within the black code are Article 44- The black slave is declared "moveable" which means that he can be sold or passed down from generation to generation. Article 40-The black slave can be sold in an auction. Article 28- The black slave is prohibited from owning anything. Articles 30 and 31- The black slave has no right to go to court, even if he is a victim, and his testimony holds no value whatsoever. However, if a slave hits his master (Article 33), acts inappropriately towards a free person (Article 34) or steals a horse or a cow (Article 35), he is to be killed. Article 38- The runaway slave is to have his ears cut and is to have the image of a lily "fleur-de-lis" (a symbol of French Royalty) branded unto his shoulder. If he relapses, he is to have the shallow of his knee cut and is to have a lily branded on his other shoulder. After a third offence, he is to be killed. It is estimated that between 1676 and 1800, France moved a million African slaves to the West Indies. Between 1815 and 1830, almost all of Nantes Mayors had been slave owners or traders.

During the Period of Enlightenment in France however, slavery and the trade in African slaves came under intense criticism by the philosophers of Enlightenment. Montesquiev, in the spirit of the laws (1748) berated people who called themselves Christians yet practised slavery. In addition, Voltaire, in Candide (1759) lamented and denounced the appalling conditions faced by African slaves. In 1788, Société Des Amis Noir (Society of the Friends of Blacks) was founded. The sole objective was to abolish the slave trade by arguing vehemently that slavery was in fact not economically profitable.

In 1789, the declaration of the Rights of Man and of the Citizen, abolished slavery. It was only abolished in the colonies in 1794 through the efforts of the Society of the Friends of the Blacks. However, in 1802 Napoleon, having been influenced by his wife, re-established slavery, the slave trade and the Black Code. Josephine came from Martinique where she owned many assets. The re-establishment of slavery sparked off a rebellion.

Napoleon responded by sending military expeditions to Saint-Dominique and Guadeloupe to quell the uprising. The rebels of Saint-Dominique became victorious and declared independence. This is generally referred to as the Haitian Revolution. Consequently, in January 1803, the first Black Republic was founded and the name, Haiti was proudly adopted.

In 1815, Napoleon in alliance with Congress decreed that slavery was abolished. Nevertheless, slavery continued into the 1840s on Goree Island in Senegal. In 1848 with the abdication of King Louis-Phillippe, the provisional government abolished slavery in all colonies. Slavery was abolished on May 23rd in Martinique, May 27th in Guadeloupe, August 10th in French Guaina and December 1848 for reunion.

On May 10th, 2001, the French state established a law which recognised the trade of slaves as a crime against humanity. In 2006, May 10th was adopted as National Date of the Commemoration of the abolition of slavery.

RACISM IN AUSTRALIA- There are eight Acts in both state and Australian Federal Legislature on racism and discrimination. These are.......

Commonwealth Racial Discrimination Act 1975. Commonwealth Racial Hatred Act 1995.

Human Rights and Equal Opportunity Commission Act 1986. New South Wales: Anti-Discrimination Act 1977.

South Australia: Equal Opportunity Act 1984 and Racial Vilification Act 1996.

Western Australia: Equal Opportunity Act 1984 and the Criminal Code. Australian Capital Territory: Discrimination Act 1991.

Queensland: Anti-Discrimination Act 1991.

The Aboriginals, the indigenous peoples of Australia, according to Wikipedia, had lived in Australia for at least 65,000 years before the arrival of British settlers in 1788. Britain claimed Eastern Australia as her own on the basis of 'Terra Nullius' (Territory Empty). This 'doctrine' is now discredited.

Initially indigenous Australians in most states were deprived of the rights of full citizenship of the New Australia. This was on the grounds of their race; effectively, the colour of their skin, 'black'. The Australian authorities then introduced restrictive immigration laws which immensely favoured European (white) immigrants to Australia.

Decades after the Second World War, discriminatory laws against indigenous people; and multi- ethnic immigration, were dismantled. A 1967 Referendum on Aboriginal Rights, received, very encouragingly, over 90% approval from the Australian electorate. Effectively, two centuries after the arrival of the first British settlers, legal reforms from the 1970s won Aboriginal and Torres Strait Island people, rights and re-established Aboriginal Land Rights under Australian law.

The beginning of the 21st Century, revealed that Aboriginal people making 2.5% of the population, owned outright 20% of all land. However, this land ownership is mainly in the sparsely inhabited Central

Australia desert rather than the sought-after rich coastal areas.

The historic repercussions of the removal of mixed ethnicity Aboriginal children from their Aboriginal parents resulted in a bipartisan Parliamentary apology to the Aboriginal people in 2008. The practice of removal (the stolen generation) involved Australia Federal and state government agencies and church missions, under Acts of their respective parliaments. The period, roughly between 1905 and 1967 was the time of the removals of the children referred as "half caste." In some areas the practice continued into the 1970s. Official government figures estimated that in certain regions, between 10% and 33% of the indigenous children were forcibly taken from their families and communities between 1910 to 1970.

CHAPTER SEVENTEEN

SOCIAL JUSTICE AND EQUAL OPPORTUNITY

Social justice anywhere whether in Australia, America, United Kingdom, France and indeed any other country is crucial to foster harmony and national development. Social justice is defined by Wikipedia, "A concept of fair and just relations between the individual and society, as measured by the distribution of wealth, opportunities for personal activity, and social privileges." In western societies as well as other cultures worldwide, the idea of social justice refers to the "process of ensuring that individuals fulfil their societal obligations and receive in return what they deserve from society."

February 20th is the World Day of Social Justice. Humanrightscareers.com/issues website states that social justice is a concept of fairness as it manifests in society, that includes fairness in healthcare, employment, housing and more. Discrimination and social justice are not compatible. Wikipedia also informs that "Social justice originated as a religious term to acknowledge the collective nature of humanity, and our personal commitment to helping other humans." Wikipedia also describes social justice as "A state or doctrine of egalitarianism, which is defined as 'a belief in human equality especially with respect to social, political and economic affairs.' "

Social justice also means every human being's human rights are respected and promoted. Everybody should have equal opportunities. It is impossible to have a perfect society, but the society which actively practises social justice, offers everybody a fair chance to succeed in life.

Race, gender, sexual orientation, creed or religion should not impede anybody's aspirations in life. This is what Christianity promotes in its values. Other religions which I believe also value life, advance the course of the individual who, when given a fair opportunity, is capable of contributing to the common good. Social justice is simply about what is right and wrong.

The humanrightscareers.com state the social justice as a concept constitutes four principles- Human Rights, Access, Participation and Equality. These four principles relate to human factors such as, Reproductive Rights, Access to healthcare services, Access to good education, Employment discrimination, Voting discrimination and Disability discrimination.

HUMAN RIGHTS- Human rights are embedded in social justice. Over the years Civil Rights activists have shown that the two are intertwined. In a just society, everybody's human rights are protected. The United Nations state, "Human Rights are rights inherent to all human beings, regardless of race, sex, nationality, ethnicity, language, religion of any other status.

Human rights include the right to life and liberty, freedom of opinion and expression, the right to work and education, and many more. Everyone is entitled to these rights without discrimination."

ACCESS-The mark of a just society is when (basic) essentials like housing, food and education are accessible to all irrespective of race, gender, creed, religious affiliation and sexual orientation. The accessibility of these essentials provides the foundation of a meaningful and good life for all.

PARTICIPATION- The spirit and letter of social justice are served when everybody is involved and consid- ered when problems and solutions are under serious examination. Until everybody, including the vulnerable and the marginalized, is heard, the process of problem- solving and decision- making, are rendered meaningless. Participation should be encouraged to rein in those who were previously not heard or silent to express their points of view: Even if these views appear divergent to what are considered 'standard' or 'norm' by the majority.

EQUITY-It is the application of the principle of social justice to ensure that everybody has a level playing field. The human rights website aptly uses the analogy- Three people are trying to see over a fence. One of them is already tall and able to see. He represents the most privileged in society. The other can just barely see and the last person, the most vulnerable in society can't see at all. 'Equity' means that everyone gets a box to stand on, even though the tallest doesn't need it and it still doesn't allow the shortest person to see. Real 'Equity' doesn't give the privileged any boxes. Instead, the middle person gets one box and the last gets two. Now everyone is at an equal level.

Millions of Africans were taken to the Americas and the Caribbean under duress from 1619 to 1865, the year slavery was abolished in America. The Africans worked very long hours in the plantations under harsh conditions, exacerbated by the most draconian supervision imaginable. Two hundred and forty-six years without pay, these Africans created the wealth which underpins the American economy and will forever be enjoyed by generations (white and black) to come.

Four centuries on, two decades into the 21st, Century and African Americans in their millions are denied social justice in modern and 'better enlightened' United States. The endemic problem regarding the treatment of African Americans was already entrenched from the onset as initially established in these pages. Advancement in technology-smart mobile phones-has uncovered concealed atrocities against African Americans whose ancestors spilt blood and many dying under bondage, laid the economic foundation for the leading global economy, the US. More disturbingly, in recent decades, in some countries, especially in the United States, a minority but hardcore members of law enforcement, has been brutal in dealing with African Americans. The Criminal Justice system, arguably, has woefully failed them. Public institutions, charities and majority in the white population have incessantly added their voices to an urgent and just reforms to foster a durable fair playing field for all.

Majority of people work hard and seek justice for all but there are skeletons in the cupboards in many countries. An example is the unethical human experimentation in the United States. According to Wikipedia a considerable number of experiments performed on human test subjects in the US were later deemed unethical. This is because they were performed "illegally or without the knowledge, consent or informed consent of the test subjects. The experiments included the exposure of humans to many chemicals and biological weap- ons (including insertion with deadly or debilitating diseases) human radiation experiments. Injection of toxic and radioactive chemicals, surgical experiments, interrogation and torture experiments, test involving mind-altering substances, and a wide variety of others. Many of these tests were performed on children, the sick and mentally disabled individuals often under the guise of 'medical treatment.'

Considerable number of these 'victims' were poor, racial minorities or prisoners. Many of these experi- ments contravened US law. Some were "sponsored by government agencies like the Centre for Disease Control (CDC), United States military and the Central Intelligence Agency (CIA) or by private corporations involved with military activities." Wikipedia added, "The research programs were usually highly secretive and performed without the knowledge or authorisation of Congress, and in many cases information about them was not released until many years after the studies had been performed."

"Public outrage in the 20th, Century over the discov- ery of government experiments on human subjects led to numerous Congressional Investigations and hear- ing including the Church Committee and Rockefeller Commission both of 1975 and the 1994 Advisory Committee on Human Radiation Experiments, among others," Wikipedia stated. Amid the Covid19 pan- demic, such a history makes the task of encouraging minorities and the vulnerable in society to take the vaccine, very difficult indeed. We are all aware of the uphill struggle by prominent African Americans and leading figures in the medical field, some churches; in encouraging blacks and other minorities to accept the safety and efficacy of the current nationally approved Covid19 vaccines.

CHAPTER EIGHTEEN

INEQUALITIES IN SOCIETY

In England, there is the 'North and South Divide,' which indicates the marked difference in wealth, job opportunities and the general pace of progress between the two regions. The South, with the magnetic pull of the national capital-London- is richer than the North. We all know about the legendary King Arthur's Round Table. The legend which originated possibly in Wales, revealed that the elite who sat at the table were supposed to be of equal status enjoying the best on offer. Those people away from the round table and the rest of the populace; not so fortunate.

In Italy, the north is richer than the south. Northern Italy has the industries producing 90% of Italy's exports. The region has at its borders, France, Switzerland and Austria.

In the United States, during slavery there were the Southern States and those in the North. The slaves in the North were reported to be better looked after, therefore enjoyed a better status than their fellow Africans in the south.

African slaves in the plantations who lived closer to the slave owner's property were reported to be better cared for than those living in structures in the fields.

Inequalities abound, sometimes even within close-knit families. Sometimes inequalities cannot be helped, but genuine and consistent efforts should be made to address the differences. It is alarming however in a society when minorities or a section of the population remain constantly at the negative end of the scale. Racial inequality or inequality affecting the poor and the vulnerable, breeds resentment and division in society.

Inequalities in many countries were marked even long before the coronavirus. Watching TV, reading the newspapers, hearing stories about other people's difficulties and my personal observations, paint a picture of misery not known for generations. Under the headline, 'Virus Hits the Poorest People the Hardest,' the Daily Mirror's Deputy Political Editor, in the August 25th, 2020, issue wrote about the daily hardships faced by many in the UK, "They can see there is no money. I'm trying to sell my things, my jewelry. Also, for the 19 years old, I don't want her to know everything, because she gets very bad panic attacks and anxiety. I try to hide as much as I can, but they know."

"I suffer with mental health issues but continue to work as I can't afford not to. This has such a significant impact. if I'd been able to reduce my hours. I possibly wouldn't be in this situation, but this was not possible due to finances."

The above points are just a couple of unnamed quotes featured in the double spread article. Alison Garnham, Chief Executive of the Child Poverty Action Group commented among other issues, "If the pandemic has revealed anything, it's that our social security net- work has become threadbare after years of cuts and freezes. It is no longer fit for the job of protecting us when times are tough. People want a system that's compassionate and robust."

Under the headline, 'Meanwhile Tory fat cats cream off millions.' In the same Daily Mirror double spread, the Mirror listed a number of well - connected people to the party who had benefitted enormously through lucrative contracts. "Conservative supporters won £180m worth of contracts to supply the government with PPE (Personal Protective Equipment) during the pandemic. Mellor Designs won seven contracts worth £65m to produce vital kits such as gloves, masks and hand sanitizers. Tory donor David Meller who has given £65,000 to the party over the last ten years co-owns the business." The paper continued, "Gloucestershire Firm P 14 Medical run by Tory Councillor Steve Dechan, was awarded two contracts worth £120m to supply face masks, shields and has two more contracts in the pipe-line. Another firm Clipper Logistics funded by Steven Parkin who has donated more than £500,000 to the Tories, won a £1.3m contract to supply PPE."

The information the Mirror obtained through The Register of Members' Interests was "Tory MP and Ex-Minister, Owen Paterson has been a consultant for Randox since 2015. He has been paid £8,333 for 16 hours work per month since 2017." The Mirror stated, "The Tory-linked firm Randox has been allowed to keep £113m Covid testing contract after 750,000 unused kits were recalled over safety concerns."

In the September 12th, 2020, issue again of the Mirror, under the heading, 'Lords- A Reaping' and 'Taxpayers Fork Out £2m to Keep Peers' Bars and Restaurants Running,' a Mirror reporter spelt out another shameful inequality in society. She wrote, "Nearly £2m of Taxpayers' money subsidised exclusive bars and restaurants for peers at the House of Lords last year." Peers are paid £313 a day for attending the Lords. One of them (not named) was reported to have complained earlier on in the year that the sandwiches at the Bishop's Bar had too much lettuce but the smoked salmon portions were too "modest." Harry Fone, of the Taxpayers Alliance was quoted on the twnews.co.uk/GB-news website, "While I don't begrudge members a decent meal, the taxpayer should not be expected to help pay for it."

During the summer of 2020, Manchester United footballer, 22 years old Marcus Rashford's persistent campaign eventually forced the government to rescind its decision to stop free school meals to needy children in the summer. In responds to Rashford's campaign, Prime Minister Boris Johnson announced that food vouchers worth £15 a week would be available during the summer holidays, for about 1.3 children to spend in supermarkets. Rashford had already raised £20m to provide 3m meals for children during the covid19 lockdown.

Tory MP for Thirsk and Malton, Kevin Hollinrake tweeted on September 6th, 2020, "where they can, it's a parent's job to feed their children," to which Marcus responded in another tweet, "I would urge you to talk to families before tweeting. To this day, I haven't met one parent who hasn't wanted or felt the responsibility to feed their children." On September 2nd, 2020, it was announced that some of UK's largest grocers and suppliers have signed up to a new Poverty Task Force set up by the young Manchester United footballer. Marcus Rashford made the proposal on September 1st, 2020, to set up the Task Force and received the immediate and resounding response from leading retailers including Tesco, Asda, Co-Op and Iceland. Kellogg's was reported to be "partnering with Marcus to ask the government to act."

There are three policy recommendations of the food strategy-" including the expansion of free school meals, ensuring holiday provision for those on school meals and increasing the value of 'healthy starts' vouchers.

Kellogg's is known as a seasoned contributor to the needy. The company "has spent more than 20 years trying to tackle childhood hunger, through its support for breakfast clubs and food banks."

'Children Hungry in Class,' was the heading inside the pages of the September 17th, 2020, issue of the Daily Mirror, "One in five children are at risk of going to school hungry, a study revealed." The report continued, "It found 28% of teachers responded that more kids coming to school on empty stomachs last year- rising to 43% in poorer areas. The study was conducted by Heinz which launched 'Silence the Rumble' Breakfast Club supported also by Marcus Rashford." He was quoted by the Mirror, "Breakfast Club played an integral part in my life." The paper concluded that the partnership with 'Magic Breakfast' will provide the all- important morning sustenance for children before school starts.

"I would urge you to talk to families before tweeting. To this day, I haven't met one parent who hasn't wanted or felt the responsibility to feed their children." Yes, to quote Marcus Rushford again and underscore the benevolence of a young man whose certitude has put to shame adults who should have known better. It would be deceitful on my part to state that the indifference which sometimes sadly borders on callousness is confined to one party. Certainly not! However, it seems some members of one party in this land are prone not only to expressing these sentiments but more likely to act on them. When Margaret Thatcher became the Education Minister of Science in Edward Heath's government, children up to the age of eleven were receiving free milk at school. In 1971, she reduced the age to seven, and earned the nickname, 'Margaret Thatcher the Milk Snatcher.' Consequently in 1985, a chance to be given an honourary degree from Oxford University was not granted. The Education Act 1944 stipulated that local education authorities should provide meals and milk. Two years after, the separate School Act 1946 provided free milk (a third of a pint daily) to all children under eighteen.

Some members of the electorate regarded the nickname unfair because in 1968, Labour's Edward Short, Secretary of Education and Science had reduced the age from eighteen to eleven. In my opinion that was unfortunate since a considerable number of children come from poor homes. Reducing the age by four more years (Margaret Thatcher) is even more unfortunate since the younger children need more nourishment to cope in their formative years.

In 1977, Labour's Shirley Williams abolished school milk for children from above seven. It is a fact that politicians for obvious reasons are reluctant to raise taxes. Instead, some chip away at benefits for the poor and vulnerable to fulfil campaign promises or 'balance the books.' If that was so in the case of these three Education Ministers, why did they not tell the public from the onset that they were going to 'snatch' the free school milk from the poor and innocent children?

Files released by the National Archives revealed that nineteen years later, Mrs. Thatcher, then Prime Minister was "horrified" when her Health Secretary, Kenneth Clarke "proposed finally ending free milk for nursery school children as well."

In society there are some people (hopefully not many) who look in the mirror every morning and wallow in the fact that they are up there, and others are many pegs down the order. However as Civil Rights leader, Jessie Jackson was quoted in the Guardian on May 18th, 2020, "If the poor aren't protected, the rich are in jeopardy."

Inequalities exist in all societies even those occupied by a single race. In even Arab countries awashed with oil dollars, inequality is part of the fabric of soci- ety. Arguably in multi-racial countries minorities espe- cially black people suffer the most. Inequality cannot be eradicated because of many factors, notably per- sonal circumstances and the environment where one is raised. It is however the moral obligation for succes- sive governments to continue and make conditions as bearable as possible for all.

In my opinion, majority of people fighting for racial equality are not looking for affirmative action or hand- outs, but the same privileges as those in the majority. "Just give me the opportunity, if I squander it, it would be my fault and nobody's," remarked an irritated black gentleman after yet, a 'failure' to secure a position for which he was more than academically qualified. During a previous endeavour, he was commended for his qualifications, ability and experience but frankly informed, "You will not fit into the culture in this office."

Well, what culture? He has a family to feed, educate; and pay his bills just like any responsible human being.

What an opportune time to reflect on what some journalists write at the slightest hint of affirmation action. They rightly point out that it devalues the true credentials of qualified and capable black people. However, until all prospective employers cast off the cloak of prejudice during interviews behind closed doors, affirmative action, unfortunately remains the only way for some organizations to tackle this perennial social injustice. When qualification, competence and experience could not be used as compelling reasons for a candidate failing a job interview, some prospective employers would conjure an excuse to deny a person the opportunity to work and earn a living; a basic right for everybody.

If sports were exclusively in camera- behind closed doors- Jessie Owens, Mohammed Ali, Ed Moses, Serena Williams, Daley Thompson, Linford Christie, Tessa Sanderson and countless others would never be known, if some people in society had their way. Therefore, if interviews like sports, were 'open' for all to witness, evaluate and form a judgment, injustice in employment opportunities would have been significantly reduced. There would be no need for affirmative action by some organizations.

On equality in all societies, it is apt to quote the late Joint Holder of FIFA Player of the Century, Diego Maradona, "Poverty is bad, it's difficult, I know it well. You want lots of things and all you can do is dream about them. It would be nice if those who have a lot had a little less, and those who have a little, had more." Simply but effectively expressed. Well, done!

One principal term which has been proven to also pro-mote inequality in society is 'institutional racism.' It is defined as, "A form of racism that is embedded as a normal practice within society or an organization. It can lead to such issue as discrimination in criminal justice, employment, housing, healthcare, political power and education among other things. "According to Hugh of the Guardian the term was first used publicly in 1967 by the African American activists, Stockey Carmichael (later known as Kwame Ture) and Charles V. Hamilton in their book, Black Power: The Politics of Liberation. In England, after the murder of Stephen Lawrence in 1993, Sir William Macpherson's in 1999 described insti-tutional racism as, "The collective failure of an organ-isation to provide an appropriate and professional service to people because of their colour, culture or ethnic origin." In the recent review report about the Windrush Generation, the Home Office was branded, "institutionally racist" over the department's "hostile environmental policy towards immigrants."

In addition to institutional racism, the term unconscious bias needs to be defined. "Unconscious biases also known as implicit biases are the underlying attitudes and stereotypes that people unconsciously attribute to another person or group of people that affect how they understand and engage with a person or group." According to the website, bing.com, "Bias is defined as stereotypes, prejudices or deeply held beliefs which lead us to favour one thing, person or group over another, in a way that is unusually considered unfair. This bias may be held by an individual but it can also be held by an entire group."

The differences, Conscious Bias is self -explanatory, when we are doing something intentionally. When we know that we are being bias, for instance towards a particular person or a group. Example, one prefers working with men more than women; or one does not like working with people of a different colour of skin or culture. Laws and policies are in existence "to prevent prejudice based on race, age, gender identity, physical abilities, religion, sexual orientation and many other circumstances."

Unconscious bias, this bias is "carried out unconsciously." It is doing something without actually realising the impact on people around you. If it happens to adversely affect a certain group of people or a certain individual, it is not deliberate and therefore no malicious intent. It holds on to stereotypes and will disregard anyone who fits into these groups."

Unconscious Bias Training in the workplace helps participants to identify bias, avoid discrimination and support a healthy culture of diversity.

Unconscious bias training for managers focuses on the implicit bias which can affect issues like recruitment, performance management and 'team dynamics.'

Unconscious bias dwells on the impact on customer service interactions with particular emphasis on the micro behaviours which are not "necessarily under one's conscious control."

In the September 22nd, 2020, Guardian, reporters Simon Murphy and Amy Walker stated, "Every parliamentarian should undertake Unconscious Bias Training if asked, so they can do their jobs better, according to a leading anti-racism campaigner who spoke out after it emerged that up to forty Tory MPs are expected to refuse to take part in classes." Simon Woolley, a crossbench Peer who founded Operation Black Vote, was quoted as being "appalled" that any MP would say no to the training. Tory MP, Mansfield Ben Bradley was reported to have written in the Conservative Home, "In my view we should be unabashed in our cultural conservatism, sticking up for free speech and the right to make my own bloody mind up, thank you very much, and stepping in to block this unconscious bias nonsense."

Lord Woolley was reported to have called on Party leaders to make the training mandatory, saying that he was "astonished" any MP would oppose it. He was quoted, "For all parliamentarians, this is the longest hanging fruit to understand our new inbuilt prejudices. I am appalled that so many MPs from whatever party would refuse." Lord Woolley referred to the Black Lives Movement and the need for parliamentarians "to make an honest appraisal about our often-inbuilt prejudices, it would help them to be better politicians." The reporters quoted a 16 -year- old constituent of Mansfield, "If (MPs) educate themselves then they can educate others, not all racism is overt and I think lots of people I know in my generation get it. It wasn't really a thing in Mansfield, but I saw lots of people I know joining the protests in Nottingham in the summer." Sue Burrell, another Mansfield constituent was quoted, "I think it is a little bit short sighted, training can't hurt."

The reporters stated that the Labour leader Keir Starmer was committed to undertaking the Unconscious Bias Training "and said all his staff would too." The reporters added that a Labour spokesman confirmed that Labour MPs will also undertake the training. A House of Commons spokesman was quoted, "Following requests from MPs, we have made Unconscious Bias Training available on a small pilot basis."

Daily Mirror September 25th,2020, heading 'Black Barrister Mistaken for The Accused Three Times by Court Staff.' Tom Pettifor, the Mirror's Crime Editor reported that the black barrister, Alexandra Wilson was asked by a security officer to check her name "against the list of defendants." Ms. Wilson was quoted, "I tried to shrug it off as an innocent mistake." Secondly, she was challenged by a journalist as she went into court and told, "Only lawyers can go in." Thirdly the editor stated, "Inside, a solicitor or barrister told her to wait for the usher to call her for her case, despite the usher standing right next to her." Finally, when Ms. Wilson "walked toward the prosecutor to discuss the case, a court clerk ordered her out." Ms. Wilson was quoted, "I AGAIN explained that I am a defence barrister."

Kevin Sadler, Acting Chief Executive of Her Majesty's Courts and Tribunals Services stated that it was "totally unacceptable behaviour" and he would conduct an investigation. Chair of the Bar Council, Amanda Pinto QC, was quoted, "I fear Alexandra's experience is not a one-off." This case on each occasion may appear an "innocent mistake" but sadly it is far- reaching and unequivocally underscore the prejudice and entrenched racism in society,

On the washingtontimes.com website, Stephen Dinan reported on the website with a photo taken on February 11th, 2015, "Dozens of unidentified Los Angeles police department officers learn to recognise unconscious prejudices and how they can impact behaviours on the street at a class at the Museum of Tolerance in Los Angeles. The department which expects to send more than 5,000 officers of the Museum's course in the next seven years, is working to weave implicit bias lessons into existing training." The course is funded by the US Immigration and Customs Enforcement (ICE).

The reporter stated that the Tolerance Museum Training was one of two programs being axed to comply with President Trump's September Executive Order instructing the government to examine its training programs and get rid of any that promote "divisive concepts" such as inherent racism in all people of a certain race. This is grossly misleading. In fact, it is poppycock. Abraham Lincoln and William Wilberforce were white people who with other white human beings stood out and showed moral courage.

In fact, without the fortitude and humanity of countless white people; (amid continued racism) in terms of equality and social justice, blacks would have been scores of years behind in society, if not a century.

Instinctively any fair- minded person will say that banning the Unconscious Prejudice Training is a tragic mistake. In these pages I have written about genuine mistakes by law enforcement officers (human beings) which sometimes could lead to tragic consequences. If anything, Unconscious Prejudice Training is primarily structured to create (unearth) awareness and therefore reduce if not (totally) eliminate some of the avoidable fatalities over the decades. These courses are not "divisive concepts," to say so is fallacious.

In my opinion, no police officer says goodbye to a spouse in the morning and says to him or herself, 'I am going to make the life of any black person hell today.' Anybody who remotely harbours that toxic thought is not fit to don the police uniform and put on the badge in the first place. We have witnessed the damage, both in life and property the behaviour of the minority in law enforcement, has caused over the decades. The unilateral decision to ban the training smacks against the tragic scenes the world has witnessed repeated over the years especially in America. In my opinion, the appropriate course to take is to conduct a secret survey among law enforcement officers who have completed the training and working on the streets. In the survey these officers would not disclose their names but would give an honest opinion regarding the unconscious training exercise and their experiences back on the streets. The results of the 'secret' survey would determine whether the training should continue or not.

It should not be forgotten that prejudice or bias is a human factor. It is not confined only to white peo- ple. If black police officers (or in any public positions of authority) were considered disproportionately and tragically targeting white citizens in the population, they should be put on an unconscious bias/preju- dice training, if it is proven to be useful. Bias training is scrapped 'because it doesn't work,' was the headline in the Daily Mail by Jonathan Coles in one of the issues in the third week of December 2020. Mr. Coles wrote, "Training in 'Unconscious Bias' will be scrapped in government departments after an official study found no evidence that it worked." He wrote about the cost, "The Department of Works and Pensions spent £112,500 on the training, providing courses for 720 people at an average cost of £156 each." It sounds costly however we should consider a few facts out of a countless number of incidents emanating from prejudice and outright racism. Rioting, looting and arson, over 20 American states, which ensued the George Floyd tragedy was reported to have cost insurance companies $20 billion. The Jacob Blake shooting in Kenosha, Wisconsin resulting in widespread protests and looting cost $50 million. The Los Angeles Riots in 1992, attributable to the brutal beating of Rodney King, after four police officers were acquitted, also cost a lot of money. In comparison, the £112,500 (Bias Training Cost) quoted above is a spit (spittle) in the Atlantic.

However much, much more importantly what about casualties? Gorge Floyd lost his life, one person was reported dead in Kenosha where Jacob Blake was partially paralysed and according to the britannica. com/eventslos-angeles website, over 50 human beings were killed, 2,300 injured and thousands arrested. The above are just a few facts but are more than compelling to empower all authorities and indeed the general public to find solutions to reduce immensely the corrosive effect of racism in society. Racism cannot be eliminated but can be reasonably managed with moral courage and political will.

Until the 1980s or so, in England many Africans were deemed disrespectful mainly because when spoken to by white people in authority and the elderly they looked away and did not look directly at the faces of the individuals speaking to them. In recruitment and in other situations many Africans suffered without knowing the reason. However, the fact is in many African countries when speaking to parents, the elderly and people in authority, one puts his hands at his back bows his head and does not look directly at the individual's face. It is a mark of respect. This underlines the importance of training like unconscious bias. However, this training on its own is not enough to significantly reduce the negative impact of racism. There are other factors, the most important being moral, which sadly is innate and therefore cannot be taught. "Do unto others as you would like them do to you." The Golden Rule in the Bible.

CHAPTER NINETEEN

RACIAL AND SOCIAL INJUSTICE

In my opinion, the only way to approach this seemingly intractable human factor, is through moral lens. Politicians in power and with considerable influence should normally have been the engines of change for the better. Sadly history, prevailing and unfolding events are testimony that many failed, have failed and woefully are failing at the dawn of every blessed day. Some politicians have scant regard to racial and social justice as long as they pander to the wishes and whims of some rich, powerful and influential people, in order to win or cling on to power.

The judiciary is a noble profession, which is an independent body; so, it should be. Sadly, again for minorities and the vulnerable in many countries, some individuals within the profession have often deplorably allowed their prejudices to suppress their probity. History is littered with these inexcusable human failings. It is still happening in many countries, some more than others.

TWO PRINCIPLES AND A CORE IDEA OF THE POLICE SERVICE-To use physical force only when the exercise of persuasion, advice and warning is found to be insufficient to obtain public cooperation to an extent necessary to secure observance of the law or to restore order, and to use only the minimum degree of physical force which is necessary on any particular occasion for achieving police objective.

SECOND PRINCIPLE - To recognize always the need for strict adherence to police executive functions, and to refrain from even seeming to usurp the powers of the judiciary of avenging individuals or the state, and of authoritatively judging guilt and punishing the guilty.

CORE IDEA- The police earn public support by respecting community principles. Winning public approval requires hard work to build reputation. Enforcing the law impartially, hiring officers who represent and understand the community, and using force only as a last resort.

Evidently the above stated are the sixth and eighth principles and the third core idea respectively of Sir Robert Peel and his associates' concrete plan to forge a congenial relationship between the police and all members of the community. All the professionals of the police services cannot rest on their laurels even if 99% of the populace are very satisfied with their service: As against the 1% dissatisfied- the tiniest of margins. It is unmiskeningly evident in Sir Robert Peel's nine principles and the core ideas that the police need to win the confidence and support of all in the community in order to discharge their public duties as expected.

This is without exaggeration, a monumental challenge. It is almost impossible, but I believe majority of the police membership, perform to the best of their abilities. Regrettably, the good and acceptable service of the majority is undermined by a minority within the ranks.

The stark reality therefore which minorities and the vulnerable face is a powerful political elite, in some countries, governments showing indifference at best and at worst using the police or law enforcement officers to crack down into submission, voices expressing bla- tant racial and social injustice. The judiciary as already stated contains some individuals, whose conduct in interpreting the law and passing judgment, have not been honourable.

Now about the police which was formed in the UK in 1829; and many years after, copied around the world. Some officers do not adhere wholly to the principles and core ideas. Sometimes their behaviours put their colleagues to shame and crucially in harm's way.

When the three machinery- executive, legislature, and judiciary- of state fail to address racial and social injustice satisfactorily, whom are the minorities and vulnerable going to call? Of course, not the Ghost Busters. Stand up and be counted, members of the Fourth Estate. Their pens are proverbially referred to as "mightier than the sword." The media is a powerful tool, the bane of dictators, rouge governments and unscrupulous politicians the world-over. Journalists have a mammoth task, for in the pursuance of bringing politicians to account, they are sometimes referred to as the enemies of the people. In some countries, some are fatally attacked. These days when journalists unearth cov- er-ups and serious operational mistakes, their material is dubbed 'fake news.'

Majority of the time the media rises to the occasion, at times however individual journalists allow their prejudices to take hold. A laudable example of fair journalism was the Daily Mail's persistent pursuit of justice for the Stephen Lawrence family after the death of their son in the hands of racists.

On the September 27th, 2020, issue of the Observer, in the Comment and Analysis section was the heading, 'Relentless pursuit of the truth that made him the greatest of editors.' Of course, the heading was referring to the Sunday Times editor in the 1970s, Sir Harold Evans who died on September 23rd, 2020 aged 92. "A good deal of his reputation rests on his relentless pursuit of a series of truths that were deeply uncomfortable to the British establishment: Exposing Kim Philby as a Soviet spy; revealing the full story of the Bloody Sunday killings in Derry; and indelibly campaigning for justice and compensation, over eight years, for the 10,000 people damaged before birth by the morning sickness drug Thalidomide." Sir Harold Evans was a giant of the Fourth Estate.

In the Sunday Times on the same day, under the heading, 'Investigations mattered to Evans and they matter to us,' the Comment section stated, "Everybody in the Sunday Times family mourns his passing, as do many others. To newspaper professionals, he was the superb technician who changed the way papers looked, more than that he was the editor who took on the Establishment because he knew he had right on his side." Also included was the statement,"Harry, driven by a passion to see a big wrong righted, did not get bored."

In the same pages of the September 27th, issue of the Observer, the former editor of the paper, Donald Telford, stated (Sir Harold Evans), "His journalistic credo was 'keep digging, the truth is down there somewhere.' "In the case of the Black Lives Matter movement, some journalists have not even scratched the surface.

They are deliberately and unashamedly barking the wrong tree. In the 'New Review' of the same Observer, Marilynne Robinson, author of Gilead was quoted, "Vast crowds of every kind protested everywhere in the country. This is good grounds for hope. The very irresponsible people running the country now are treating the demonstrations as criminal disorder, turning the focus away from the criminal police violence, that provoked the protests. The ugly intentional defeat of progress."

The factors which underpin journalism are truthfulness, accuracy, objectivity, fairness, and public accountability. Some pieces of advice instilled into the aspiring journalist from the beginning include, "Don't take things on face value," "Always look behind the scene," "Don't leave any stone unturned" and "Delve into the story." In psychiatry, one is expected to ponder, "Why did the patient say this?" Or "Why did the patient behave like this?" An appropriate case history is likely to provide the answer. Having ascertained the facts or got a considerable measure of the patient's history, the responsible nurse will carefully formulate a care plan which will help manage the patient with understanding and compassion.

Returning to the media, if only all journalists upheld the ideals of their profession, a sense of fairness would prevail across all sections of society. On the September 21st, 2020, issue of the Guardian, under the headline, 'Right Wing Media Slurs Will Not Halt Black Lives Matter,' columnist Nesrine Malik wrote, "The purpose of this propaganda is clear: To diminish the moral power of demands for racial and social justice so they are easier to extinguish."

Referring to the reaction of sections of the public and the press over the BLM-themed dance by Diversity on ITV's 'British Got Talent' show, Nesrine Malik wrote, "There is then a sort of free word-association exercise in the media that hangs over the movement, darkening it with suspicion. The Telegraph has called its supporters 'Lockdown busting statue toppling anarchists.' 'Far-left agitators' stuck in a Marxist echo chamber,' says the Express. Mention Black Lives Matter enough times in the company of Marxism, lawlessness, boycotting Israel and abolishing the police, and the movement becomes defined by terms that push people away and bury its main cause." The Sun newspaper was reported describing the BLM founder as "trained Marxist" who had links to a "pro-Chinese Communist Party Liberal Group."

I stated from the beginning of this chapter that the only way to approach this seemingly intractable human factor (racial and social injustice) is through a pair of moral lens. The journalists who wrote these in the three national papers were intentionally skipping over a vital point. If the founding members and protesters are all that and even arsonists, the important thing is that the law is there to deal with people who cause public disorder and opportunists alike.

This is irresponsible journalism. It is a deliberate ploy to mislead, confuse and accentuate an already divided society. It is dangerous. If positions were reversed, would these reporters focus on the background of organisers or dwell on the actual (human) story behind a movement to seek racial and social justice for a minority of white citizens within a largely dominant black population? If the US or UK were a single race country, would some members of the Fourth Estate and some people in public approve or remain silent if a group within the same population is treated differently?

These journalists should be upholding the integrity of the national newspapers they represent by asking themselves and examining meticulously what prompted the formation of the Black Lives Matter movement, a mere eight years ago. Ignore the commotion or the hullabaloo and "look behind the scene, young man, you will learn a lot," as I was told in Journalism tutorials by an elderly white gentleman almost five decades ago.

Why was the BLM movement formed? What is the essence of the movement? What is the story or the message behind the slogan? Through the moral lens as well, Why was the BLM formed only eight years ago?

These are just a few pertinent questions which need careful examination rather than a smear campaign against the founders and mainly peaceful demonstrators of a movement yearning in pain for just basic human requirements, racial and social justice. The founders of the Black Lives Movement have no sole prerogative over the human story behind the movement they have created. My timeline from 1619, shedding light over just a small sample within a multitude of inhumane treatment till the present, indicate that blacks and for that matter some whites were harbouring the same sentiment scores of years even before the BLM organisers were born. The credit to the found- ers of BLM is that their slogan, vividly captures how fair-minded people of all races have felt for generations and continue to feel.

When one considers the negative reactions to the Black Lives Matter movement, it appears that some people in society want black people to remain quiet and continue to endure the suffering which has been going on for four centuries. Some want blacks to keep quiet when the knee is firmly on our necks: Not even to murmur, "I can't breathe," when our last breath   is being siphoned out of our bodies: And not to pro- test our innocence by raising our hands to say, "Don't shoot." We should not forget that the Black Lives Matter Movement gained rapid global recognition because the essence of the movement resonates with minorities and vulnerable people in diverse societies throughout the world. Humanity everywhere is yearning for racial and social justice: nothing complicated. It is every- body's human right. Yes indeed! Every human being's life matters. Absolutely! Yeah man!

On January 6th, 2020, far- right supporters of President Donald Trump attacked Capitol Hill as Joe Biden's victory was formally being ratified. Prior to that, the mob had been incited allegedly by the President who falsely claimed that he won the 2020 Presidential elec- tions "by a lot." In the January 8th, 2020, issue of the Daily Mirror, under the heading, 'Incompetent Cops In a Den Of Cowardice,' Christopher Bucktin, US Editor in Washington wrote, "The senior chiefs responsible should hang their heads in shame and hand in their badges. Images of their officers humiliated policing around the world; cops posing for selfies with rioters, opening gates to invite them in and standing idly by as trouble flared was shameful." The Editor contrasted," In the summer the same force met peaceful BLM (Black Lives Matter) protesters with rubber bullets and tear gas outside the White House to clear the way for Donald Trump's photo op with military leaders and a Bible at a nearby church."

In fact, Trump held the Bible upside down in the "photo op" in front of the church. In the summer of 2020, during the Black Lives Matter protests which was largely peaceful, Trump described the movement a "symbol of hate" and "part of mob rule." However, when his mob was involved in 'the Siege of Congress,' after hours of intense pressure from aides, he told them, "Go home, we love you. You are very special." What double standards! It is immoral and outrageous. Many law enforcement officers were brutal towards even young BLM protesters in the summer but during the 'Capitol siege' Trump supporters mingled freely around some law enforcement officers.

One officer was seen helping a female protester by tenderly holding her hand to negotiate a flight of steps. The attack on Capitol Hill ended with the death of five human beings. One was police officer Brian Sicknick.

These were precious lives. Police officer Sicknick's family had the right to except his safe return home no matter how difficult the profession he had chosen for a living. Every life matters, whether it is that of a demonstrator or a public officer. What was it all about? Even a broken leg would not have been worth it. It was a dangerous and futile exercise to assuage the grandiose ego of one human being. Indefensible!

According to the History Channel about 1.2 million African Americans served in the United States Army during the Second World War. In some quarters these black American soldiers were referred to as the Invisible Soldiers. On YouTube, the black soldiers are described as Silent Heroes. In September 1940, when the Selective Training and Service Act became America's first peacetime draft, Civil Rights leaders put pressure on President Franklin D. Roosevelt to allow African Americans the chance to register and serve in integrated regiments. Black Americans had taken part in every conflict from the Civil War as a segregated unit. Roosevelt's Secretary of War, Henry Stimson, was reluctant to deviate from the 'norm.' The need to increase the size of the army became crucial as the war in Europe raged. The President approved the registration of blacks for the draft, but they would remain in a segregated unit. It was also decided that the military hegemony would have a ruling on the "proportion of blacks inducted into the service."

Despite the willingness of black Americans to lay down their lives for their country, in all the bases and train- ing facilities, many of which were located in the south, the Jim Crow laws persisted. This happened in all the branches of the Armed Forces. Irrespective of any region, there were separate blood banks, hospitals or wards, medical staff, barracks and recreational facilities for black soldiers. Even in Europe and areas in Asia, in difficult conditions, segregation was the order of the day. The accommodation and other facilities for blacks were sub-standard compared with their white compatriots.

In both the United States and abroad, the blacks were not treated well. Matthew Delmont, a history professor at Dartmouth College and author of 'Black Quotidian: Everyday History in African American Newspapers.' Stated, "The experience was very dispiriting for a lot of black soldiers." He added, "The kind of treatment they received by white officers in the army bases in the United States was horrendous. They described being in slave-like conditions and being treated like animals. They were called racial epithets quite regularly and just not afforded respect either as soldiers or human beings."

The military leadership thought that the African Americans were not fit for combat or leadership roles. Consequently, they were tasked with working as cooks, mechanics, building roads, ditches and unloading supplies from trucks and airplanes. The few African Americans who achieved officer rank were restricted to leading only black soldiers. In 'Fighting for America: Black Soldiers- Unsung Heroes of World War Two,' Christopher Paul Moore wrote, "Black Americans carrying weapons, either as infantry, tank corps, or as pilots, was simply an unthinkable notion. More acceptable to southern politicians and much of military command, was the use of black soldiers in support positions, as non-combatants or labourers." Delmont also wrote, "The black press was quite successful in terms of advocating for black soldiers in World War Two. They point out the hypocrisy of fighting a war that was theoretically about democracy, at the same time having a segregated army."

In 1942, the black newspaper, the Pittsburgh Courier received a letter from James G. Thompson, a 26 -year- old black soldier. In the letter, Thompson wrote, "Should I sacrifice my life to live half-American?" This launched the 'Double V' campaign. The slogan which stood for "victory for democracy overseas and a victory against racism in America," was touted by black journalists and activists to rally support for equality for African Americans." The campaign also underscored the positive contributions the black soldiers made "in the war effort and exposed the discrimination that black soldiers endured while fighting for liberties that African Americans themselves didn't have."

There were many successes by African Americans on the battlefield. Notable were the 761st Tank Battalion African American heroes who courageously fought the Nazis. In October 1944, they were the first African

American tank squad to see combat in the war. They were dubbed the Black Panthers. The History Channel stated, "And by the end of the war, the Black Panthers had fought their way further east than nearly every other unit from the United States, receiving 391 decorations for heroism.

They fought in France and Belgium; and were one of the first American battalions to meet the Russian Army in Austria. They also broke through Nazi Germany's Siegfried Line, allowing General S. Patton's troops to enter Germany." The 761st Tank Battalion was also praised for their exploits during the 'Battle of the Burge.' Their contribution helped in the victory of the Allied Forces.

According to the American World War Two - com/articles/patton-loved-hated, which described Patton as a bigot, stated, "he was the only major American General to request more black soldiers, the first American General in history to integrate Rifle Companies, and the first to use black tank units, 'I would never have asked for you if you weren't good,' Patton told the all-black 761st Tank Battalion." General Patton added, "I have nothing but the best in my army."

Another Black American success on the battlefield was the 92nd Infantry Division. They were the first black infantry division to see combat in Europe during the war. They were part of the Fifth Army fighting in the Italian Campaign. The group was highly praised by all. Their mascot was a Black Buffalo.

The courage of Africans in American over four centuries is not in question. However, racism has always been the tool to stifle, underplay or even erase the achievements of blacks. When it is not a job interview behind closed doors where facts could be distorted, the evidence is there for all to see. On January 6th, 2021, during the infamous siege of Capital Hill, 41 years old African American, Eugene Goodman, law enforcement officer and army veteran did all humanity proud. Goodman's bravery in the face of the baying mob on a flight of steps and corridors of the building created a period, short but precious time of delay to offer senators the chance to flee to safety. Threats were made to the lives of senators and especially then Vice President Mike Pence and the Speaker of the House, Nancy Pelosi.

Senator Mitt Romney was alerted by officer Goodman in the nick of time. Romney stated, "I expressed my appreciation to him for coming to my aid and getting me back into the path of safety and expressed my appreciation for all that he did that day."

On Friday, 12th of February, the Senate gave officer Goodman a standing ovation as it unanimous passed a law to award the African American the Congressional Gold Medal. It is the highest honour the Senate can bestow on any American. Senate Majority leader, Chuck Schumer who introduced the bill stated, "In the weeks after the attack on January sixth, the world learned about the incredible bravery of officer Goodman on that fateful day." Minority leader, Mitch McConnel concurred by praising "a group of heroes whom we in Congress were already proud to call our colleagues and to whom we owe a great debt." He added, "If not for the quick thinking and bravery of officer Eugene Goodman in particular, people in this Chamber may not have escaped that day unharmed."

In this chapter I hasten to add a scandal in British education. The May 20th, 2021, issue of the Daily Mirror, previewed a program on BBC1 captioned 'Subnormal: A British Scandal.' The paper stated, "The shocking documentary explores one of the biggest scandals in history of British education, with some poignant first-hand interviews. In Britain in the 1960s, black children were disproportionately sent to schools for the so-called 'educationally subnormal. 'They were labelled as having a lower intelligence by the state, but in truth, immigrant children were dispersed to different schools after white parents complained that black immigrant children were holding their kids back and a 30% maximum quota was introduced."

"I was told I was stupid, that I was a dunce", says a 54-year-old Londoner Noel Gordon, who was sent to a school for 'slow learners' based on no evidence of any learning difficulty. It had an enormous impact on Noel, who has since gained 13 qualifications, including a post grad certification in education". The Mirror con- cluded the preview, "This gripping film tells the story of how black parents, teachers and activists banded together to expose injustice and racism, and to ulti- mately force the education system to change."

I watched the program on that Thursday night and was highly impressed by the academic and professional achievements of many of those interviewed. However, the psychological scars of such a policy resonated throughout the hour-long viewing. The despairing effect of such a policy on innocent (black) children can only be described as a 'scandal.' The irony of the whole story is that while the poor black children were considered as having lower intelligence by the British state, their parents were becoming key workers in the British Railways, the buses and diverse factories throughout Britain; not forgetting the all-important NHS

(National Health Service). Come to think of it a few years ago, a Nigerian family was dubbed 'The Brainiest Family In Britain.' Truth is like a cork, in water. It can never be suppressed. It always comes up.

In the United States Black schools, referred in the past as "Colored" schools have been beset by under-funding from time immemorial. The Rethink Schools Magazine revealed- "Over the first three decades of the 20th Century, the funding gap between black and white schools increasingly widened." Public schools in the US get their funding from the Federal, state, and local sources. Nearly 50% of the funds come from local property taxes.

Invariably, the affluent communities generate sub-stantially more funds than the less affluent. The dispar-ity therefore in school funding between the rich and poor communities is huge. The future of every country depends on the youth, the leaders of the future. Why should governments of different complexions con-done, play lip service, or turn a blind eye to the chronic underfunding of black schools?

According to Wikipedia, another significant factor to this racial and social inequality, emanates from the late 1860s "during the Reconstruction Era when Southern States under biracial Republican governments estab-lished public schools for former slaves." Unquestionably those schools were segregated. When conservative whites took control across the south after 1877, they maintained the schools but at a significantly lower funding rate than the white schools.

The National Association for The Advancement of Colored People (NAACP) studies of unequal expenditures in the mid-to-late 1920s revealed that in Georgia only $4.59 was spent annually on an African- American child, as compared to $36.29 on a white child. A late 1930s study by Doxey Wilkerson, a black education expert, author, editor and Civil Rights activist found that only 19% of 14–17-year-old African- Americans were entered in high school.

In 1968, when the Civil Rights Act was signed, 76.6% of black students and 54.8% of Latino students attended public schools where the majority of learners were non-whites. According to the website, topmastersineduca-tion.com/school-funding-post-racial-us, "The number of students of color in majority-minority schools has remained virtually unchanged since 1968, with only 2.5% less black students attending these schools over the past 45 years."

The authors of a 2003 Havard-study on resegregations, stated that the steady departure of white teachers from predominantly black schools was as a result of Federal court decisions limiting former methods of Civil Rights' Era protection, such as busing and affirmative action in schools' admissions. Other examples teach-ers and principals cite included economic and cultural barriers in schools with high rates of poverty as well as teachers' choices to work closer to home or in higher performing schools. In some areas, black teachers were reported in the study to be leaving the profession thus creating teacher shortages.

On February 27th, 2019, Jay Croft of CNN quoted an education advocacy group, "Predominantly white school districts in the US get $23billion a year more than districts that educate mostly non-white children."

A report from EdBuild, which promotes equity in public schools reported that the average white school district got $13,908 for every student in 2016, compared to $11,682 per student in districts which predominantly serve people of color. The report also revealed that white districts "enroll over 1,500 students- half the size of the national average- while non-white districts serve over 10,000 students, about three times more than that average."

I had a look at an array of sayings, poems and verses of hymns to capture if not all but a considerable part of what I have written in these pages.

Having gone through a protracted and intense deliberation, I settled for Verse 2 of the Methodist Hymn,

'Lord Your Church on Earth Is Seeking,' by Hugh Sherlock (1905-1998).

FREEDOM GIVE TO THOSE IN BONDAGE, LIFT THE BURDENS CAUSED BY SIN.

GIVE NEW HOPE, NEW STRENGTH AND COURAGE, GRANT RELEASE FROM FEARS WITHIN:

LIGHT FOR DARKNESS; JOY FOR SORROW, LOVE FOR HATRED; PEACE FOR STRIFE. THESE AND COUNTLESS BLESSINGS FOLLOW AS THE SPIRIT GIVES NEW LIFE.

There are countless and appropriate verses and lines to quote from the same Methodist Hymn Book, 'Singing the Faith,' but I will add just two more... 'Let Love Be Real in Giving and Receiving,' by Michael Forster.

1. 'Give me your strength when all my words are weakness. Give me your love in spite of all you know.'

2. 'As God loves us, so let us love each other: with no demands, just open hands and space to grow.'

I have written and I will repeat, I believe in humanity. However, the machinery of state- elected government, the legislature, the judiciary and law enforcement, lacks the political and moral will to uphold at all times racial and social justice. Individuals within these public bodies have betrayed not only the genuine objectives of the majority within their ranks; but have repeatedly and woefully failed, due to inherent prejudice to address inequalities in society which disproportionately affect blacks, other minorities and the vulnerable. The Fourth Estate, the only body which is not part of the state machinery, has a unique and powerful independent position to bring everybody to account. The media is therefore morally tasked with the role of seeking the welfare of the weak, the disadvantaged, the victim, the oppressed and the marginalised.

Deplorably, a minority within the 'Estate' again saddled by their own biases, has on countless occasions failed miserably to uphold the integrity of the noble profession. When it comes to protests against racial and social injustice, the opportunists, the hooligans will always show up, but the majority of protesters will remain peaceful and focused on their objectives. How many column inches do some journalists use to attack public officers whose prejudice, recklessness, ignorance, and sheer irresponsibility perpetuate the incidents in the first place: Giving the opportunists and so-called anarchists the chance to cause mayhem and social disorder?

Instead, minority of members of the media use pages even double spreads continuously ignoring the real human stories behind the protests but attacking movements (e.g., BLM) which have legitimate and genuine grievances. How many times have some journalists also attacked some politicians and members of the judiciary whose prejudice or innate racism has sparked off protests and riots leading to loss of life, injury and damage to property and business?

Who is expected to be more responsible, the paid public official or ordinary Joe Bloggs on the street? Cause and effect- discriminatory policies, reckless behaviour, injustice, and police brutality are all incendiaries to serious public disorder and loss of precious human life. These are just a few examples.

1. WATTS RACE RIOTS- On August 11th, 1965. The riots of Los Angeles were caused by "frustrations about poverty, prejudice and police mistreatment," according to The Kerner Commission. The Advisory Commission on Civil Disorders concluded that white racism was the fundamental cause of the riots. Most of the 34 deaths were black. There were more than 1,000 people injured and more than $40m worth of property destroyed.

2. BRIXTON RIOTS UK- Between April 10-12, 1981. Police officers injured-299, so were 65 members of the public. Sixty-one vehicles and 56 police vehi- cles were destroyed. Twenty-eight premises were burned and 117 damaged and looted. According to Wikipedia, the causes of the riots were poverty, alienation, and systematic racist abuse from the police.

3. THE BRIXTON RIOTS OF 1985-The mailonline stated," 'I can't breathe', 40 years before George Floyd, this

is what one black boy heard his mum gasp after she was shot by a white police officer in their Brixton home and now Cherry Groce's son tells how he finally won justice."

In fact, it was on September 28th, 1985, 36 years ago when 11 years old Lee Lawrence saw how his mother was accidentally shot by an officer of the Metropolitan Police during a raid to arrest her 21 years old son Michael who was suspected of being involved in a robbery. Cherry Groce was paralysed at 36 years old. She died of kidney fail- ure in 2011. The shooting led to the second Brixton Riots. Fifty people were injured, and more than 200 arrests were made by police.

4. RODNEY KING- In March 1991, Rodney King an African American was beaten and humiliated by three white officers of the Los Angeles Police Department. They had chased and arrested him for drink –driving. Sixty- three people died during the ensuing riots. This included 9 killed by law enforce- ment and one killed by guardsmen. An estimated 2,383 people were injured, according to Wikipedia. Rodney King died on June 17th, 2012, aged 47.

5. GEORGE FLOYD's death on May 25th, 2020. The num- ber of people killed during the riots vary between 17 to 23. According to the Daily Mail's website on June 3rd,2020, during protests in the first week of riots 11 people died including a retired officer, an ex-college athlete and a restaurant owner. In all 700 police officer were injured during nationwide protests. Riots in 140 cities after his death is esti- mated to cost insurance companies $2b.

6.   JACOB BLAKE-On August 23rd,2020, 29 years old African American Jacob was shot seven times in the back by 31 years old white police officer, Rustein Sheskey. Two people were killed and a third was injured during the third night of protests and unrest in Kenosha, Wisconsin US. Damage to property and businesses was estimated at $50m.

This is the reality for blacks after four hundred years and counting of racial and social injustice. Having lived in the UK for almost five decades, reading, hear- ing, watching TV and experiencing issues about race, I think it is safe to conclude that blacks and other minori- ties do not want sympathy but empathy. We do not want enmity: But amity as a bonus, in our relationship with the majority white population, will do nicely. If I may, to quote the African American, the late Maya Angelo, "Human beings are more alike than unalike." Amazing Grace!

Yes, we know and believe that it is the minority in society who are perpetrators of racial and social injustice. The majority in all societies should stand up and be counted, else be charged with complicity. There are many examples I can list to testify that there is hope yet for humanity. I will however settle for two.

During the various protests and demonstrations in the summer of 2020 about police brutality and racial injustice, many white people especially young adults stood shoulder to shoulder with their black brothers and sisters. In some cases, they suffered as much as meted out to the black protesters. What a vivid and sincere demonstration to let us know and feel that they feel and share our pain.

"I am my brother's keeper." During a counter protest against the Black Lives Movement in London on June 15th,2020, a BLM activist 50 years old Patrick Hutchinson was pictured carrying on his shoulder, an injured white man- 55 years old Bryn Male- from the opposing camp to safety. Mr. Hutchinson was ably supported by a number of his black friends to ensure that the injured human being did not suffer further injury during the violent clashes. This was extensively covered by both the national and international media. Give Sarah Vine her due, she rightly featured the powerful image in her column. She praised Patrick and his colleagues.

Well, done, Sarah. Under that powerful picture, the headline by Rosie Kinchen in the November 8th, 2020, issue of the Sunday Times was, 'If we put our backs into it, we can make this a fairer country.' Profuse thanks, Rosie.

My Christian Duty

It was a cold winter evening.
Snow covered the ground and rooftops.
The Croydon street was deserted
but for a frail solitary figure.

A statue, she appeared from a distance.
Closer proximity revealed otherwise.
In her seventies, she stood in a trance.
I could barely see her sad face.

Icy snow had capped her flower hat.
The cascade, slanted hat, had claimed one eye.
The other blinked feebly to indicate life.
She was cold and soaked to stupor.

Snow had covered the bus stop sign;
only the pillar to betray that identity.
No bus in sight to offer solace:
only my wading Metro for salvation.

I slowed down to help a fellow human being,
but recalled the day's headlines, "Black Muggers";
and ruefully drove on negating my Christian duty.
She was white, I am black.

WHO IS HIS BROTHER'S KEEPER?

A picture of US law enforcement officer Derek Chauvin with his knee on George Floyd's neck: And BLM activist Patrick Hutchinson carrying injured right- wing protester Bryn Male to safety.

CHAPTER TWENTY

SLAVE OWNERS IN THE AMERICAN PRESIDENCY

Social justice appeared irrelevant when even American Presidents occupying the White House were slave owners. They were Thomas Jefferson, James Madison, James Monroe (5th President), Andrew Jackson, John Tyler, James K. Polk and Zachary Taylor. African slave labour was used in building the White House. Initially there was a plan to bring in workers from Europe. However, when the idea did not materialise, the African slaves were 'recruited.' They were trained to quarry stone and brick besides helping to build the actual structure. The White House took eight years to build starting from 1792. The African slaves also built fifteen other famous landmarks in America. These include The US Capitol Hill in Washington, The Statue of Freedom Atop The Capitol, The Smithsonian Institution D.C., Wall Street in New York, Trinity Church in New York, Fraunces Tavern in New York, Faneuil Hall in Boston, Fort Sumter in South Carolina, Harvard Law School Massachusetts, Castillo De San Marcos Fort in Florida, Georgetown University in Washington D.C., The University of North Carolina in North Carolina, Monticello in Virginia, Montpelier in

Virginia (home of former President-James Madison) and Mount Vernon in Virginia.

In addition to the benefit of about 250 years of free African labour to the general American public, occupants of the highest office in the land personally gained from slavery. No doubt it took more than two centuries for the inhumane practice to end in 1864. If there was strong political will and more importantly ingrained moral will, it would have been stopped much sooner. Even after abolition, the American economy still benefited because there was no parity in wages with the rest of the population for the freed Africans.

THOMAS JEFFERSON- (1801-1809). He was the 3rd President of the United States. He was reported to favour the eventual freedom of all slaves yet had hundreds of slaves in the White House during his tenure in office.

JAMES MADISON- (1809-1817). The two very import- ant events during James Madison's presidency were the war of 1812 and the writing of the 'Star-Spangled Banner' by Francis Scott Key. It was reported that Paul Jennings one of the many slaves at the White House wrote a "detailed memoir" about his time in Washington D.C.

James Monroe- (1817- 1825). James Monroe, the 5th President was a slave owner from Virginia. He had slaves in the White House. In 1820, when he won his second term, he "outlawed slavery" in the Northern states.

ANDREW JACKSON- (1829-1837). Andrew Jackson is regarded as one of the most controversial Presidents ever. He practised nepotism. He "handed thousands of government jobs" to his friends. He had hundreds of slaves in the White House. It was reported that "slaves built his Hermitage Estate" in Tennessee.

JOHN TYLER-(1841-1845). John Tyler was regarded as the most pro-slavery on the list of American Presidents who owned slaves. He was reported to have "owned slaves throughout his life." He defended slavery and vehemently opposed anti-slavery measures of James Monroe's presidency. He appointed pro-slavery, John C. Calhoun as his Secretary of State, according to "presidential history geeks." Undoubtedly, there were many slaves in the White House during his four-year tenure.

JAMES K. POLK- (1845-1849). James Polk was pro-slavery and therefore intensely appalled abolitionists. He owned slaves "his whole life." His presidential salary enabled him to buy more slaves. This was a period close to the American Civil War, with slavery, a polarising political topic.

ZACHARY TAYLOR – (1849-1850). He was reported to have relied on slaves at the White House to help keep the place running during the briefest of tenures. Irrespective of being a slave owner, he was not a keen defender of slavery. He "vowed to start a war with Southern secessionists over his slavery policies."

GEORGE WASHINGTON-(1789-1797). George Washington was described as a "Founding Father who was torn on the subject of slavery." He became a slave owner at the age of 11. Despite having been a long- standing slave owner for 56 years, he was known to have struggled with the institution of slavery and spoke frequently of his desire to end the practice. In his 1799 will, he made the decision, and all his slaves were freed before he died. He was the only Founding Father to do so.

MARTIN VAN BUREN-(1837-1841). Martin Van Buren was Vice President to Andrew Jackson (1829-1837) who was pro-slavery. Van Buren however, was opposed to the practice. He did not have slaves in the White House but in his entire life he owned only one slave.

WILLIAM HENRY HARRISON-(1841) William Harrison who was a "slave owner and a slavery lover," did not have any slaves in the White House. He scarcely had the chance to settle in -he died a month after his inauguration-on March 4th, 1841.

ANDREW JOHNSON-(1865-1869). Andrew Johnson was a slave owner, but he did not have slaves in the White House. He became President after Abraham Lincoln was assassinated. He was reported to lack the same humanity his predecessor had towards the freed slaves. In his impatience to rebuild the nation after the Civil War, his "lenient reconstructionist polices" allowed the Southern States oppress the newly freed slaves.

ULYSSES S. GRANT- (1869-1877). Ulysses Grant was a Union General during the Civil War. His wife Julia owned slaves whom he was supposed to control. Grant owned only one slave whom he "freed in 1859" before the Civil War started.

ABRAHAM LINCOLN- He often expressed moral opposition to slavery both in public and in private. He stated, "If slavery is not wrong, nothing is wrong." He went on, "I cannot remember when I did not so think and feel." The thorny issue was what to do about it and how to end it considering it was entrenched in America's constitutional framework and the economy of the country. Lincoln never owned a slave but was married to Mary Todd Lincoln, the daughter of a slave owner from Kentucky. Considering his marital connections and the economic importance of slavery to America, President Lincoln's stance on the immoral practice was morally and politically courageous; and therefore laudable. The complex and politically challenging matters, compelled Lincoln to dwell on the practical objective of preventing the creation of new slave states and particularly stopping the expansion of slavery into the new Western Territories.

CHAPTER TWENTY-ONE

THE ACADEMIC AND PROFESSIONAL ACHIEVEMENTS OF AFRICAN AMERICANS

Many Americans, especially those in the southern states regarded the African slaves only fit to work in the fields and be exploited endlessly. They worked in bondage –free labour, almost for two hundred and fifty years to lay the foundation of the American economy. Many hurdles were put in their way in their quest to be educated and acquire a profession of note. White sympathisers were discouraged to educate blacks, with threats of fines, flogging and even imprisonment.

George Washington Carver was born in Diamond Grove, now Diamond, Missouri, on July 12th, 1864, a year before the abolition of slavery. He was an African American, a colossus of a human being and refuted the deep- seated derogatory perceptions of the intellectual ability of the black man. He studied Botany at Iowa State Agricultural College (now Iowa University) in Ames. He started in 1891, the first black student at Iowa State. His Bachelor's thesis for a degree in Agriculture was, "Plants as modified by man."

George Washington Carver became an American agricultural scientist and inventor who promoted alternative cross to cotton and methods to prevent soil depletion. He was arguably the most renowned black scientist in the early 20th, Century. When he was two years old, he, his mother and a sister were kidnapped. He was eventually rescued but his mother and sister were never found.

Carver was a scientist who avidly studied diseases. He made more than 300 products including soap and ink from peanuts. He was called the Peanut Man. He made 118 products including flour and candy from potatoes. He made 75 products from pecans and building materials for walls from cotton stalks. He was a mine of ideas extremely beneficial to humanity.

When he was at Tuskegee Institute as a professor, Carver developed techniques to improve soil depletion caused by repeated planting of cotton. He wanted poor farmers to diversify by growing other crops like peanuts and sweet potatoes as a source for personal consumption and improve their quality of life. According to Wikipedia, the most popular of his 44 Practical Bulletins for farming contained 105 food recipes using peanuts. However, despite years of developing and promoting numerous products made from peanuts, none became commercially successful.

Among his many pursuits was showing leadership in promoting the environment. He received many awards including the Spingam Medal of NAACP (National Association for the Advancement of Coloured People). Despite an era of entrenched racial polarisation, Carver's fame went beyond the black community. His achievements and talents were well recognised within the white community which held him in high esteem.

The Time Magazine called him the "Black Leonardo." In 1896, at the invitation of Booker T. Washington, the first President of Tuskegee Institute, Carver became the Head of the Agriculture Department. He taught methods of crop rotation and introduced diversification. He initiated research into crop products (CHEMURGY) and taught a host of black students, farming techniques for self-sufficiency.

President Theodore Roosevelt openly admired Carver's work. He also met Presidents Calvin Coolidge and Franklin Roosevelt. The Crown Prince of Sweden studied with him for three weeks. Former professors taught by Carver at Iowa University, were appointed to positions as Secretary of State. An example was James Wilson, a former dean and professor served from 1897 to 1913. A couple of George Washington Carver's saying are, "It is simply service that measure success," and "Where there is no vision, there is no hope." He was referred to in a biography as 'Man's slave becomes God's scientist, George Washington Carver', He also stated, "The Lord has guided me; he has shown me the way just as he will show everyone who turns to him." Alleluya!

His special prayer to those he knew as well as for the many strangers the Lord would bring into his life was, "May the God ever bless, keep, guide and continue to prosper you in your uplifting work for humanity, be it great or small, is my prayer. And may those whom He has redeemed, learn to walk and talk with him, not only daily or hourly, but momentarily, through the things that He has created."

He died on January 5th, 1943, at the age of 78 after a bad fall down a flight of steps. His epitaph read,"He could have added fortune to fame but caring for neither, he found happiness in being helpful to the world."

FIST UNIVERSITY- The free Coloured School opened on January 9th, 1866, a year after the abolition of slav- ery: And shortly after the American Civil War. The founding members were John Ogden, Erastus Mild Cravath and Edward Parmelee Smith of the American Missionary Association for The Education of Freedmen in Nashville. Fisk is one of several schools and colleges which the Association helped to establish in the southern states devoted to educating freed slaves after the Civil War. The school is named after Clinton B. Fisk, a Union General and Assistant Commissioner of the Freeman's Bureau of Nashville. Fisk is the oldest higher education institute in Nashville, Tennessee.

The website reads," Fisk University is committed to maintaining a diverse community in an atmosphere of mutual respect and appreciation of differences. Fisk, in its educational program and activities including students and employees, does not discriminate on the basis of race, colour, national origin, sex, religion or age." According to US News and World Report, Fisk is the sixth among historically black universities. Fisk College was the first African American institution to gain accreditation by the Southern Association of Colleges and Schools (SACS). Accreditations for specialised programs were soon granted.

In a creative move to raise funds for the financially strapped institute, the Treasurer and Music Professor, George L. White formed a Nine-Member Singing Group called 'Fisk Jubilee Singers.' The National Fundraising Tours started on October 6th, 1871. States outside the South were for the first time introduced to 'Negro Spirituals' and Christian songs created by African American former slaves. The group captivated the imagination and won the hearts of many white audiences. They were able to earn enough money to cover their expenses and send much needed funds back to Fisk College. October 6th, is annually celebrated by Fisk University as "Jubilee Day." In 1872, they sang at the World Peace Festival in Boston. The President, Ulysses S. Grant invited them to the White House at the end of that year.

In 1873, The Jubilee Singers toured Europe. They performed for Queen Victoria of England who commissioned a portrait of the singers as a gift from England to Fisk College. The funds raised from the European tour enabled Fisk to construct its permanent structure known as The Jubilee Hall. In 1975, the United States Department of the Interior designated Jubilee Hall as a National Historic Landmark. Fisk University has a long history of activism in racial equality in the United States. In 1942, Dr Charles S. Johnson formed the Race

Relations Institute at Fisk. The end of legal segregation in Nashville during the Civil Rights Movement was partly due to the activism of the students from Fisk. In the winter and summer months of 1960, demonstrators staged a successful sit-in campaign targeting segregated businesses in downtown Nashville. The annual one-week seminar at Fisk of scholars from diverse backgrounds, offers the opportunity for racial dialogue.

Past prominent scholars of Fisk include W.E.B. DuBois co-founder of NAACP, Booker T. Washington, who was an educator, author, orator and adviser to many US Presidents. He was influential between 1890 and 1915. Other prominent students were US Congressman John Lewis, Civil Rights activist Diane Nash, former Washington D.C. Mayor, Marion Barry, Matthews Knowles (Beyonce's father) and Alma Powell, audiologist, and wife of Military General and former US Secretary of state, Colin Powell. In 1823, Alexander Lucius Twilight, graduated from Middlebury College and became the first negro to be a college graduate.

In all countries around the world, especially in a racially divided country like America, education is a lifeline to the poor, minorities and those marginalised in society. It helps immensely to alleviate poverty and enhances the ability to participate in a meaningful manner in affairs of the community or even the state. The academic standards of some African American boys remain a concern. A 2012 survey indicated that African American boys had significantly lower scores than white boys in reading and mathematics. Stimulus which is needed through the interaction with people of different walks of life and other social experiences needs considerable elevation. The realisation of this gap and hopefully the related discussions it has evoked, will help improve the lot of those African American boys and even some white American children from poor families.

In a 2019 publication study by Tanisha Shirelle Pruitt and Sharon Olanike regarding the effects of eco- nomic inequality on the academic achievement of the African American males, highlighted that they disproportionately affect the poor with many living below the poverty line. In 2016, candidate Trump, in a bid to capture the African American vote stated, "What do you have to lose." He continued by telling a nearly all-white audience in Michigan that black voters "are living in poverty" and their "schools are no good." Racism, inequalities in society and many other fac- tors are attributable to the lot of some African Americans in these modern times. In that vein, for anybody, let alone somebody aspiring for the presidency to say this, is unfortunate and irresponsible, to say the least.

Any fair-minded citizen should bemoan a national 'fail-ure' like this rather than exploiting it for personal politi-cal gain. The national 'failure' is also utterly disgraceful because these African Americans' ancestors laboured tirelessly in bondage, endured unimaginable inhu-man treatment and laid the economic foundation for America.

Conversely a 2015 survey and information indicated that 86.4% of African immigrant children born in America aged 25 and older, have a high school degree or higher compared to 78.9% of Asian born immigrants and 76.5% of European born immigrants.

The difficulties African slaves endured in two hundred and forty-six years before the abolition of slavery in 1865 was unprecedented. Arguably in terms of inhumane treatment against fellow human beings, there is still no comparison. President Abraham Lincoln stated, and I repeat, "If slavery is not wrong, nothing is wrong. I cannot remember when I did not so think and feel."

Emancipation, the main thrust or essence of the post abolition period was an illusion for almost all the freed African slaves; for the social, legal and political shackles persisted. We are in the 21st, Century and deplorably unfolding events are indicators of the residual effects of slavery. They may be residual but remain potent; and because of racism, hurdles remain.

Therefore, any achievement by an African American is commendable. The awareness of the achievements of African Americans was heightened in 1926 when Carter G. Woodson started the Negro History Week, which took place in the second week in February. Four decades on in 1969, African American academics at Kent State University suggested that the whole month of February should be considered Black History Month. In 1970, Kent state celebrated its first Black History Month. The following six years saw other establishments follow suite. In 1976, President Gerald Ford showed his approval and officially recognised Black History Month.

There are countless African American heroes and heroines known, unknown or forgotten whose achievements dislodged some hurdles and paved the way for modern-day trail blazers. Dr Martin Luther King was one of many who took on the mantle with moral and physical courage and sadly eventually paid for it with his life. Countless others with admirable moral and physical bravery stood out to be counted and suffered stated-sponsored police brutality. One such person was the late Congressman John Lewis who with all the required attributes including tenacity, championed the cause till his dying days.

I would gladly shed light on all the African American heroes and heroines, but it is impossible hence I will list just a fraction of one percentage point. My list comes from the African American History Month website.

1. JOHN MERCER LANGSTON- (December 14th, 1829, to November 15th, 1897). He was abolition- ist, attorney, educator, activist, diplomat and a politician. He became the first Dean of the Law School at Harvard University and helped create the department.

2. THURGOOD MARSHALL- (July 2nd, 1908, to January 24th,1993). He was an attorney and a Civil Rights activist. He served as Associate Justice of the Supreme Court of the United States from October 1967 until October 1991. He was the Court's first African American Justice.

3. HIRAM RHODES REVELS- (September 27th, 1827, to January 16th, 1901). He was a Republican US Senator, Minister in the African Methodist Episcopal Church and a college administrator. He was born as a free person in North Carolina. He later lived and worked in Ohio, where he voted before the Civil War.

4. SHIRLEY ANITA CHISHOLM- (November 30th, 1924, to January 1st, 2005). She was politician (a Democrat) an educator and author. In 1968 she became the first black woman elected to the US Congress. She represented New York's 12th, Congressional District for seven terms from 1968 to 1983. Shirley was the first

African American to make a bid for the presidency as a major party black candidate.

5. MADAM C.J. WALKER- (December 23rd,1867 to May 25th,1919). She was an entrepreneur, philan-thropist, and a political and social activist. She was considered the wealthiest self-made woman in America at the time of her death in 1919.

6. HATTIE McDANIEL-(June 10th, 1893 to October 26th, 1952). She was an actress and a singer who was the first African American to win an Academy Award. She received the honour for her performance as 'Mammy' in 'Gone with The Wind' in 1939. She acted in other films including 'Colonel' and 'Alice Adams.' both in 1935.

7. ROBERT F. FLEMING JNR- (July 1839 to February 23rd, 1919). He was an American inventor and Union sailor in the American Civil War. He was the first crew member aboard the USS Housatonic to spot the HL Hunley before it sank the USS Housatonic. He became a music teacher. On March 3rd, 1886, he invented the Euphonic Guitar.

8. ALVIN AILEY JNR-(January 5th,1931 to December 1st,1989). He was an American dancer, director choreographer and activist. He founded the Alvin Ailey American Dance Theatre (AAADT). He cre-ated AAADT and the affiliated Ailey School as suit-able places for up-and-coming black artists. He was an advocate for expressing the universality of the African American experience through dance.

9. MISTY COPELAND- (Born September 10th, 1982). She is a ballet dancer for American Ballet Theatre (ABT)

which is one of the three leading classical ballet companies in the US. On June 30th, 2015, she became the first African American woman to be promoted to principal dancer in ABT's 75-year history.

10. GWENDOLYN BROOKS (June 7th, 1917, to December 30th, 2000). She was a poet, author, and a teacher. Her work mainly dealt with the per- sonal celebrations and struggles of ordinary people in her community. She won the prestigious Pulitzer Prize for poetry on May 1st, 1950, for 'Anne Allen.' It made her the first African American to receive a Pulitzer Prize.

11. COUNT BASSIE- (August 21st,1904 to April 26th, 1984). He was an American jazz pianist, organist, bandleader and composer. He formed his own jazz orchestra -The Count Bassie Orchestra- in 1935. The band did its first recording in Chicago in 1936. He was the first African American to win a Grammy Award in 1958.

12. ROBERT LEROY JOHNSON- (May 8th, 1911, to August 16th,1938). He was an American Blues guitarist, singer and songwriter. His renowned recordings in 1936 and 1937 depicted a combination of sing- ing, guitar skills and song writing talent. His musical prowess was emulated by many and those who came after him.

13. ROBERT LOUIS JOHNSON- (Born April 8th, 1946). He is an American entrepreneur, media magnet, executive, philanthropist, and investor. He is the founder of BET (Black Entertainment Television) which was acquired by Viacom in 2001. He also founded R L J Companies, a holding enterprise which invests in

various business sectors. He became the first African American billionaire in 2001.

14. NINA SIMONE-(February 21st, 1933, to April 21st, 2003). Nina's musical career spanned over four decades from her first hit in 1959, the Top 10 classic 'Loves You Porgy' to 'Single Woman.' She wrote songs addressing racial discrimination against African Americans. Some popular ones are, 'Mississippi Goddamn,' 'Why (The King of Love is Dead)' and 'Young Gifted and Black.'

15. JOSEPHINE BAKER -(June 3rd, 1906, to April 12th, 1975). She was an American-born French entertainer, French Resistance Agent, Freemason and Civil Rights Activist. She became very popular in Europe especially in France during the 1920s. Despite giving up her American citizenship in 1937, Josephine became an activist in the Civil Rights Movement. She made her mark by adopting twelve children of all different races to demonstrate that people can live together peacefully. They were dubbed 'The Rainbow Tribe.'

16. DR GUION STEWART BLUFORD-(Born November 22nd, 1942). He is an American aerospace engineer, retired US decorated Air Force Officer and Fighter Pilot. In 1983, he became the first African American to go to space.

17. DR MAE JAMIESON- (Born October 17th, 1956). She is an American engineer, physician, professor and former NASA Astronaut. She became the first African American woman to travel into space. She served as a mission specialist aboard the space shuttle 'Endeavour.'

18. THE THREE FEMALE AFRICAN AMERICAN MATHEMATICIANS- The collective contribution of Mary Jackson, Dorothy Vaughan and Kathleen Jackson was invaluable in America's quest for dominance in the space race.

(A) Mary Jackson was born on April 9th, 1921. She died on February 11th,2005. Mary was a mathematician and aerospace engineer at the National Advisory Committee for Aeronautics (NACA). This was replaced in 1958 by the National Aeronautics and Space Administration (NASA). Mary took advanced engineering classes and in 1958 became NASA's first black female engineer. Having worked for 34 years and achieved the most senior position available, she accepted a demotion and became a manager of both the Federal Women's Program in the NASA office of equal opportunity programs and of The Affirmative Action Program. She was instrumental in the hiring and promotion of women in NASA's science, engineering and mathematical careers.

In 2019, she was posthumously awarded the Congressional Gold Medal. In 2021, the Washington D.C. headquarters of NASA was renamed Mary W. Jackson NASA Headquarters.

(B) DOROTHY VAUGHAN was born on September 20th, 1910. She died on November 10th, 2008. Dorothy, as a mathematician was dubbed 'The Human Computer.' She worked for NACA and then NASA. In 1949 she became Acting Supervisor of the West Area Computers. She was the first African American to gain promotion and supervise a group of staff at the centre.

Dorothy's 28 years career which started in 1943 as a mathematician and a programmer in the Langley Research Centre involved specialisation in calculations for flight paths, the Scout Project and computer programming. In 2019, she was also awarded posthumously, The Congressional Gold Medal.

(C) KATHELEEN JOHNSON was born on August 26th, 1918. She died on February 24th, 2020. Kathleen's role as a mathematician involv- ing calculations of orbital mechanics at NASA were crucial to the success of the first and sub- sequent US manned space missions. During her 33 years career with both NACA and NASA, "She earned a reputation for mastering com- plex manual calculations and helped pioneer the use of computers to perform the tasks. The Space Agency acknowledged her 'historical role' as one of the first African American women to work as a NASA scientist."

"Johnson's work included calculating trajectories, launch windows and emergency return paths for project mercury spaceflights, including those for astronauts, Alan Shepard, the first American in space; and John Glenn, the first American in orbit, and rendezvous paths for the Apollo Lunar mod- ule and command module on flights to the moon," according to Wikipedia. Johnson's calculations were also crucial to the start of the space shuttle program. She also worked on plans for a mission to mars.

In 2015, President Obama awarded her The Presidential Medal for Freedom. The following year, she was presented with The Silver Snoopy Award by NASA astronaut, Leland S. Melvin, and a NASA Group Achievement Award. In 2019, she was awarded The Congressional Gold Medal by the United States Congress. In 2021, she was inducted into The National Women's Hall of Fame.

The 2016 film, 'Hidden Figures' recounted the extraordinary story of these three African American women, whose invaluable contribution helped American win the space race. The film is also described as 'How Black Women Did the Maths That Put Men on The Moon.' Hidden Figures is a box office success.

19. LEXA IRENE CANADY-(Born November 7th, 1951). She is a retired American Medical Doctor who specialised in paediatric neurosurgery. She was the first African American in the United States to become a neurosurgeon.

20. DANIEL HALE WILLIAMS- (January 18th, 1856, to August 4th, 19310. He was an American physician and founder of Provident Hospital in Chicago. The hospital staffed with African American doctors, was the first interracial hospital to open in the US. In 1893, this African American cardiologist performed the first documented, successful pericardium sur- gery in the US to repair a wound.

21. DR CHARLES R. DREW-(June 3rd, 1904, to April 1st, 1950). He was an American surgeon and medical researcher. He researched in the field of blood transfusions, developed improved techniques for

blood storage and applied his expertise in developing large-scale blood banks in the early part of the Second World War. In 1941, he led another effort in blood bank storage for the American Red Cross. He worked on developing a blood bank to be used for the US Military personnel. Early on in his endeavours, he became naturally frustrated with the military request for segregating the blood donated by African Americans.

22. BASSIE COLEMAN-(January 26th, 1892, to April 30th, 1926). She was the first African American and also the first Native-American to hold a pilot licence. She could not enter flying schools in the US because of her colour. She learned French and went on finally to achieve her objective. She was an early American aviator. In 1922, she became the first African American woman to stage a public flight in America. Her high-flying skills always thrilled her audience. She specialised in stunt flying parachuting. She earned a living in barnstorming and in performing aerial tricks. She remains a pioneer for women in the field of aviation. On April 30th, at only 34, Coleman was tragically killed when an accident during a rehearsal for an aerial show, sent her falling to her death.

23. ELLA JOSEPHINE BAKER-(December 13th, 1903, to December 13th, 1986). In 1940, she worked as a secretary for the NAACP and then served as a director of branches from 1943 t0 1946. She was inspired by the historic bus boycott in Montgomery, Alabama in 1955. Subsequently she founded the organisation, 'In Friendship' to raise funds to fight against Jim Crow laws in the deep South.

24. DR GLADYS MAE WEST- She is 89 years old and according to Wikipedia, she is known for her "contri- bution to the mathematical modelling of the shape of the earth and her work in the development of the satellite geodesy models that were eventu- ally incorporated in the Global Positioning System (GPS)." She was born in 1930 in a family of farmers and naturally grew up working in the fields. The toil on the farm started before daybreak and through the scorching afternoon sun. She regarded educa- tion as crucial in elevating her out of the drudg- ery of farm work. She worked hard and secured top grades in all her subjects. Her family did not have the money to send her to college but being academically assiduous, helped secure a scholar- ship to study at Virginia State University where she graduated as the highest -ranking member of her class in 1948. Having gained her bachelor's degree, she taught science and mathematics in Waverly, Virginia for two years.

She returned to Virginia State University and com- pleted her masters in 1955. The following year she was appointed as a mathematician at The US Naval Proving ground in Dahlgren, VA (now called Naval Surface Warfare Centre). She was only one of four African American employees at that time. This was written about Dr West, "At first she was a human computer, doing the math out longhand herself, but then she transitioned to programming computers, the machines." In the early 1960s she worked on an astronomical study that proved the regularity of Pluto's motion relative to Neptune's.

It proved that every two orbits Pluto makes, Neptune makes three: A phenomenon called

'Orbit Resonance,' according to David Falkner, President of the Minnesota Astronomical Society.

Dr West retired in 1998 after 42 years of working at Dahlgren. She suffered a stroke five months after retirement. In a bid to rebuild her strength and recover her mobility, she attended classes with her husband at a local YMCA. It was reported that she was "motivated by a big goal; to finish her remote PhD program in Public Administration, which she received from Virginia Tech in 2018."

25. PRESIDENT BARACK HUSSIEN OBAMA-(Born August 4th, 1961). An American attorney and politician. He was born in Honolulu, Hawaii. He graduated from Columbia University in 1983. He worked as a Community Organiser in Chicago. In 1988 he enrolled at Harvard Law School. He graduated with (magna cum laude), the second highest honour in 1991. He taught Constitutional Law at University of Chicago Law School for twelve years; as a Lecturer for four years (1992-1996) as a Senior Lecturer for eight years (1996-2004). The courses he taught included voting rights, racism and law. He was Illinois Senator before becoming the 44th, President of the United States in 2008. This was a feat of historic and monumental proportions con- sidering where the African American stood at the turn of the 17th, Century-1619, to be precise. Two hundred and forty-six years of the bondage of the African and the aftermath of undoubted system- atic racism.

"They cannot take it away from you," so says the adage. Education from the onset, was one of the hurdles in the way of the African. Indeed, after

almost two hundred and fifty years since the abolition of slavery, there are many black areas and yes,
some white areas where the standard of education leaves much to be desired. A national 'failure.'
It is therefore remarkable to learn of the extraordinary achievements of African Americans in the
field of education and diverse professions in a relatively short time. Of course, the cherry on the cake
is the elevation of the African to the American presidency in the personality of Barack Obama in 2008.
No doubt this historic achievement was achieved
with the resounding support of majority of the white
Americans especially the younger generation.

Now returning to our adage, in sports and entertainment in general the African American has excelled
from time immemorial. Ability, like a cork always remains
afloat defying suppression. It is not like a job interview
behind closed doors where one could be termed a
failure when indeed one has excelled. The importance
of African American sports people and entertainers in
lifting the spirits and spurring other brothers and sisters
to excel in their respective disciplines, is invaluable.

1. JACKIE ROBINSON- He was an American National
    Hero because of his exploits in the game of base-
    ball. He was also reported to have performed well
    in other college sports like basketball. He became
    the NCAA champion in the long jump. He also
    reached All-American football status. He served as
    a Second Lieutenant in the Second World War. He
    did not experience combat because he refused to
    move to the back of a segregated bus and there-
    fore expelled from the military. He played his first
    major league game in Ebbets Field for the Brooklyn
    Dodgers on April 15th, 1947. Robinson was cho-

sen as the Rookie of the Year in the same year. In 1949, he was named the National League's Most Valuable Player (MVP). In 1955, he helped his team to win the World Series. He was the first African American to play major league baseball. He was also the first to be included in the baseball Hall of Fame.

2. JACK JOHNSON- He was known as 'The Galveston Giant'. He was the first African American to win the coveted World Heavyweight Boxing Crown in 1908. He defended it until 1915.

3. ATHEA GIBSON- She was the first African American to play in and win in tennis at Wimbledon and the US National championship in 1956.

4. MARLIN BRISCOE- In 1968, in the colours of the Broncos, he became the first African American quarterback to start a professional football game.

5. JESSIE OWENS- A four-time Olympic Gold Medallist at the 1936 Berlin Olympics. He also set a record of 26 feet 8.25 inches in the long jump at the 1935 Big Ten championships.

6. WENDELL SCOTT- One of the first African American drivers in in NASCAR and first to win a race in the Grand National Series, NASCAR'S highest level.

7. NATHANIEL ADAM COLE- Known professionally as 'Nat King Cole,' an African America singer and jazz pianist. He recorded over hundred songs which became global hits. He acted in films, on TV and performed on Broadway. He became the first African American man to host an American

Television series. He had in her daughter, Natalie Cole, a renowned singer-songwriter.

8. MICHAEL JEFFERY JORDAN- He is also known by his initials 'MJ.' He was born in 1963. His playing career spanned fifteen seasons in the NBA (National Basketball Association) winning six championships with the Chicago Bulls. He is the principal owner of the Charlotte Hornets of the NBA. His biography on the official NBA website reads, "By acclamation, Michael Jordan is the greatest basketball player of all times." He was a key personality in making basketball popular globally in the 1980s and the 1990s. On September 11th, 2009, with four others, Jordan was enshrined in the Naismith Memorial Basketball Hall of Fame.

9. EDWIN CORLEY MOSES- Popularly known as Ed Moses, born in 1955 is an African American former track and field athlete. He won gold medals in the 400 metre hurdles at the 1976 and 1984 Olympic Games. In ten years, between 1977 and 1987, Moses won 107 consecutive finals -122 consecutive races- setting the World Record in the event four times. In 2000, he was elected the first Chairman of the Laurels World Sports Academy, an international service organisation of world-class athletes. Edwin Moses attended Morehouse College in Atlanta where he earned a BSc in Physics. He later gained a master's degree in Business Administration in Pepperdine University.

10. HANK AARON- (February 5th, 1934, to January 22nd, 2021). Full name, Henry Louis Aaron. He made baseball history in 1974 when he hit the 715th home run of his career breaking the 39-year-old record set by Babe Ruth. He endured racist abuse

and death threats while chasing down and breaking Babe Ruth's all-time home run record. He was regarded by many as "base ball's legitimate long ball king," the New York Post reported. In his 1991 autobiography, he wrote, "The Ruth chase should have been the greatest period of my life, and it was the worst. I couldn't believe there was so much hatred in people." He was receiving 3000 letters a day, most were supportive, but a considerable number were not. Some of those vicious ones contained the n-word with a typical warning, "If you hit one more home run, it will be your last. My gun is watching your every black move." When Aaron hit the historic home run in Atlanta on April 8th, 1974, besides the excitement of his teammates and the jubilation among baseball fans, his mother hugged him tightly. She was later reported to have said that she wrapped her body around "as protection in case he was targeted by a sniper," the Times obituary column reported on January 26th, 2021.

Aaron whom the Times described as a reserved and discipline baseball player, hit a record 755 home runs which stood for 33years. It was broken by Barry Bonds in 2007 with 762 runs. President Biden was quoted, "When I watched Henry Aaron play baseball, I knew I was watching someone special. It was not just about watching a gifted athlete master his craft on the way to a Hall of Fame career, as one of the greatest to ever play the game. It was that each time Henry Aaron rounded the bases, he wasn't just chasing a record, he was helping us chase a better version of ourselves."

Vin Scully, now 93, a white American sportscaster said on air when Aaron broke the record, "What a marvellous moment for baseball, what a marvellous moment for Atlanta and the state of Georgia, what a marvellous moment for the country and the world. A black man is getting standing ovation in the Deep South for breaking the record of an all-time baseball idol. And it is a great moment for all of us." In his memoir, Hank also wrote about the fans, "I never wanted them to forget Babe Ruth, I just wanted them to remember Henry Aaron." It must be noted, because of segregation, blacks were not allowed to play in the Major League Baseball until 1947.

11. MOHAMMED ALI- (January 17th, 1942, to June 3rd,2016). Mohammed, the incomparable global idol mesmerised spectators and audiences with his unique boxing skills, poetry, wit and fast-talking. Ali was also an activist and a philanthropist. He changed his name from Cassius Clay to Mohammed Ali in 1961 when he converted to the Muslim religion. Affectionately called 'The Greatest,' because he was widely regarded as one of the most important and celebrated figures of the 20th, Century and one of the finest boxers of all times.

In 1960, at 18 years old, he won the Light Heavyweight Olympic crown. He moved to the higher professional weight and became the first person to win the World Heavyweight title on three different occasions. He successfully defended his title nineteen times. On April 28th,1967, he refused to be inducted into the US Army and was immediately stripped of his Heavyweight title. He cited religious reasons for his refusal to fight in Vietnam. He famously said on TV, "Ain't get no quarrel with those Vietcong." He then added that they "did not call me nigger."

On June 20th, 1967, Ali was convicted of draft evasion, sentenced to five years in prison, fined $10,000 and banned from boxing for three years. He stayed out of prison as he had a successful appeal and resumed his boxing career in October 1970, knocking out Jerry Quarry in Atlanta in the third round.

CHAPTER TWENTY-TWO

PROVIDENCE ALWAYS PROVIDES

The United States benefited immeasurably from free African labour from 1619 for almost two hundred and fifty years. The main European countries which were reaping rewards from the vile trade were Britain, France, Netherlands, Portugal and Spain. They all benefited from the expansion of industries and the related economic growth. Almost all the establishments including even the church enjoyed the economic benefits. Surely there were numerous pockets of dissenting voices within the populace of these European countries. Humanity knew, even among those with their enormous ill-gotten gains that slavery was (and still is) wrong. If not, then the wealth stifled their humanity. "If slavery is not wrong, then nothing is wrong," to quote yet again, American President Abraham Lincoln.

The enslaved, Africans in their singing-Negro Spirituals-yearned desperately for the protective care of God. Three centuries on, in 1946, amid grave consequences to his family and himself, Oskar Schindler, a German Industrialist defied the nefarious Nazis and saved 1,200 Jews from the dreaded German concentration camps.

In England, the mother country to America, the African slaves' fervent prayers were answered by William Wilberforce and his associates- James Ramsey, Granville Sharp and Thomas Clark. Countless others supported their humane call. The Abolition of Slavery Movement was started by the Quakers (Historical Christian Denomination) and Non-Conformists, but the Test Act of 173, prevented them from becoming Members of Parliament. The noble cause was therefore taken up by William Wilberforce, an Independent MP in the Commons. He became the parliamentary spokesperson for The Abolition of Slavery Movement.

In Britain, Wilberforce's conversion to Evangelical Christianity in 1784 spurred him on in pious pursuit of this social reform. Wilberforce's Slave Trade Act 1807 prohibited dealing in slaves. Britain used its influence to persuade other countries around the world to abolish the slave trade. Countries were encouraged by Britain to sign treaties to enable the Royal Navy's West Africa Squadron to "interdict slaving ships." Irrespective of Britain's move, the British economy continued to bene-fit from slavery for many years. Undeniably, the trade in slaves which underpinned the economy, will continue to benefit generations to come.

In France in 1788, Jacques Pierre Brissot founded the Society of the Friends of the Blacks (Société Des Amis Noirs) to work for the Abolition of Slavery. France granted the freed slaves full citizenship after the (French) Revolution on April 4th, 1792. In France, the first elected assembly of the First Republic (1792 -1804), in April 1794, under the leadership of Maximilien Robespierre, abol-ished slavery in law in France and all its colonies.

The Society of the Friends of the Blacks and Abbe Gregoire, a French Catholic Priest, worked tirelessly in galvanising anti-slavery sentiment in the cities. The initial article of the law stated, "Slavery was abolished in the French colonies." The second article stated, "Slave owners would be indemnified," with financial compensation for the value of their slaves. The French Constitution, passed in 1795 included in the Declaration of the Rights of man that slavery was abolished.

The Hague, Netherlands on September 9th, 2020, Netherland marked 157 years since the country abolished slavery on July 1st, 1863. The solemn event also reflected the Black Lives Matter Movement which received recognition after the death of George Floyd on May 25th, 2020.

Dutch merchants and ships were also involved in slave-trading. Plantations owners in Dutch colonies in the Caribbean benefited enormously through free slave labour. On September 9th, 2020, Protesters who vandalized statues of historic figures, demanded their removal.

Spain abolished slavery in 1861. The abolition of slavery in Spanish West Indies happened much later. In fact, they were the last to abolish slavery. Spain abolished slavery in Puerto Rico and Cuba in 1873 and 1886 respectively. Denmark was the first nation to abolish the slave trade. It officially ended in 1792. However, the slaves in the West Indies were not liberated until 1848; that was fifteen years later than the British slaves.

Across Europe, slavery was known to be going on especially in the United States and the Caribbean. In America and Europe, it is highly debatable whether the populace actually was aware of the full extent of the suffering the African slaves were enduring, day after every blessed day.

The Quakers, William Wilberforce and associates, Abbe Gregoire and Society of Friends of the Blacks: And other like-minded humanitarians across Europe were rowing against a titanic wave of financial avarice. Even some of the churches had their hands in the till. I believe in humanity, had ordinary people known more and ear-lier about the plight of the African slaves especially in the plantations, the vile trade in human beings would have been stopped sooner in Europe, the Caribbean and the United States. There are countless stories of many freed slaves supported by white European and American humanitarians who helped to turn the tide towards total abolition. Space will not allow, therefore a selected few will suffice.

1. JAMES SOMERSET - a 17 -year- old slave was brought to England from Jamaica in 1769. He escaped and appealed to the British courts to stop his owner from taking him back to Jamaica. In 1771, 19 years old James was supported by lawyer Granville Sharp who called for 'habeas corpus' to be applied in James's case. The legal term means, 'A prisoner has to be brought before a court, so it can decide if that person's imprisonment is lawful.' There were then an estimated 15,000 slaves in England, but because James had been put in chains to be returned to Jamaica, Granville Sharp argued that James was a prisoner. It was a crucial test case with Sharp challenging the law to see slaves as human beings and not another person's property. Lord Mansfield, The Lord Chief Justice- highest judge in England- agreed and James Somerset become a

free man. Lord Mansfield described slavery as "odious" and that the English courts could not accept it.

2. MARY PRINCE- She was born into slavery at about 1788 in Bermuda in the Caribbean. According to the bbc.co.uk/newsround website, she was taken away from her family at the age of ten. She was forced to work on many West Indian islands making salt. Years of tireless work in the scorching tropical sun caused blisters on the "exposed parts of her body and painful sores on her legs." In 1828, her owners brought her to England from Antigua. Slavery was still legal in the West Indies and not in Britain. In London, Mary left her owners and joined a group called, Anti-Slavery Society. The main aim of this society was the abolition of slavery in the British Empire. Mary told her life story to the supporters of the society and was helped with the publication of her book-The History of Mary Prince- in 1831.

3. FREDERICK DOUGLASS- An African slave in the United States escaped at the age of twenty. In 1838, he married, changed his surname and joined the Anti-Slavery Movement. He became a leading campaigner for abolition. He wrote two books about his experiences and travelled to Ireland and the UK. He was encouraged by the greater number of free black people in the United Kingdom as compared to the United States.

4. OLAUDAH EQUIANO- He was known much of his life as Gustavus Vassa.

He was born on October 16th, 1745, in the Eboe Province in the West African Kingdom of Benin, an area which used to cover present day Southern

Nigeria. He was kidnapped and sold into slavery as a child. Olaudah was taken to Barbados and sold to a Royal Navy officer. He was later taken to Virginia in the United States. In America his new owner was Michael Henry Pascal who travelled all over the world with him. Olaudah admirably managed and saved enough money which enabled him to buy his freedom in 1766 at the age of only twenty-one. He settled in England the following year. He became a leading Anti-Slavery campaigner and wrote a book about his life, published in 1789.

The book, 'GUSTAVUS VASSA THE AFRICAN,' was first published in London. It is about his time spent in enslavement and his attempts to become an independent person, through his study of the Bible, his eventual success in becoming a free man and subsequent business undertakings. In the year the book was published he moved to 10, Union Street (now 17, Riding House Street). In April 1729, Olaudah married a local woman called Susannah Cullen at the St Andrews Church, Soham, Cambridgeshire. When he died on April 7th, 1797, he was living in Paddington Street, Westminster.

5. CHARLES IGNATIUS SANCHO- He was born at about 1729 on a slave ship in the Atlantic middle passage. He was known as 'The Extraordinary Negro' and 'The Man of Letters.' He became a British actor, composer and writer. According to Wikipedia, he was the only Briton of African heritage known to have been eligible and voted in an 18th, Century General Election through "property qualifications."

Sancho's mother died not long after his birth in the Spanish colony of New Grenada. His father was reported to have committed suicide rather than live as a slave. When he was two years old, his owner took him to Greenwich, London, England. He was left in the care of three unmarried sisters. He lived in Greenwich from about 1731 to 1749. John Montagu, the Second Duke of Montagu of the first creation (1690-1749) was highly impressed by Sancho's intellect, frankness and friendliness. The Duke lent him books from his personal library in Blackheath. Sancho ran away to the Montagus in 1749. He worked as a butler for Mary Montagu (Nee Churchill) Duchess of Montagu at the Montagu House. He concentrated his attention to music, poetry and writing. He was a leading campaigner of the abolition of slavery and became "a symbol of the humanity of Africans and the immorality of the slave trade." In the 1970s he married a West Indian woman called Anne Osborne. They had seven children. Sancho died on December 14h, 1780.

6. CHLOE COOLEY- She was a young black woman held as a slave in Fort Erie and Queeston, Upper Canada. According to Wikipedia the area was then being occupied by loyalties from the United States. In 1793, her owner with the assistance of two other men forced her into a boat to sell her across the Niagara River in the US. Several people witnessed the incident and "petitioned the Executive Council of Upper Canada." This incident is widely quoted as attributable to the "passing of the Act Against Slavery in Upper Canada in 1793." It prevented "the importation of slaves into the Province and provided a gradual abolition of slavery within a generation among those held there."

Cooley's owner was a loyalist, Adam Vrooman, a white farmer and Sergeant with the Butler's

Rangers. The Executive Council of Upper Canada filed charges against Sergeant Vrooman for disturbing the peace. He petitioned against the charges which were subsequently dropped on the grounds that Cooley was his property.

Chloe Cooley's story is proof that did the populace know exactly the magnitude of the plight of the African slaves, multitudes would have vehemently campaigned and most likely achieved the abolition of slavery a considerable period earlier than the official declarations. We should not forget that even in the United States, many white Americans took risks of being lynched themselves by trying to help innocent African slaves about to be mercilessly lynched by mobs. In terms of education, some states used flogging, fines and even imprisonment as penalties for white Americans who dared educate the African slave.

PHILLIS WHEATLEY PETERS- (1753-December 5th, 1784). In Phillis, the white Wheatley family showed humanity irrespective of the dire consequences of educating an African slave. Phillis is reported to be the first African (American) slave author of a published book of poetry. Phillis was born in West Africa, probably in Senegal or Gambia. She was kidnapped at the age of seven or eight, sold into slavery and taken to North America.

John and Susanna Wheatley of Boston became her owners. They taught her how to read and write. When she showed promise in writing, they actively encouraged her. Mary Wheatley, the couple's 18 years old daughter was credited to have contributed considerably to Phillis's education. Her brother Nathaniel also helped. The Wheatley's treated Phillis like their own daughter. They spared her the drudgery of slave work and focused more on her education. Under the tutelage of the whole Wheatley family, Phillis started reading Greek, Ancient History and Latin Classics in their original languages in addition to tackling difficult passages in the Bible at the age of twelve. Her first poem was published in the Mercury, a Rhode Island newspaper at the age of fourteen.

Phillis was familiar with and read the works of literary personalities like Alexander Pope, John Milton, Homer, Horace and Virgil. Wikipedia stated that Phillis had "unprecedented education for an enslaved person and one unusual for a female of any race." When she was seventeen, an elegy she wrote to Rev George Whitefield was published in the Massachusetts Spy. In 1773, at the age of twenty, she was accompanied to London by Nathaniel Wheatley seeking the publication of her work. She met prominent people like the Lord Mayor of London. Some became patrons to her literary work. On September 1st, 773, still twenty, her book of poems covering topics in religion and morality was published.

Consequently, Phillis became famous in England and the American colonies. In a poem of his own, fellow African American poet Jupiter Hammond wrote and praised Phillis.

In 1775, at twenty-two Phillis wrote a poem about George Washington and sent it to him with a letter (produced below). This happened when George Washington was about to take office as the First President of the United States. Thomas Jeffery, the Third President, was also reported to be a reader and admirer of her poetry. He wrote that Phillis's verses were "beneath criticism."

The Wheatleys set Phillis free after the publication of her book. Sadly, Susanna died in 1774 followed four years after by her husband John. It was reported that Phillis drifted into poverty. Marriage did not reverse her fortunes. Her husband John Peters was a free black grocer. The death of two babies and poor living conditions had their toll. In 1784, her husband was jailed because of unsettled debts. Phillis Wheatley Peters took up a job as a scullery maid in a boarding school. This was a job she was not experienced to do as the Wheatleys did not subject her to the toil of domesticity. "She died in poverty and obscurity" at the age of thirty-one due to complications in childbirth. Sadly, as well, their sickly infant son died shortly after her death.

Phillis's story unearthed and underlined many facts as it dispelled many myths and assumptions. Just a few notable points. When anybody is treated fairly and equally, for example in education, that person's natural ability comes to the fore. Sometimes some people do not even need equal opportunity, they need just "a shot" to bring out the best they can offer society. The white Wheatley family exemplarily demonstrated that kindness does not discriminate. Colour is not an issue, for we are all humanity: And to put a religious favour on it, 'We are all God's children.'

[Letter to George Washington from Phyllis Wheatley]

To His Excellency George Washington

Sir,

I have taken the freedom to address your Excellency in the enclosed poem, and entreat your acceptance,

though I am not insensible of its inac-
curacies. Your being appointed by the
Grand Continental Congress to be
Generalissimo of the armies of North
America, together with the fame of
your virtues, excite sensations not easy
to suppress. Your generosity, therefore,
I presume, will pardon the attempt.
Wishing your Excellency all possible
success in the great cause you are so
generously engaged in. I am, Your
Excellency's most obedient humble
servant,

Phillis Wheatley 1776

Cambridge, February 28, 1776.

***

To His Excellency, George Washington
Celestial choir! enthron'd in realms of light,
Columbia's scenes of glorious toils I write.
While freedom's cause her anxious breast alarms,
She flashes dreadful in refulgent arms.
See mother earth her offspring's fate bemoan,
And nations gaze at scenes before unknown!
See the bright beams of heaven's revolving light
Involved in sorrows and veil of night!
The goddess comes, she moves divinely fair,
Olive and laurel bind her golden hair:
Wherever shines this native of the skies,
Unnumber'd charms and recent graces rise.

Muse! bow propitious while my pen relates
How pour her armies through a thousand gates,
As when Eolus heaven's fair face deforms,
Enwrapp'd in tempest and a night of storms;
Astonish'd ocean feels the wild uproar,
The refluent surges beat the sounding shore;
Or thick as leaves in Autumn's golden reign,
Such, and so many, moves the warrior's train.
In bright array they seek the work of war,
Where high unfurl'd the ensign waves in air.
Shall I to Washington their praise recite?
Enough thou knows them in the fields of fight.
Thee, first in peace and honours, —we demand
The grace and glory of thy martial band.
Fam'd for thy valour, for thy virtues more,
Hear every tongue thy guardian aid implore!

One century scarce perform'd its destined round,
When Gallic powers Columbia's fury found;
And so may you, whoever dares disgrace
The land of freedom's heaven -defended race!
Fix'd are the eyes of nations on the scales,
For in their hopes Columbia's arm prevails.
Anon Britannia droops the pensive head,
While round increase the rising hills of dead.
Ah! cruel blindness to Columbia's state!
Lament thy thirst of boundless power too late.

Proceed, great chief, with virtue on thy side,
Thy ev'ry action let the goddess guide.
A crown, a mansion, and a throne that shine,
with gold unfading, WASHINGTON! be thine.

***

[Letter from George Washington to Phyllis Wheatley]

Mrs. Phillis [sic],

Your favour of the 26th of October did not reach my hands 'till the middle of December. Time enough, you will say, to have given an answer ere this. Granted. But a variety of important occurrences, continually interposing to distract the mind and withdraw the attention, I hope will apologize for the delay, and plead my excuse for the seeming, but not real neglect.

I thank you most sincerely for your polite notice of me, in the elegant Lines you enclosed; and however undeserving I may be of such encomium and pan- egyrick, the style and manner exhibit a striking proof of your great poetical Talents. In honour of which, and as a tribute justly due to you, I would have published the Poem, had I not been apprehensive, that, while I only meant to give the World this new instance of your genius, I might have incurred the imputation of Vanity. This and noth- ing else, determined me not to give it place in the public Prints.

If you should ever come to Cambridge, or near Head Quarters, I shall be happy to see a person so favoured by the Muses, and to whom Nature has been so liberal and beneficent in her dispensations.

I am, with great Respect, etc. [General George Washington]

CHAPTER TWENTY-THREE

WORLD-WIDE REACTION TO GEORGE FLOYD'S MURDER

Centuries after the premier of all American Presidents-George Washington, we live in an era when some public officials and even a former occupant of the White House (Trump) show open hostility towards black people. One single act of unimaginable brutality to typify the era is the daylight lynching of poor George Floyd. The murder of George Floyd, the justifiable public revulsion and protests, projected the Black Lives Movement into a global brand. Besides widespread protests in the United States, England and European countries, the movement was hailed in India, Palestine, war-torn Syria and of course African countries. Surprisingly, there are some strands of backlash from some members of the public and sections of the media. Some individu- als, even in TV debates, started using the slogan 'White Lives Matter.' In United States in particular some right-wing activists added. 'Blue Lives Matter.' This refers to the police or law enforcement officers.

Of course, All Human Lives Matter as the Good Lord intends. What had been (and still is) a torn in the fresh of black people until 2013 was that for almost 400 years the black man suffered all manner of atrocities and injustices from every quarter. Even some polices of governments of different shades, shackled the progress of blacks.

In America especially, behind the scene, police bru-tality towards blacks was rife. This brutality was felt and well known within the black community, but not so much within the majority white community. However, the widespread availability and usage of smart phones brought into the public domain, the systemic police brutality towards mainly blacks. The turning point occurred with the killing of 17 years old Trayvon Martin by 36 years old George Zimmerman in Sanford, Florida on February 26th, 2012. It was an example of white civilians killing blacks seemingly at will besides those of law enforcement officers across America. Zimmerman's acquittal was the last straw which led to the formation of the movement, Black Lives Matter on July 13th, 2013. How can any fair-minded person begrudge the black community for saying or emphasising that black lives matter after almost 400 years of inhuman treatment and systematic racism?

The media, as expected, covered extensively the Black Lives Matter movement after the death of George Floyd. Overall, the coverage was fair but there were aspects which need critical examination. On the 10th of June 2020 issue of the Daily Mail, under the heading, 'I fear for Britain's future if we erase the past (good and bad).' The columnist Sarah Vine wrote about slavery, the dismantling of statues and the repercussions of George Floyd's murder.

On the whole Sarah Vine's article was fairly balanced but a few points need scrutiny. First and foremost, the heading can be described as alarmist. She wrote, "and the consequences, and as we have seen over the past few days, are spilling out onto our streets. The killing of George Floyd was an abomination, but the way his family's tragedy has been used on both sides of the Atlantic to fan flames of hatred and fuel division is devastating." Sarah, the hatred and the division were not brought about by the black community. It was and still being perpetrated by racism: And the only denominator is the mere colour of one's skin. Not the content of one's character.

Socio-economic and racial injustices create divisions in society. The Black Lives Matter Movement is a notable symptom of decades of entrenched racial injustices and inequalities.

Outrageous and fallacious statements-intentionally or otherwise by people with important platforms exacerbate these divisions in society. Sarah's fear is unfounded. An example of unfounded fear borne out of prejudice is 'The Rivers of Blood' speech given by the Tory soothsayer, MP Enoch Powell on April 20th, 1968. It is over five decades now: He envisaged "The

River Tiber foaming with much blood." I do not know about River Tiber, but the River Thames is not foaming with human saliva let alone blood. What cannot be refuted in many decades is the blood of defenceless black men and women in the hands of mainly police officers; on especially the streets of some American cities and indeed in the UK.

How many times have some sections of the press and for that matter, columnists written about former Republican President Trump's divisive rhetoric, fuelling hatred and blatant racism towards black people and other minorities? Sarah and columnists who think like her should dwell also on some politicians and some members of law enforcement, whose actions are the root causes of some of the ills in societies today.

On May 1st, 1989, as already stated in these pages, Donald Trump paid thousands of dollars for full page advertisements in some of New York city's popular newspapers condemning the so-called 'Central Park Five' and for the return of the death penalty. The four blacks and one Latino were all aged under 16 years when a white woman was attacked in the park. Having served some years in prison, they were acquitted after a prisoner admitted being responsible for the horrific sexual attack on the white woman. Trump did not apologise then and even when he became US President, did not. Had it been President Obama being cruel and dividing society he would have been front-page news for days on end in some sections of the media.

On December 12th,2020, under the heading, 'US execution rush begins,' the Daily Mirror reported, "The US has executed the first of five federal inmates as Donald Trump rushes through their deaths before he leaves office." The paper continued, "Brandon Bernard, 40, was given a lethal injection in Indiana on Thursday after last-ditch clemency pleas were rejected. He was convicted of two murders in 1999 when he was a teenager and is the youngest offender to be executed in almost 70 years." The paper concluded, "Four more executions are due to take place before January 20-the end of Trump's presidency."

On January 16th,2021 the Mirror US editor, Christopher Bucktin reported under the headline, 'Trump's Land of Execution Spree'- His 12th Victim and 1 More Doomed.' Fifty-two years old murderer Corey Johnson was given a lethal injection on January 16th, 2021. He had been on death row for 28 years for seven murders, among a host of further charges related to drug trafficking and acts of violence in Virginia. Johnson expressed remorse before receiving the lethal injection, "Sorry for my crimes." He added, "On the streets, I was blind and stupid. I am not the same man that I was." The editor ended, "The pro-death President resumed federal executions assuring that last year, for the first time in history, the US government executed more people than all 50 states combined."

On January 16th, 2021, indeed, Dustin Higgs became the final and 13th to be executed on death row during Trump's presidency. Forty-eight years old Higgs was convicted for killing three women in 1996. He was executed in the federal prison in Terre Haute, Indiana.

Sarah Vine also wrote in her article, "In particular, the notion that all white people need to apologise for their very existence (exemplified by one little girl, aged maybe six or seven, whose mother posted a picture of her holding up a sign proclaiming her 'white privilege') and the idea we are all racists" This is the most outlandish statement I have read for a long, long time. Polls which are just samples and may not be always accurate, do provide a measure of what people are thinking and saying. Sara failed to provide proof to back her claim. We should not forget the courage and moral bravely of William Wilberforce, Baptist Minister William Knibb and all their white associates who fought to end slavery. It is almost two centuries now since slavery was abolished in the UK, US and France, yet there are consistently many white men and women seeking social justice and equality for the black man. We should not forget white Americans risking being lynched for being "nigger lovers."

Sarah Vine compared the removal of statues to the behaviour of "ISIS Jihadis who torched the library at Mosul, or flattened the Temple Baal in Palmyra, felt they were pursuing righteousness in eliminating the evidence of past regimes they despised." She added, "In reality, they were like that mob in Bristol, merely indulging in cultural vandalism." What I can simply say is that one does not have to be black to have a measure of the emotions these statues evoke in majority of blacks. History shows that the comparison with ISIS is woefully hollow, therefore does not hold water.

Since George Floyd's death, there have been more shootings of black people by law enforcement officers in America. The glaring example is the shooting-seven times- of Jacob Blake by police officer, Rusten Sheskey in the presence of his three young children 3,5 and 8 years old. Surely the white law enforcement officer saw the young children at the back of the car. Without under playing the severity of Jacob's injury,(para- lysed waist down), let us turn our attention just momentarily on the children. It will be interesting to know how many papers both in the UK and the United States have dwelt, may God forbid, on the trauma which could affect these poor children in years to come. One does not have to be a psychologist or a therapist to know. What are required are understanding, maturity and humanity. Specifically, how many female columnists have shed light on the plight of the Blake children? Are the Blake children different? Do not these innocent and poor children deserve any consideration? Or do black lives not matter?

Another journalist who wrote about the repercussions of the George Floyd murder, was John Humphreys, former BBC TV broadcaster and Radio 4 presenter. His detailed article was published in the Mailonline on June 12th, 2020. Yes, like Sara Vine, John Humphreys's article was balanced in parts, others sadly not so. Some relevant points in his article In the second chapter, referring to opening a new TV bureau in South Africa, he stated, "I would not become one of those ghastly privileged whites who expressed their disgust for apartheid but enjoyed its benefits. I would not, for a start, have black servants." Fair enough. What Mr. Humphreys failed to realise was that once a white person stepped on the soil of then apartheid South Africa, he/she was immersed from head to toe in white privilege, whether it was sought for or not.

Mr. Humphreys wrote about the Robert Mugabe regime promising "black people democracy and dignity in the new Zimbabwe." Yes, majority of Africans were disappointed and condemned the brutal regime. We should however not distort the essence of the Black Lives Matter movement. It is an open secret that opportunists on the fringes would exploit it to their own advantage likewise dissenters or opponents who would indulge in vandalism to soil the reputation of the movement. Linking the atrocities of Mugabe's regime does not disguise the fact that human beings are being killed especially in America because of the mere colour of their skin. Mr. Humphreys there is no 'tribal racism' in African countries.

There is tribalism, it is everywhere, even here in the UK. We have the English, Welsh, Irish and the Scottish. If there are no blacks in the UK, one of these groups would be the whipping boy of the Union. It is sadly, a human factor.

Mr. Humphreys also stated the corruption in Nigeria. Perhaps the corruption in the UK, US and other white democracies is innocuous hence has a less intimidating sound, "fraud." Corruption may not be as blatant in these countries as it is regrettably in African countries, but it is still corruption. Is the recent distribution of covid-19 contracts by the British government for the purchase of PPE, executed without any blemish?

Brutal regimes and corruption in African countries should not be condoned by any African; but they should not be categorised with the senseless killing of blacks by law enforcement officers in the US or UK.

Mr. Humphreys referred to white privilege and stated, "fair enough, except that I haven't always been privileged. My education ended at 15 and I know what it is like to be poor. And anyway, I can't help being white any more than someone else being black. It does not automatically confer guilt." No! It does not. What Mr. Humphreys failed to realise was that if he were black, with his education ending at 15, displaying the same ability and motivation, it is not an exaggeration to state that it would have been a miracle to get to where he is now. There are countless black people of Mr. Humphreys's age who went beyond 15 and gained excellent academic qualifications. How many of these hardworking blacks would have 'climbed the ladder' as far as Mr. Humphreys? On the website bing.com, he was reported to have been "paid between £600,000 and £649,999 in 2016/17. He is one of six male stars who have agreed to earn less after revelations about differences between men's and women's pay." How many black people have taken the same career path as he and can boast of earning even £400,000 annually? I am afraid the colour of one's skin, not only makes the difference, It Matters!

Mr. Humphreys wrote about employment in the BBC and elsewhere, "In more enlightened institutions (yes including the BBC) you hear young white men complaining about that they'd have a better chance of promotion if they were black." In my opinion, this assertion does not hold water. It is a fallacy and disgraceful on his part. How many people are employed in the BBC? What percentage is black, of course including the cleaners? How many are in middle management not to mention top management? Where are the statistics to support the claim? In the September 16th, 2020, issue of the Mirror, in the 'BEEB'S' Top 20 earners of 2019/20 from Gary Lineker at £1.75m to Laura Kuensberg at £290,000, I could only identify broadcaster George Alagiah as a member of the BAME community with a salary of £325,000.

He went on, "How long before there are marches behind banners declaring 'White Lives Matter?' Note that the odious Tommy Robinson and his followers are making an unwelcome appearance." I do not know whether I could state that unconscious bias has made Mr. Humphreys suffer from myopia. What I can state and inform is that the Black Lives Matter movement was formed in 2013. A mere eight years ago. Mr. Humphreys should reflect on the history from 1619 to 2013; 394 years of (total) silence, (blatant) denial and (implied) complicity. Yes, that collectively is the root cause and therefore the emergence of the Black Lives Matter movement. In my opinion it is painfully and tragically centuries overdue. We need empathy, maturity and humanity, for goodness' sake!

Mr. Humphreys, if the BBC reports a positive fact concerning the Black Lives Matter movement, the corporation is not taking a political stance. What is politics anyway? It is not about inanimate objects. It is about human beings. During a debate on TV about the Black Lives Matter movement, John Humphreys asked at the end about the situation concerning white work- ing-class boys. Indeed! However, the implication of Mr. Humphreys's statement, "my education ended at 15 and I know what it is like to be poor," is that if he could make it there is no reason why blacks could not make it as well. He wanted the focus to be on white work- ing class boys as well. Fair enough. If he was not suffering from unconscious bias, he would initially have grouped the working-class boys of both races and raised concern about their problems in society. Yes, inequalities in society are some of the factors which prevent working class white children from achieving their aspirations. If social conditions were fair, majority of them could use education as the key to lift them out of the doldrums. White working-class boys still have advantages over black working-class boys. Giving both groups of boys opportunities to do their best, could only help society at large. As we provide shelter, sustenance and education for our children, we should spare a thought for the parents of both black and white children who are genuinely struggling to provide these basic essentials. They would rather provide for their offspring than be told by a flint-hearted politician that they should not rely on the state.

If ever there is a case for the restructuring and the reintroduction of the 'Unconscious Bias' program, this is a classic example. Some in the media refer to themselves as liberal. However, on certain topics on race the material they put out can be damaging. One female columnist who blamed the Black Lives Matter movement for the vandalism and injury to a police officer in the summer, recently referred to racism as "fading." The sad thing is that some of these journalists think that they have the facts, but the gulf between what they know, and reality is immense.

Their material inadvertently (not intentionally, unconsciously) is damaging, hence the urgent need for the reinstitution of an effective Unconscious Bias program.

Finally, I want to inform both Sarah Vine and John Humphreys, not all black people think that all white people are racist. I believe both Sara and John are Welsh. In my humble capacity as a semi-lay preacher at my church, I shared a story I read in the August 12th, 2019, issue in the Daily Mirror about the generosity of a Welsh teenage girl who went to Uganda in 2008 on a placement scheme. Christiana Ramsey, now 31, on her return to Wales raised money to replace the shack which the then 11 years old Julius Muyomba lived with his family. It is a heartfelt story every human being should read. The Mirror stated, "At 11 Julius was picking up litter in Uganda for 70p a day but meeting a kind British teen changed his life. She fought to give him an education and 10 Welsh families clubbed together to make it happen. Now a decade later, this inspirational young man is a university graduate. "In fact, he graduated at Bangor University, Wales.

I share this story and other kind deeds by white people especially towards blacks whenever the opportunity arises. We have a congregation made up of both white and black worshippers. The congregation appreciates these moving true stories.

In June 2016 ABC in the US gave a report about Matt White in his early thirties, meeting a 16 years old African American called Chauncy Black. The "straight A" black teenager wanted to help Mr. White with his shopping in exchange for a few coins to buy doughnuts. He told him that he was looking for a part-time job to look after his sick mother. Having correctly assessed the situation, Mr White bought the black teenager some groceries and drove him home, where he met his mother. He later stated, "He and his mum had nothing. They didn't have the best of furniture."

Mr. White quietly went away and secretly raised $341,000 through the Go Fund Me scheme. He helped them buy a new house. Mr White even managed within the amount raised and bought the teenager a lawn mower to start his own small business. The black teenager and her mum were extremely grateful. The gentleman said, "As I was leaving, I gave him a hug and told him how much God loved him and that he was going to grow up to be an incredible man. I'll never forget that hug. It meant more to me than any possession I have. Our God is awesome, and we can never be thankful enough for the blessings we have." And their surnames? Mr White and Mr Black. One cannot make it up if one tried. Our God is Wonderful! John Bunyan, the author of 'Pilgrim's Progress' wrote, "You have not lived today until you have done something for some- one who cannot pay you back." Alleluya! Praise God.

Nothing can be more disheartening for a young black man from tropical Ghana to arrive in a cold coun- try like Britain and receive a hostile reception from the host. My experience and majority of friends and acquaintances in the BAME community paint a picture of warmth and acceptance. In Hertfordshire where we trained as psychiatric nurses, black colleagues and I played football in the hospital team. We were warmly received in almost all the venues we played in Herts and Bedfordshire. The hospital was the largest employer in the county, with a spacious Social Club which provided the opportunity for interaction and genuine socialization of human beings of all walks of life. Within the first month of arriving in the hospital to start our nursing training, four fellow Ghanaians and I saw four young girls aged between probably 8 and 10. Their precocious 'leader' on seeing us said with an infectious smile, "We like darkies, don't we?" The rest responded in unison, "Yes, we do." My friends were amused by their boldness and innocent charm.

On my third 'placement,' I worked in a Geriatric Ward staffed mainly by blacks. One old dear sat in pensive mood. Suddenly she asked one of my female colleagues who was expecting, "Have you got other children?" My colleague cheerfully responded, "Yes, I have two young ones, a boy and a girl." The old dear, after a moment's pause enquired, "Are they black as well, poor little ones."

There you have it. What does the age spectrum above throw up? My interpretation is this, the young white girls wanted to assure us that if it seems others did not like blacks, they did not share that feeling. Grandma in the Geriatric Ward on the other hand, felt sorry for the "poor little ones" born into a world which at times appears hostile to certain people because of the mere colour of their skin.

I have countless personal examples to recount but just two will suffice. Having qualified, I worked in a leading hospital in Kent. I worked with many kind older and some elderly white ladies. One of the older ones, Mrs. Owen treated me like a junior brother. Of the elderly ones, Mrs. Macdonald treated me like her own son. She saw how hardworking I was and advised me on what steps to take and buy my own property. I followed her advice and within a relatively short time, I achieved that. Among many others, she bought a special coin for us when our first child was born. It is just over four decades now, it should be worth a few bob now.

When I was in petrol retail management in the 1970s to mid- 1980s, one of my customers was the renowned Sports Broadcaster, Harry Carpenter of Blessed Memory. He always made a point of saying "Hello" even some-times when I was behind closed doors in my office. He once returned from the US and spent some time telling me about the interview he had with "the Great Man" Mohammed Ali, no less. I found Mr Carpenter person-able; no doubt he got on well with Frank Bruno. 'You know what I mean?'

The above is just a testimony of how kind human beings are, therefore for anybody to imply or state that all blacks think that all whites are racists and for whites to "apologise for their own existence" is "nonsensical nonsense," to quote a frustrated, elderly African traveller at Heathrow Airport.

On June 22nd, 2020, Richard Littlejohn wrote in the mailonline, "Just stop these stupid protests, it's getting silly." Reading his article, I concluded that he did not address properly recent years of atrocities and blatant racial injustices, let alone the pain and tragedy of four centuries.

What is "silly" to Mr Littlejohn is life or death to another human being who happens to have a black skin. No level-headed black person would condone the destruction and wanton vandalism which occurred in the US and UK after the death of George Floyd. It should also not be forgotten that some right-wing groups 'chipped' in to make the situation even worse for the Black Lives Matter movement. What about the 'Cause and Effect' factor. How many column inches have some journalists devoted to the minority of police officers who are catalysts of these very serious public disorders? Had a black man not been lynched in broad daylight, there would not have been opportunism, vandalism, rioting, injuries to police officers and civilians alike and sadly loss of life in some cities, as it happens often in the US and to a lesser extent the UK and other places.

On reading both Sarah Vine and John Humphreys's articles I wrote to three national papers. I have reproduced them at the end of this chapter. My response also relates to Mr Littlejohn's article. He was not happy about, "raging Roy Kean" show-casing Black Lives Matter on TV. Mr Littlejohn referred to, "Manchester City Raheem Sterling expressing his political opinions…" If Raheem Sterling was expressing his political opinions, then young Marcus Rashford, of Manchester United, by his stance and statements since summer, is doing likewise. What is politics anyway? I have already stated in these pages that it is not about inanimate objects, it is about human beings, for goodness sake! One does not have to be black to have a considerable measure of how adversely social issues affect blacks and others in society. We need, I repeat, empathy, maturity and humanity.

The BBC's stance on race is a moral one. When Mr Littlejohn's employers, The Daily Mail fought tirelessly for the prosecution of those who murdered the black teenager, Stephen Lawrence, they were not taking a political stance, they were "expressing" and taking a moral stance.

Mr Littlejohn went on and wrote about Trevor Phillips, former Equalities Commission Chairman. He stated, "Here how assured, a man of Guyana heritage, who has spent his whole life fighting racism with every fibre of his being, is now slandered as Uncle Tom by preening white middle-class onanists." Phillips was quoted, UK, "is the best country in Europe to be black." I whole heartedly concur. However, I think some sections of the media look at other countries to evaluate UK's standard or progress in racial equality. Nobody forced the UK to embark on humane policies to make it the best country in Europe for blacks and other minorities. In compliance with true Christian values, successive British governments, and the kind British public especially, created conditions, which may never be perfect, but congenial enough for outsiders including blacks. Please do carry on at the appropriate pace to uphold your own values. We all know what has been happening in America especially in the last four years.

Using that as a barometer would engender compla-
cency and set the UK back many years in race relations. Please do not rest on your laurels.

In Mr Phillip's article, I cannot recall reading the facts
which made UK "the best country in Europe to be
black." In my opinion, Britain's acceptance (willingly)
of her moral obligation (Scramble for Africa, Slavery
and Colonisation) coupled with the humanity of the
British people, is attributable in creating the right atmosphere for blacks and other minorities. Even without the
moral obligation, I have experienced enough in almost
fifty years, heard a lot and avidly read a lot to be convinced of the humanity of the British. I have followed
Trevor Phillips in the media for decades. I do not want
to question his probity, but I found his article in the Daily
Mail on the Black Lives Matter protests, one sided. He
stated some good points like, "The fact that what we
loosely call the 'Black Lives Matter story' simply will not
go away is a good thing. People of all back grounds
and colours who previously would not have devoted a
second thought to racial and religious inequality...." In
my opinion, Trevor dwelt too much on those who
exploited the protests to cause "mayhem" than centuries of racial injustices and police brutality which gave
rise to the movement just a mere eight years ago. In
journalism, you cover both sides of the coin equally to
the best of your ability and let the readership form their
own judgment.

In my opinion, the founders of the Black Lives Matter
movement have no prerogative over the term of the
slogan. They admirably and aptly captured the sentiments of human beings everywhere concerned about
the needless loss of life, especially unarmed black
people in the hands of law enforcement officers. They

have been accused of propagating radical views, principally defunding or even disbanding the police organization. Arguably many supporters of the movement, black and white alike do not agree. Many point to retraining or having social workers embedded in special law enforcement groups, as the way forward. I am sure that before the Black Lives Matter movement was formed in 2013, whenever a fatality in the hands of law enforcement was announced, blacks agonised within themselves, "Don't our lives matter at all?" I did share that agony as a black person, and I am sure so did majority of white people. I believe in humanity, some white people might not have said it openly but did share the sentiment. Even within the police service, when the minority let their colleagues down, many in this group would be musing, "Not again." Why should a police officer serving the public, come out from the safety of his own home in the morning in trepidation, not knowing what may unfold?

In America despite the injustices and suffering by black people, there are a few blacks who have allowed themselves to be exploited by the right and unashamedly turn their backs on their own people. These people used to be called 'Uncle Toms,' but in case Mr Richard Littlejohn does not know, the term has run its long four-century course. The new term is 'Useful Idiot.' Mr Trevor Phillips, in my opinion is far from being called that, but I hope in future he balances the scale accordingly.

The following are articles I sent to three newspapers after the death of George Floyd.

CONFRONTING INJUSTICES IN OUR WORLD

George Floyd's death on the 25.05.2020, has awakened once again the conscience of the world. Many people have reflected and candidly admitted what I can describe as unconscious bias, tacit racism, blatant prejudice, or outright racism. In the field of psychiatry in which I have been for over four decades as a registered nurse, many professionals have also been candid. This is laudable.

Our 'perceptions' and 'prejudices' become barriers in the delivery of care to our patients (black and white) with compassion. Using a colour to describe a person is just a label. None of the colours –white, black, brown, yellow or red, accurately describes the human skin. These colour-labels are just for easy identification and therefore should not be used to define who a person is as a human being. Perception is not a fact until proven.

Strip away the labels and you see humanity. Dr Martin Luther King stated, and I quote, "I look to the day when people will not be judged by the colour of their skin, but the content of their character."

George Floyd's death, seen in graphic detail the world over; not only underscores the suffering of African-Americans, it is a testimony of a human being's wickedness towards another human being.

The world has had many wake-up calls over many decades. Emmitt Till, Michael Brown, Steve Beko (Apartheid S. Africa) and Eric Garner, to name a few. In the interest of all humanity, this call should continue to reverberate and hold.

This is my contribution to the Black Lives Matter debate.

George Floyd laid down his life to lay bare all forms of injustices in our world.

He died to recount how Mother Africa cried and hae-morrhaged in the 17th Century.

He died to retell the history of bondage of Africans in the Americas.

He died to reopen the debate of four centuries of pain and suffering of the African American.

George Floyd laid down his life to resurrect the pain inflicted by Apartheid on African soil.

He died to shed light on the forgotten plight of Aborigines in Australia and Native Americans.

He breathed his last breath to underscore the suffering of Minorities and the Vulnerable.

He lost his life to portray the complicit silence of the majority to the inhuman acts of the minority.

George Floyd's death uncovers the wilful intent of dic-tatorships and some legitimate regimes in our world.

His loss reopens the wounds of families who have lost loved ones to police and state- sponsored brutality.

His death challenges humanity to re-examine its con-science and show compassion.

George Floyd laid down his life to remind the world that Mother Africa is still wailing and bleeding in the 21st Century.

Humanity is unique; the iniquity of man should not have a place in this Wonderful World.

Humanity is not complete without each and every race on our Planet. 'Do to others as you would like them do to you,' Luke Chapter 6 verse 31. 'Love thy neighbour as yourself,' James Chapter 2 verse 8.

RACISM-THE DEBATE

I was disappointed to read the BBC Broadcaster, John Humphrys's article on Mail-On-Line regarding the repercussions of the senseless murder of George Floyd in America. He raised some valid points but the only part I whole-heartedly agree is the last paragraph. He wrote and I quote, "My own experience is that when children choose their friends the colour of their skin is irrelevant. Surely, we must look to the future rather than the past." The tail end needs a bit of clarification, 'Mr Humphrys, we must look to the future but must not forget the past to help us navigate carefully and safely as events unfold.'

Majority of blacks do not think majority of whites are racists: Neither do we think that "white people need to apologise for their very existence," as Sarah Vine stated in the Mail 10.06.2020 issue. Since slavery, without the help of numerous white people, blacks would not have been where we are now. William Wilberforce, William Knibb, Abraham Lincoln, Father Trevor Huddleston, to name a few, all led the fight for justice. In this country we have not forgotten the dogged campaign by the Mail newspaper for justice when Stephen Lawrence was murdered.

The media has not ceased reporting the kindness of people of all races. Exactly four years ago, a white American in his early thirties, had pity on a teenage African American who just wanted to help him with his shopping for a few coins to buy doughnuts. The gentleman, having interviewed the teenager, whom he described as, "most amazing person," bought a load of grocery for the boy, drove him to his rented house and was appalled by the state of the house and the health of the mother. He went away and privately organised a GO-FUND scheme and raised $341,000 for a new house for the African Americans who were extremely grateful. The white gentleman stated, "Our God is an awesome God, and we can never be thankful enough for the blessings we have." The surname of the white person? White: And the black teenager? Black. Yes! Our (Humanity's) God is wonderful.

A young white female student from Wales went to Uganda a few years ago. On her return she helped raise money to replace the shack a bright African was living in with his family. She was also instrumental in the African getting a private secondary education in her school, leading on to graduation in a Welsh University.

A young white English student went on a work- placement in Kenya. She "fell in love" with a baby African orphan. She raised money online to adopt the baby. I am glad that my organisation- The George A. Amarteifio Foundation 'cheerfully' contributed towards such a compassionate course. During the George Floyd protests, young adult white males and females stood in solidarity receiving blows to the stomachs and other parts of their body from the police. In fact, the majority of the protestors were white, as we all witnessed.

The list is endless. I always use these noble acts of kindness when I get the opportunity as a semi-lay preacher to lead the Sunday service at my church.

Majority of blacks are not saying that all whites are racist. What we hear vehemently from majority of our black brothers and sisters is that the silence of the majority is tantamount to complicity.

We all have platforms; whether in public or in private; we should use them judiciously and conscientiously.

Of Course All Lives Matter

I agree with anybody who now says, 'All Lives Matter,' but this call is perplexingly, frustratingly and regrettably long overdue. We should reflect on the lot of the African in the last four centuries in America. Just a few facts.

1. The slightest insurrection by African slaves in the plantations was met with brute force ending in the slaughter of many including the innocent.

2. Lynching of African slaves was happening in the American South on average, two a day. Petty offence or often a fabricated story ended with an African slave being lynched. Even families brought along their children to watch the 'event' and celebrate.

3. During the span of fourteen hours between 31st May and 1st June 1921 (Juneneeth) a white mob descended on the prosperous black district (Black Wall Street) of Greenwood, Tulsa, Oklahoma, massacred 300 African Americans and destroyed properties. The financial loss was put at $1.47m, about $20m in today's money. Adding insult into injury, the National Guard arrested thousands of African Americans and held them prisoner for eight days. The whole sad episode was triggered by what was later established as a false accusation by a 17-year-old white female lift operator of sexual assault by a19 year-old African American shoe shiner, who had stepped on her foot. No doubt there was also an element of envy by the mob towards the success of the Africa-Americans in Greenwood district.

4. On 28th August 1955, Emmett Till a 14-year-old African American from Chicago was accused of offending a white woman in her family's grocery shop. The boy was lynched and dumped in the Mississippi.

5. During the Civil Rights demonstrations in America in the 1960s, the police often used brute force to disperse or quell largely peaceful demonstrations. Countless number of African Americans suffered horrific injuries.

6. On November 22nd, 2014, a 12-year-old African American, Tamir Rice was shot and killed by a white police officer, Timothy Loehmann who "feared" for his life, after seeing what turned out to be a toy gun held by the boy in a playground. The officer was not charged.

7. The murder of numerous blacks by the American police culminated in the gruesome murder in broad daylight on 25th May 2020 of George Floyd and on the 13th of June 2020, the senseless murder of Rayhard Brooks.

The 'Black Lives Matter,' movement was formed on the 13th, July 2013 just eight years ago. Prior to the formation, where were the people who are now saying 'All Lives Matter' or even 'White Lives Matter.?' Undoubtedly both Black and White Lives Matter.

Had those dissenters, before July 2013, raised in the media and society at large that 'All Lives Matter (ed),' they would have stolen the wind off the sails of any movement to be called, 'Black Lives Matter.' In fact, it is highly likely that the organisers of the 'Black Lives Matter' and the black community as a whole would have understood the essence of that slogan and supported it.

The African in America has suffered since 1619. People who are offering counter slogans are disingenuous. Humanity is incomplete without each race on our planet. We should all be our brother's keeper.

On the 17th, June 2020, a 49-year-old black man was reported to have saved a 55-year-old white man, Bry Male from a very serious injury during a counter demonstration at Waterloo Station, London.

Silence by the majority until now has been construed as complicity. In future to avoid such a tag, all humanity should consistently condemn all inhuman acts by the few. Every human life MATTERS.

CHAPTER TWENTY-FOUR

REPARATION

The reparation for slavery has been made for centuries by African and Caribbean countries. In addition, there have always been establishments and distinguished public figures advocating for victims of slavery and their descendants to receive compensation. These are the Global Reparations Movement in the Caribbean, The National Coalition of Blacks for Reparation in America, The National African American Reparations Commission, The European Reparations Commission and similar groups in Canada and the UK.

Despite the countless calls for reparation, starting mainly after abolition of slavery, no financial nor material compensation has been received by any of the countries or groups in the United States, Africa or the Caribbean. In the summer of 2020, the United Nation's Human Rights chief, Michelle Bachelet urged countries to confront the legacy of slavery and colonization. The dailymail.co.uk website reported on June 18th, 2020, that the Church of England and Bank of England apologised over their historic links to slavery through high-ranking directors of their establishments in the 19th Century.

On September 3rd, 2001, under the heading, 'Britain Blocks EU Apology for Slave Trade,' the guardian.com website reported that Britain and a small number of allies, "are being accused of jeopardising the UN's Anti-Racism Conference by blocking the European Union from issuing a straightforward apology for the Transatlantic Trade in slavery." Under intense pressure, the British delegation could only express "regret." A European source was quoted," Britain is the stickiest on this." The source continued, "The majority of EU delegations are willing to make a compromise on an apology, but some are still unable to accept this." The EU delegates agreed that they were not prepared to call slavery a crime against humanity, as it could have legal implications leading to the payment of reparation. Britain stated that "even an apology could have damaging consequences."

A draft wording on slavery agreed by foreign ministers in July 2001 stated, "The European Union profoundly deplores the human sufferings, individual and collective, caused by slavery and the slave trade. They are among the most dishonourable and abhorrent chapters in the history of humanity.

The (EU) condemns these practices, in the past, present, and regrets the suffering they have caused."

The African delegates protested vehemently by demanding that the African block wanted slavery to be described as "barbaric," of "enormous magnitude" and unparalleled in its dehumanising of so many people. British governments have not been willing to apologise for slavery, however on November 27th, 2006, Labour Prime Minister, Tony Blair, made a partial apology for Britain's role in the African slave trade. Wikipedia however, reported that African Rights Activists, con-demned it as "empty rhetoric" which failed to address the issue properly. PM Blair again apologised on March 13th, 2007. On August 24th, the same year, the new Mayor of London publicly apologised for London's role in the African slave trade. He was quoted, "You can look across there to see the institutions that still have the benefit of the wealth they created from slav- ery." Mayor Ken Livingstone was reported as breaking down in tears as he made the statement and point- ing towards London's financial district. The Mayor was praised by the American Civil Rights Activist, Rev Jessie Jackson.

On August 20th, 1999, the BBC reported that the African World Reparation and Reparation Truth Commission, meeting in Accra, Ghana made demands for the West to pay $777t (Trillion) to Africa within five years.

Reparation demands as already stated have been made for centuries. Sadly, and ironically in this "barbaric" treatment on an "enormous magnitude," the wrong side has been compensated, in many cases, handsomely. This is racial injustice on a monumentalscale.

On October 6th,2020, in the Guardian newspaper, under the heading, 'The Long Road,' the historian, Mary Lewis was reported to have detailed, "In the 18th and 19th Centuries, the policy of paying reparations to former slave-owners was standard practice among colonising Europeans and American states. In 1792, the dawning of the Haitian Revolution, when masses of enslaved people revolted against French colonial power, destroying plantations and constructing their own government, the French state began to pay exiled former slave-owners the secours or a state- funded compensation for their property losses. The assistance was offered not only to former slave-owners, but also to their descendants. It was paid by successive French governments for more than 100 years ending in 1911."

The report added that the former slave-owners were not satisfied with their lot but demanded "reparation" directly from the impoverished Haitians.

Astonishingly, the French government succumbed to this flint-hearted request. In 1825, the French government stationed 14 warships off the Haitian coast threatening the destruction of the main port cities unless a huge sum of reparations-'The indemnite'- was paid. Eventually over more than 120 years, the Haitian government was forced to pay 90m gold Francs, an additional 135m gold Francs in bank interest and fees to France. This ended in 1947.

The British, as already stated in these pages, awarded a total of £20m in 1833 to former slave-owners. It was reported as "The largest reparations bounty of all to its former slave-owners." The sum was 40% of the national budget, "along with statutory re-enslavement, or 'apprenticeship,' of emancipated people for a subsequent four years." It was estimated that more than 44,000 former slave-owners in the Caribbean and Britain benefited. The financial burden of the reparations for 180 years was borne by the British taxpayer ending just six years ago, 2015. Another irony, black taxpayers of African and Caribbean descent in the UK also contributed to the 'bounty' which went to these individuals. Talk about rubbing our bantu noses in it.

The United Nations state in their basic principles that, "states are under legal obligation to provide reparations for gross violations attributable to them." The UN defined the parts of the plan for reparation as restitution, rehabilitation, compensation, satisfaction (apologies) and guarantees of non-repetition. In September 2016, a report in the Nation stated the United States owes African Americans reparations for slavery. It stated that the UN working group of experts on people of African descent pointed out that compensation was necessary "to combat the disadvantages caused by 245 years of legally allowing the sale of people based on the colour of their skin." The group warned that the US had not confronted its legacy of "racial terrorism."

In 1989, House Representative John Conyers introduced a Bill to establish an exploratory committee on reparations. He reintroduced it ever year until his resignation in 2017. In 2019, the House Sub Committee on the Constitution, Civil Rights and Civil Liberties held a hearing on resolution calling for a commission to investigate reparations and provide recommendations.

On January 12th, 1865, getting to the end of the American Civil War, according to the Guardian (The Long Read) black leaders in Savannah, Georgia met the victorious anti-slavery Union army chief Maj-General, William T. Sherman. The army chief enquired what the black leaders wanted after emancipation. They then made a reparation pitch," Slavery is receiving by irresistible power, the work of another man, and not by consent." The redress they asserted should be "to have land and turn it and till it by our own labour......so we can maintain ourselves and have something to spare."

In response, three days later, the sympathetic and considerate army chief's order, known as Sherman's Field Order No 15, "redistributed 400,000 acres of coastal land, stretching from Charleston, South Carolina to the St John's River in Florida, to black families in 40-acre plots." However just four months after in May 1865, barely enough time to see a tomato seed germinate, President Andrew Johnson, a former slave-owner, intervened, abrogated the considerate grant and ordered the return of all plantation lands to the former enslavers. Consequently, blacks seeking reparations set up mutual aid societies, black churches, community schools and grassroots saving banks for fellow blacks.

In the 1950s through the tireless work of Audrey Moore, dubbed the Queen Mother of reparations movements, reparations attained a truly global status. Audrey who grew up in New York was born in 1898 to sharecroppers in Louisiana. She was quoted among others, "We're Africans, no matter where we are born. Just remember, whatever you are." In the centenary year-1963- of the Emancipation Proclamation, 65 years old Audrey Moore submitted a petition with more than one million signatures to President Kennedy. The trust of the petition- the US government pay no less than $500 Trillion over the course of four generations as a partial payment of what was owed to African Americans. The money should be controlled by the black community and was to "benefit the whole people," through the reconstruction of the infrastructure, industry, educational institutions, and health services. The Guardian stated, "Moore's epic reparations demand made it as far as Kennedy's secretary, then stopped. Silence is power."

In 1993, Bernie Grant a Labour MP for Tottenham joined forces with a Nigerian reparations leader, Chief Mko Abiola and the OAU (Organization for African Unity) to hold a Pan-African Conference in Abuja, Nigeria. The proclamation stated, "The damage sustained by the

African peoples, is not a thing of the past; but is painfully manifest in the damaged lives of contemporary Africans from Harlem to Harare in the economies of the black world from Guinea to Guyana, from Somalia to Suriname." The conclusion, "recognize that there is a unique and unprecedented moral debt owed to the African peoples which has yet to be paid."

Having returned from Abuja, Grant brought a motion before the British parliament on May 10th, 1993, to ratify the Abuja Proclamation. It was the first time that the subject of reparations had been discussed as part of the British parliament's official business. Three years later Grant collaborated with the Human Rights lawyer Anthony Gifford QC and the reparation topic was raised, and so far, the only time in the House of Lords.

On July 15th, 2020, the London Borough of Lambeth, led by Green Party representative, Scott Ainslie, became the first local authority to pass a successful motion calling for a Parliamentary Reparations Commission to address the impact of slavery on current racial inequalities in the UK."

In Europe some states followed Britain's example of using state funds and substantial government loans to compensate former slave owners. The Danish and Swedish governments paid reparations to enslavers through their own "compensate emancipations." The Dutch state paid £1m in 1863 to its 5316 former slave owners. The state "guaranteed" the continuation of slavery in Suriname for more years after abolition.

According to the Guardian website, in Spanish Puerto Rico "enslavers were showered with reparatory gifts: money, bonded black labour and land grants."

In the US enslavers in states like Rhode Island, Connecticut and New York were given reparation deals "in the form of right to the ongoing involuntary labour of enslaved black children for up to 28 years in addition to guaranteed pensions." A classic case involved a minister called Reverend Thompson who had title to an enslaved boy called James Mars in Connecticut after the abolition of slavery in the state. The law allowed the Reverend to keep Mars enslaved until he was 25. He could even send Mars to Virginia where he owned land and could enslave him for life. This inhuman outcome was averted when James Mars's own parents "stole" him and fled to somewhere in New England for them to stay together as a family.

Under the heading, 'The town that finally made preparations a reality,' Kris Manjapra (in the Guardian's Long Read) stated, "In a suburb of Chicago, the world's first government-funded slavery reparations programme is beginning. Robin Rue Simmons helped make it happen but her victory has been more than 200 years in the making." In February 2019, Simmons then 43 years old was in the second term as an Alderman for the Evanston City's historically Black 5th Ward. She sent an email to the nine-member Equity and Empowerment Commission of the Evanston City Council. The heading was reported as, 'Because Reparations Make People Uncomfortable.' She stated,"Hello Equity Commission, thank you for the work you are doing. You have the most difficult work of all the commissions because the goal seems impossible.... I realise that No1 policy or Proclamation can repair the damage done to black families in the 400th year of African American resilience. I'd like to pursue policy and actions as radical as the radical policies that got us to this point."

Eventually the benefit of Simmons email to some of the six million blacks who over the decades left the post-plantation south "to fill the growing labour vac- uum across the industrial north; and to escape the intensifying white supremacists for retribution and racial rule; came nine months after that bold request." On November 25th, 2019, the Evanston City Council, "passed the United States' first, indeed the world's first legalised and funded reparations program to acknowledge and address the intergenerational disparities of racial slavery. The $10m fund will be resourced by the new Municipal income tax on can-nabis. There is justice in this too, since the unequal enforcement and prosecution of marijuana prohibi-tions have served as a major mechanism by which black youth are criminalised and shoved in the US's prison-industrial complex."

Simmons was quoted, "We are focused on breaking the racial wealth divide. My hope is that the fund grows tenfold as other institutions and other donors follow our lead." It must be stated that Evanston reparation suc-cess was attributable also to the active commitment of white allies, such as Nina Kavin.

This may be a small success in America and indeed globally; but it is a major break through which should be applauded. All parties especially the "white allies" are a credit to humanity. Reparations Sub-Committee Chair, Ald. Robin Rue Simmons stated, "This is a tremen-dous program that has been supported by the City of Evanston, the City Council, the residents, largely. This is not to replace Federal reparations or HR 40." She added, "This is one step towards repair that we are years ahead of any other municipality."

SETTLED REPARATIONS IN HISTORY- The most notable was Germany paying reparations to Holocaust survivors after World War Two. According to Broomsberg, the reparations varied in amount and form. It is estimated that Germany has made over $80 Billion in social welfare payments to Jewish people who suffered under the Nazis.

In 1995, through the deliberations of the Truth and Reconciliation Commission, which laid bare the atrocities of the Apartheid Regime, the South African government paid reparations to 18,000 victims who gave testimony.

In 1988, the US gave $20,000 to each of the 82,219 Japanese Americans who survived interment during the Second World War. In America Republican Senate Majority leader, Mitch McConnell argued that white Americans should not have to pay for acts which predated their birth.

Many Republicans hold this view. Tim Scott, the only African American GOP Senator seconded McConnell's stance.

This is gross injustice which can be supported by countless statements and declarations. I will however quote a passage from the root.com website. It stated, "From 1619 until 1865, this country transformed itself from a colonial outpost into the biggest economy in the world. A lot of that was because of free labour. We like to think about the riches we received from industries like cotton, but even people who didn't own slaves benefited from slavery. Northern shipbuilders made fortunes building boats for exporting cheap American products. Retailers profited from the goods that slaves produced. America enjoyed cheap food and clothing because slavery made labour cost zero."

The website added, "The military became the world's strongest partly because farmers could leave plantations to fight for their country without worrying about their farms failing. The sons of farmers went to college and became educated instead of staying at home and working the fields, creating a new class of intellectuals and industrialists. Everything that America was, is, or will be, is partially due to the fact that this country had the advantage of sustaining itself using two-and-a-half centuries of free labour. Not only have the people responsible for building this country not benefited from their own labour, but they have been oppressed because of it."

On December 13th, 2020, in an exclusive report by Paul Lashmar, Jonathan Smith in Barbados and Alan Selby, in the Sunday Mirror, it was reported, "A super rich Tory MP is raking in cash from a Caribbean sugar plantation where thousands died during the colonial slave trade." The 621-acre estate was reported to be in the name of Richard Drax, "A Lord of the Manor worth an estimated £150m." The estate has been dubbed a "kill- ing field" because of its notorious and shameful past. The demand for reparations is led by Sir Hilary Beckles. He was quoted, "Driving through Drax Hall Land, I feel a sense of being in a massive killing field..." It was reported that today's workers face a different plight, "allegedly earning as little as £24 a day, half the average in Barbados."

Some of the key facts in the report are...

1. For 200 years the Drax Hall workforce comprised up to 327 enslaved people, brought from Africa in grim conditions.

2. Campaigners in Britain and the Caribbean are urging the MP to pay compensation to aid impoverished local workers.

3. Plantations were "criminally enriched" exploiting enslaved people, said a critic.

4. Workers on the site claim their modest retirement bonus has been axed.

5. Barbadian authorities value the plantation and buildings at £4.7m.

Sir Hilary Beckles, the Chair of the Caribbean Community Reparations Commission said, "Black life mattered only to make millionaires of English enslavers and the Drax family did it longer than any elite family." The aristocrat Tory MP, 62 years old Drax lives in his ancestral seat in Dorset, England. He holds the Lordship of Longburton and is the "largest individual landowner in Dorset with 13,870 acres." Clement Simpson 72, ex-plantation worker was quoted, "They used to give a little extra to the people who retired, but I ain't had nothing"

Document from Barbados Companies House reveals that the Tory MP registered the Drax Hall Plantation Business this year in his full name, Richard Grosvenor Plunkett Ernie Erle Drax and pays tax due on the property personally. A follow-up on the above appeared on January 3rd, 2021, Sunday Mirror with relevant headings- 'Tory MP owns up over slave past property,' and 'Drax finally lists colonial farm in Commons index.'

The three original reporters stated, "There is precedent for compensating descendants of slaves. Oxford and Glasgow Universities gave £100,000 and £20m respectively to Caribbean counterparts after it emerged they received donations linked to slavery."

The report continued, "Ex-Lib Dem leader, Vince Cable said, 'I hope the recently further enriched Mr Drax pays some attention to polite representations from the Caribbean Community Reparations Commission. He could donate his inheritance to the island on which it stands and still have plenty of property left.'" Mr Drax was reported to have described his ancestors' role in slavery, "deeply, deeply regrettable." He was quoted, "I have updated my entries to include the property in Barbados, although that disclosure is not necessary until it has been legally transferred to me." He added, "In reviewing the entries I realised an agricultural property transferred from my mother to me after my father's death had not been included on the register. My parents died in short succession and administration of both estates is ongoing." He ended, "The process has been complicated, which led to this accidental oversight."

AMERICAN PRESIDENTS ON REPARATIONS- On July 9th, 2019, the Washington Post reported that in an interview in August 2008, candidate Barack Obama rejected reparations by arguing that the political will did not exist to provide them. He favoured "pursuing more practical political goals." In the interview with African American author, Ta-Nehisi Coates, Obama stated that a powerful case could be made that continued slavery, Jim Crow laws and discrimination are primary causes which have beset "the black community as a whole and black families specifically." He stated, "Society has a moral obligation to make a large, aggressive investment, even if it's not in the form of individual reparations checks, but in the form of a Marshall Plan" to make amends.

Candidate Obama doubted the practicality of executing reparation in a population with the majority prepared, "to take a big chunk of the nation's resources over a long period of time to make it right." When Obama cited post-war Germany where reparations were paid to Holocaust victims and families, Coates intervened, "They lost the war." Obama agreed and appeared to underline why it was practical, "small population, finite amount of money that it was going to cost, not multiple generations but people, in some cases, who are still alive who can point to, 'that was my house, those were our paintings, those were my mother's family jewels,' "

Obama then raised the complication that America is not just Black/White society and "it is becoming less so every year." He questioned how Latinos would feel if there was a big investment just in the African American community which would prompt the former to say, "We're poor as well, what kind of help are we getting.?" Obama added, "Or Asian Americans who say, "Look I am a first-generation immigrant and clearly I didn't have anything to do with what was taking place." Coates then rightly explained, "...many of the benefits, that you will actually enjoy are in fact I would say largely in part here because of the past. So when you want the benefits, you invoke the past, that thus you inherit the debt too..."

Candidate Obama agreed with Coates but conceded that he was "not being sufficiently optimistic or imaginative enough." Coates replied, "You are supposed to be optimistic," to which Obama responded that he was not so optimistic "as to think that you would ever be able to garner a majority of an American Congress that would make those kinds of investments above and beyond the kinds of investments that could be made in a progressive program for lifting up all people." He added, "I have much more confidence in my ability or any president or any leader's ability to mobilise the American people around a multiyear, multibillion - dollar investment to help every child in poverty in this country than I am in being able to mobilise the country around providing a benefit specific to African Americans as a consequence of slavery and Jim Crow."

Mitch McConnell, from Kentucky is currently the majority Republican leader in the Senate. His great-great grandfathers were slave owners, according to the politico.com/story website (June 19th,2019). He referred to slavery as "America's original sin." His stance on reparations is already stated in these pages. Besides implying that no living American is responsible for what happened centuries ago, he stated, "We've tried to deal with our original sin of slavery by fighting a civil war, by passing landmark Civil Rights legislation. We elected an African American President."

In the interview with Candidate Obama, Coates stated that slavery in part has benefited Americans. Unquestionably, the general benefit is evident but those who have benefited directly include people like Mitch McConnell, a descendant of slave owners. It must be stated, when Barack Obama was first appointed president, Mitch McConnell was quoted, "The most important thing we want to achieve is for President Obama to be a one-time president."

On reflection, Candidate Obama's stance on reparations was 'political.' In his interaction with Coates there were indications of his actual moral sentiments.

His reference to the Latinos and Asian American communities could be assessed this way; If positions were reversed, would the Latino or Asian community be satisfied with being grouped with African Americans for reparations? Or would Latinos or Asian Americans accept that any consideration for reparation would not proceed until African Americans were included? I doubt it.

In terms of all the views on reparations stated above, President-elect Joe Biden offers a glimpse of hope for African Americans. Equally important he included Native Americans who have also suffered in America. African slaves worked under bondage to provide about two hundred and fifty years of free labour to lay the foundation for the American economy.

Irrespective of that, a considerable number of African Americans endure racial and social inequality by the dawn of every day. This is morally indefensible. In my opinion a fair amount of financial reparation to poor African Americans is justified. The program should not stop there. The standard of housing, education and social amenities in poor African American, Native American, Latino, Asian American and indeed poor white communities should be considerably elevated to underscore America's status as being the world's leading political and economic power. It is a "win, win" situation; for whatever money is poured into these areas, is an investment which would yield a considerable measure of dividends for all America.

Sunday, the 31st of May 2021 heralded extensive media coverage marking the Centenary of one of the worst race massacres in American history, as already recounted in these pages. During a two-day mayhem, white mobs attacked black residents, burned their homes, churches, businesses, schools, libraries and other properties. Three hundred (300) blacks were murdered and 10,000 made homeless.

Three survivors of this atrocity were interviewed on CNN. The oldest is 107 years old Viola Fletcher who stated that 100 years since the nefarious act, she still smelt the burning of buildings. The second survivor who is 106 years old is Lessie Benningfield Randle and the 'baby' of the trio at 100 years old is Van Ellis whose big sister is Viola Fletcher. During the interview, Viola stated, "I still see black men being shot, black bodies lying in the street, I still smell smoke and see fire," She added, "I still see black businesses being burned. I still hear airplanes flying overheard. I hear the screams. I have lived through the massacre every day."

Despite the unimaginable inhumanity, nobody was charged. A current Reverend of one of the churches destroyed but now rebuilt stated on CNN that insurance companies did not pay compensation. The rebuilding was done through donations from parishioners. Some of the businesses were not insured.

Authorities did their utmost to keep this dreadful act under wraps. Those who spoke about it were either murdered or chased out of town.

According to reports, it was only 25 years ago when this massacre was introduced into American history books.

President Biden became the first President to visit Tulsa on the first of June and mark the anniversary of the 1921 Race Massacre. He was quoted, "We have to choose and remember." The President was reported to be "pouring $100 billion into minority-owned businesses to "root out systematic racism and getting rid of unfair housing appraisals."

Reparation for survivors and descendants of victims of the massacre has been discussed and sought for, for decades, but not a cent so far has been paid in compensation. The quest and fight for compensation go on.

A story which shared the headlines with the Tulsa Massacre Anniversary also involved the plight of black people, with Germany in the dock. It is the Herero and Nama genocide in present-day Namibia between 1904 and 1908. The German atrocities, besides the genocide included starvation, the use of concentration camps on African soil and human experimentation.

On the 28th of May 2021, the New York Times web- site reported that the German government agreed to recognise the killing of members of two ethnic groups in Namibia as genocide. Germany ruled the then German South-West African state between 1884 to 1915. Namibia was then ruled by South Africa for 75 years before gaining independence in 1990.

The German government announced a financial aid of $1.3 billion. The announcement was reported to have been made after five years of negotiations. It is understood that the sum will be paid over 30 years and should primarily benefit the descendants of the Herero and Nama people. According to VOA News, in 1904 first the Herero people, then the Namas rose up after being deprived of their livestock and land by the Germans.

In the ensuing conflict- The Battle of Waetrber August 1904, about 80,000 Hereros including women and children fled and were pursued across present-day Kalahari Desert. Only 15,000 survived; about 10,000 Namas were killed between 1904 and 1908.

"Colonial soldiers carried out executions; exiled men, women and children to the desert where thousands died of thirst; and in established concentration camps, such as the one on Shark Island," it was reported.

The Paramount Chief of the Herero people, Vekuii Rukoro described the deal between Germany and Namibia as "an insult because it did not include reparation."

And finally, I mean …finally on April 20th, 2021, 45 years old psychopathic and arrogant Derek Chauvin was found guilty in the court of law, for the murder of 46 years old George Floyd on that fateful day of May 25th, 2020. Daily Mirror April 22nd, 2021. Chauvin had "a reputation among colleagues for his ruthless nature."

No human being black or white, Jew or Gentile, should be compelled to plead for his (or her) life to be spared by another, especially if he does not pose any grave danger to that individual. Can anybody imagine how it would be, to be handcuffed behind one's back, lying not only in prone position, but having an adult male with his knee on one's neck applying pressure at will for 9 minutes 29 seconds; eventually snuffing out precious and God-given life? It is horrifying even to contemplate.

What was it all about? A mere 20-dollar fake bill. Former law enforcement officer, Chauvin had the luxury of being tried in court with his Defence Attorney in attendance. In George Floyd's case, then officer Chauvin was judge and jury; and lest I forget executioner. The only attire missing was the black hood. In the rich Western World, how much is a child's pocket money these days? What was it worth? A 10-kg Basmati rice at the Tesco Supermarket could costs about $20 (genuine of course) when a discount thrown in for good measure.

Is human life that cheap? There is no doubt some retired police officers in countries mentioned in these pages and indeed around the world, have got away with murder, because of grotesquely bias and corrupt judiciary systems. Sometimes these judiciary systems are sound but at times the repulsive behaviour of the minority make them stink to high heavens. Daily Mirror April 22nd,2021- according to data from Research Group Mapping Police Violence, since George Floyd's murder, 181 black people have been killed by the police in the US." Indefensible! Even if it is that imperative, why shoot to murder when the police could shoot to maim?

The 'guilty' retired police officers might have got off scot-free but the least they can do, if not already done, is to get down on their KNEES in the privacy of their chambers and pray earnestly for forgiveness. Our God-Yes! the God of humanity is a forgiving God.

Humanity is faced with dangers, Covid-19 and climate change; and who knows what lurks in the shadows of unfolding years and decades. The world should wake up. Human beings desperately need each other and one another; for goodness' sake! May the Good Lord continue to grant us wisdom and compassion in the daily interaction with fellow human beings.

The subject of reparation evokes many view- points. The main three groups are those in favour, those opposed and thirdly those who may incline to compensation but do not know how it could be appropriately funded even if the money is available. Many who are in favour do not even advocate for cheques to be sent in the post. Notable suggestions put forward include poverty assistance program like education grants, small business loans and low-interest mortgages for American descendants of slaves (ADOS). The opposition group includes those who argue that slavery happened centuries ago hence it is not right for current generation and those to come to contribute towards reparations. Others state that their forefathers were not slave owners, so they never benefited from slavery.

The only way to examine this contentious subject, is through moral lens. The African in their millions, under bondage toiled in very difficult conditions for almost 250 years before the abolition of slavery. The free labour contributed immensely to laying the foundation for the American economy. All Americans benefited and still do; and so will generations to come. American and the rest of the new world gained; while societies in African countries lost able bodied men and women, many of whom were heads of families and community elders, to slavery.

The seven main countries from which slaves were taken and the proportion of those enslaved in the west, were as follows, Nigeria 24%, Angola 24%, Ghana 16%, Senegal/Gambia 13%, Guinea-Bissau 11%, Sierra Leone 6% and others 6%.

According to the Gilder Lehrman Institute of American history, only 6% of African slaves were taken to North America. Majority of the slaves were shipped to the

Caribbean and South America. However, by 1825, "the US had a quarter of the blacks in the new world." Brazil had 35% (4million) of the slaves from Africa and 20% (2.5 million) went to Spanish America. It is estimated that over one million slaves were transported directly from Africa to Jamaica. Two hundred thousand of this number were redirected to other parts of the Americas. The total number of West Africans taken directly to Cuba in 300 hundred years was 600,000. Tens of thousands died during the brutal Atlantic crossing.

DEATH AND DISEASE- According to the Gilder Lehrman Institute, half of all enslaved infants died in their first year of life. "Children suffered very high mortality rates in slavery. Pregnant women were not given much of a break from their work in the fields. They still performed three-quarters or more the amount of work of non- pregnant women. Infant mortality was high, twice as high as southern white children. A majority contribution to this high mortality rate was chronic under nourishment."

Slaves were fed on low nutrition purely starch diet. Symptoms of disease among the enslaved include blindness, abdominal swelling, bowed legs, skin lesions and convulsion. The institute continued, "Common conditions among enslaved populations include beri-beri (caused by the deficiency of thiamine), pellagra (caused by a niacin deficiency), tetany (caused by the deficiency of calcium, magnesium and vitamin D), rickets (also caused by the deficiency of vitamin D), and Kwashiorkor (abdominal swelling caused by severe protein deficiency). Diarrhoea, dysentery, whopping cough and respiratory diseases as well as worms, pushed the infant and early childhood death rate of slaves to twice that experienced by white infants and children.

On August 16th, 2019, the Guardian website stated, "Approximately 600,000 to 10 million African slaves" were in the American colonies "before the slave trade- not slavery- was banned by Congress in 1808." The abolition of slavery in 1865, did not abate the suffering of Africans. World leaders, especially in the West justi- fiably criticise human rights violations in countries like Iran, Russia, North Korea; and the treatment of Uighay Muslims in China, not forgetting the clamp down and the detention of pro-democracy demonstrators in Hong Kong. Four centuries of inhumane treatment of blacks in America persists. Police brutality has com- pounded the endemic problem. The global populace has always shown empathy and expressed concern. However, the political world appears cowered into silence. An indefensible stance which could be con- strued as complicity.

© EBSEN W. AMARTEIFIO (Mr) BSc (Hons) In Business Management, Dip. In Journalism & RMN CEO/ FOUNDER- GEORGE A. AMARTEIFIO FOUNDATION.

BIBLIOGRAPHY

1. African American History Month website.

2. Wikipedia.

3. Affinity Magazine, US.

4. Humanity And The Nature Of Man.

5. Our Generation- An Anthology Of Poems.

6. Reuters.

7. The Guardian, Independent & Mirror Newspapers and websites.

8. The Times, Mail, Telegraph newspapers and websites.

9. New York Times and New York Post newspapers and websites.

10. BBC.Com/news/world Europe.

11. WWW Insider.com

12. Britannica.com

www.ingramcontent.com/pod-product-compliance
Lightning Source LLC
Chambersburg PA
CBHW020433130626
46549CB00001B/113